Microsoft Project 2002 For Dummies

Cheat Sheet

Checklist for Resolving Resource Conflicts

Here's a checklist of things to try when a resource is overallocated in your project. Your ability to use any of these suggestions depends on the circumstances of your project. (For example, you can add resources only if your budget allows it, and you can increase a resource's availability to the project only by checking with that resource and his or her boss to be sure it's okay.)

- ✔ Revise the resource's availability to the project (for example, change the person's availability from 50% to 100%)
- ✔ Modify assignments to take the resource off some tasks in the conflict timeframe
- ✔ Move a task to which the resource is assigned to a later date or modify its dependency relationships
- ✔ Add a second resource to a task that the overallocated resource is busy on to complete the task sooner and free up the resource earlier
- ✔ Replace the resource with another on some tasks (try the Resource Substitution Wizard for help with this)
- ✔ Make changes to the Resource base calendar to allow the resource to work more days in a week

Checklist for Creating a Project Plan

Here's a handy checklist that you can follow to help you build a Project schedule:

- ✔ Enter project information (such as the start date)
- ✔ Set up your work calendar
- ✔ Create tasks, entering information about durations
- ✔ Create milestones (tasks of zero duration) in your project
- ✔ Organize your tasks into phases using Project's outline structure
- ✔ Establish dependency relationships among tasks and add constraints, if appropriate
- ✔ Create resources, assigning cost/rate and Resource calendar information
- ✔ Assign resources to tasks
- ✔ Resolve resource conflicts
- ✔ Review the total duration and cost of the project and make adjustments if necessary
- ✔ Set a baseline

Now you're ready to start the project and track any progress on it, reporting progress to management using Project reports.

For Dummies: Bestselling Book Series for Beginners

Microsoft® Project 2002 For Dummies®

Cheat Sheet

Project Management Web Sites

Here are some useful project-management-oriented Web sites as well as a few sites where you can access third-party add-ins for Project or Project templates.

Microsoft Template Gallery:

http://officeupdate.microsoft.com/templategallery

Project Management Institute:

www.pmi.org

Project Management Worldwide Web Site:

www.projectmanagement.com

American Society for the Advancement of Project Management:

www.asapm.org

International Project Management Association:

www.ipma.ch/

Checklist for Saving Time

If your project is running longer than you expected, try the following methods to tighten the timing:

- Modify dependency relationships so that tasks can start sooner, if possible
- Create overlap dependency relationships where appropriate
- Reduce the amount of slack (but never get rid of it all!) on individual tasks
- Add resources to effort-driven tasks to have them finish earlier
- Consider whether you can do without certain tasks (for example, a second Q&A testing phase or a management review of a package design)
- Outsource a phase of your project when resources can't complete it because they're busy with other tasks

Shortcut Keys

Here are some shortcut keys you'll use all the time when building and working with a Project plan.

Keystroke	Result	Keystroke	Result
Insert	Inserts new task	Shift+F1	Displays the What's This cursor
Ctrl+K	Inserts hyperlink	Ctrl+F2	Links selected tasks
F7	Begins spell check	Ctrl+G	Displays the Go To dialog box
Alt+F10	Assigns resources	Ctrl+Z	Undoes the previous action
Shift+F2	Opens the Task Information dialog box	Ctrl+P	Prints
		Ctrl+N	Opens new project task pane
F1	Opens Microsoft Project Help	Ctrl+S	Saves the file

For Dummies: Bestselling Book Series for Beginners

 ™

References for the Rest of Us!®

BESTSELLING BOOK SERIES

Are you intimidated and confused by computers? Do you find that traditional manuals are overloaded with technical details you'll never use? Do your friends and family always call you to fix simple problems on their PCs? Then the For Dummies® computer book series from Wiley Publishing, Inc. is for you.

For Dummies books are written for those frustrated computer users who know they aren't really dumb but find that PC hardware, software, and indeed the unique vocabulary of computing make them feel helpless. For Dummies books use a lighthearted approach, a down-to-earth style, and even cartoons and humorous icons to dispel computer novices' fears and build their confidence. Lighthearted but not lightweight, these books are a perfect survival guide for anyone forced to use a computer.

"I like my copy so much I told friends; now they bought copies."

— Irene C., Orwell, Ohio

"Quick, concise, nontechnical, and humorous."

— Jay A., Elburn, Illinois

"Thanks, I needed this book. Now I can sleep at night."

— Robin F., British Columbia, Canada

Already, millions of satisfied readers agree. They have made For Dummies books the #1 introductory level computer book series and have written asking for more. So, if you're looking for the most fun and easy way to learn about computers, look to For Dummies books to give you a helping hand.

Wiley Publishing, Inc.

Microsoft® Project 2002

FOR

DUMMIES®

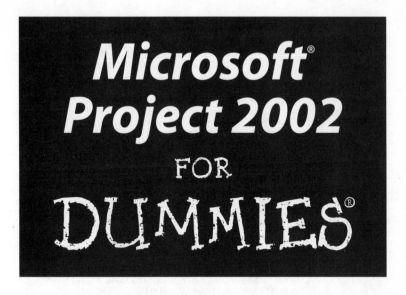

Microsoft® Project 2002 FOR DUMMIES®

By Nancy Stevenson

Wiley Publishing, Inc.

Microsoft® Project For Dummies®

Published by
Wiley Publishing, Inc.
909 Third Avenue
New York, NY 10022
www.wiley.com

Copyright © 2002 Wiley Publishing, Inc., Indianapolis, Indiana

Published simultaneously in Canada

For general information on our other products and services or to obtain technical support, please contact our Customer Care Department within the U.S. at 800-762-2974, outside the U.S. at 317-572-3993, or fax 317-572-4002.

Wiley also publishes its books in a variety of electronic formats. Some content that appears in print may not be available in electronic books.

Library of Congress Cataloging-in-Publication Data:

Library of Congress Control Number: 2002100186

ISBN: 0-7645-1628-0

Manufactured in the United States of America

10 9 8 7 6 5 4 3 2

3B/TQ/RR/QS/IN

About the Author

Nancy Stevenson has written more than 30 books on topics ranging from the Internet and desktop software applications to distance learning and motivating people. Her books include *Microsoft Project 1998 Bible* and *Microsoft Project 2000 Quick Reference For Dummies.* She has taught workshops in project management to clients including the U.S. Navy, NASA, and Ameritech. Nancy worked as a manager in software and book publishing businesses and has taught technical writing at the university level. She currently writes full time and acts as a consultant to the publishing industry.

Dedication

To my family, Graham, Bryn, Dylan, and Clawdette, for putting up with my long hours and keeping me constantly amused when I do take a break.

Author's Acknowledgments

Thanks to Terry Varveris and Jill Schorr for entrusting me with this project and to Susan Pink and Vickey Quinn for working hard to make sure my words make sense.

Publisher's Acknowledgments

We're proud of this book; please send us your comments through our online registration form located at www.dummies.com/register/.

Some of the people who helped bring this book to market include the following:

Acquisitions, Editorial, and Media Development

Project Editor: Susan Pink

Acquisitions Editor: Terri Varveris

Technical Editor: Vickey Quinn

Editorial Manager: Constance Carlisle

Editorial Assistant: Amanda Foxworth

Production

Project Coordinator: Ryan T. Steffen

Layout and Graphics: Joyce Haughey, LeAndra Johnson, Stephanie D. Jumper, Gabriele McCann, Jackie Nicholas, Jacque Schneider, Betty Schulte, Julie Trippetti, Jeremey Unger

Proofreaders: : Laura Albert, John Greenough, TECHBOOKS Production Services

Indexer: Ty Koontz

Publishing and Editorial for Technology Dummies

Richard Swadley, Vice President and Executive Group Publisher

Mary C. Corder, Editorial Director

Andy Cummings, Vice President and Publisher

Publishing for Consumer Dummies

Diane Graves Steele, Vice President and Publisher

Joyce Pepple, Acquisitions Director

Composition Services

Gerry Fahey, Vice President of Production Services

Debbie Stailey, Director of Composition Services

Contents at a Glance

Cartoons at a Glance

By Rich Tennant

page 7

page 101

page 175

page 279

page 141

page 261

Cartoon Information:
Fax: 978-546-7747
E-Mail: richtennant@the5thwave.com
World Wide Web: www.the5thwave.com

Table of Contents

Introduction

*P*roject management probably started back when a few cave dwellers got together and figured out how to work as a team to bag a wooly mammoth for their Sunday dinner. Some fellow — we'll call him Ogg — probably took the lead, so he was the very first project manager. He drew things in the dirt with a stick to help his team members understand the strategy of the hunt and communicated with them in ughs and grunts. Unlike you, he had no boss to report to, no budget, and no deadlines (lucky Ogg), but the fundamental spirit of a project was there.

Over the years, project management has evolved as a discipline that involves sophisticated analysis, projections, tracking of time and money, and reporting. Project management software — which has, let's face it, been around only about a dozen years or so — has brought a new face and functionality to project management that would have left our friend Ogg ughless.

About This Book

Microsoft Project 2002, the most recent incarnation of the world's most popular project management software, offers a tremendous wealth of functionality to users. However, it's probably not like any other software you've ever used, so mastering it can seem like a daunting process. One trick is to understand how its features relate to what you do every day as a project manager. Another is to get someone like me to tell you all about its features and how to use them.

In *Microsoft Project 2002 For Dummies,* my goal is to help you explore all that Project offers, providing information on relevant project management concepts while also offering specific procedures to build and track your Project plans. But more importantly, I offer advice on how to make all these features and procedures mesh with what you already know as a project manager to make the transition easier.

Foolish Assumptions

I've made some assumptions about you, gentle reader. I figure that you are computer literate and know how to use a mouse, a keyboard, and software menus and toolbars. I assume you know how to use most common Windows functions such as the Clipboard and many basic software functions such as selecting text and dragging and dropping things with your mouse.

I do not assume that you've used Project or any other project management software before. If you're new to Project, you'll find what you need to get up to speed, including information on how Project works, finding your way around, and building your first Project plan. If you've used an earlier version of Project, you'll find out about Project 2002 and all the new features it provides.

Conventions Used in This Book

I should explain a few odds and ends to make using this book easier:

- ✔ All project and task names are *italicized* to make them easier to identify.
- ✔ Web site addresses, known as URLs, are highlighted like this: `www.microsoft.com`.
- ✔ Menu commands are given in the order in which you select them, for example, "Choose Tool⇨Resource Sharing⇨Share Resources."
- ✔ Options in dialog boxes use initial caps even if they aren't capitalized on your screen to make it easier to identify them in sentences. (For example, what appears as Show summary tasks in the Options dialog box will appear as Show Summary Tasks in this book.)

How This Book Is Organized

This book is designed to help you begin to use Microsoft Project 2002 to plan, build, and track progress on projects, keeping in mind tried-and-true project management practices and principles. I divided the book into logical parts that follow the process of building and tracking a typical project plan.

Part 1: Setting the Stage for Project

Part I explains what Project 2002 can do for you, and what types of input you have to provide to use it successfully on your projects. You'll get your first glimpse of Project views, and master ways to navigate around them. You'll begin to build Project plans by making calendar settings, building a task outline, and then enter timing and timing relationships for those tasks.

Part 11: People Who Need People

Part II is the Project resources section: You discover all you need to know about creating and assigning resources and material costs to tasks in a project. This is also the place to explore the features of Project that help you incorporate several smaller projects into a master project, and how to share resources among projects.

Part III: Well, It Looks Good on Paper

Up to now you've been mapping out your project plan. Now it's time to see whether that plan meets your needs in terms of budget and timing. Project offers a whole toolbox of tools that help you modify resource assignments and task timing to trim your costs and meet your deadlines so you can finalize your plan.

Part IV: Avoiding Disaster: Staying on Track

As any experienced project manager knows, projects just about never happen the way you thought they would. In this part, you find save a picture of your plan called a baseline and then begin to track actual activity against your plan. You'll also take a look at methods of reporting your progress, and how to get back on track when you find yourself derailed. In the final chapter, I provide advice on how to use what you learn in your projects to make better planning choices going forward.

Part V: The Part of Tens

Ten seems to be a handy number for humans to put lists into, so in this part you'll get two such lists: Ten Golden Rules of Project Management, and Ten Project Management Software Products to Explore. The first tells you about some of the do's and don'ts that will save you a lot of grief when using Project for the first time (or the fifth time, for that matter). The second offers some ideas of add-on products and complementary software products that bring even more functionality to Microsoft Project.

Part VI: Appendixes

I've provided two handy appendixes. They're not essential to using Project, but they offer information that may help you as you put it to work.

Appendix A provides an overview of Project Server, a companion product to Project from Microsoft that makes online collaboration on projects possible. Appendix B suggests useful Web sites for anyone involved in project management.

Glossary

Earned value? Budgeted cost of work performed? Work breakdown structure? I'm not here to sell you a bill of goods: The Glossary has a lot of terms, some from the discipline of project management and some Project-specific. Definitions of key terms are included throughout this book, but when you need a refresher course, look here.

What You're Not to Read

First, you don't have to read this book from front to back (but it's not in Japanese, so don't read it from back to front). If you want to just get information about a certain topic, you can open this book to any chapter and get the information you need.

That said, I have structured the book to move from some basic concepts you need to understand how Project works through the steps involved in building a typical project. So, if you need to find out the whole shebang, you can start at the beginning and work your way through to build your first Project plan.

Icons Used in This Book

One picture is worth . . . well, you know. So, *For Dummies* books use icons to give you a visual clue as to what's going on. Essentially, icons call your attention to bits of special information that might make your life easier. Following are the icons used in this book.

This icon directs you to lots of information and even additional tools you can use with Project.

Remember icons signal either a pertinent fact that relates to what you're reading at the time but is also mentioned elsewhere in the book, or a reiteration of a particularly important piece of information that's — well — worth repeating.

Tips are the Ann Landers of computer books: They offer sage advice, a bit more information about a topic under discussion that might be of interest, or ways to do things a bit more efficiently.

Warning icons spell trouble with a capital T: When you see a Warning, read it, because it's trying to tell you that if you're not careful you might do something at this point that could cause disaster.

Where to Go from Here

Time to take what you've learned in the project management school of hard knocks and jump into the world of Microsoft Project 2002. When you do, you'll be rewarded with a wealth of tools and information that help you to manage your projects much more efficiently.

Here's where you step out of the world of cave-dweller project management and into the brave, new world of Microsoft Project 2002.

Part I
Setting the Stage for Project

The 5th Wave   By Rich Tennant

"Can't I just give you riches or something?"

In this part . . .

1 know you: Someone handed you Microsoft Project and now you have to figure out how to use it. Is this a glorified spreadsheet program or a word processor with to-do lists? Neither. Project is probably like no other software you've ever encountered.

In this part of the book, you meet Project and find out what you two have in common. You find about exactly what Project can do to make your projects more efficient. You take a walk around the software and see what it looks like. In Chapter 3, you start to appreciate how Project determines the timing of tasks with calendars, and then you build a project task by task. You see how Project's outlining feature brings order to chaos and how dependency relationships among the tasks in your project help to build a timing logic into your entire project.

Chapter 1

Project Management: What Is It, and Why Should I Care?

· ·

In This Chapter

▶ Discovering how traditional project management makes the move to software

▶ Understanding what elements of a project are managed in Project

▶ Exploring the role of the Internet in project management

▶ Getting started using New Project Wizard

· ·

*W*elcome to the world of computerized project management with Microsoft Project. If you've never used project management software before, you're entering a brave, new world. It will be like walking from an office of twenty years ago — with no fax, voicemail, or e-mail — into the office of today with its wealth of high-tech devices.

Everything you used to do with handwritten to-do lists and word processors and spreadsheets all come magically together in Project. But this transition won't come in a moment, and it will take some basic understanding of exactly what project management software can do to get up to speed. If you've used Project before, this little overview will help you refresh your memory, and ease you into many of the new features of Project 2002.

So, even if you're a seasoned project manager, take a minute to review this chapter — it provides the foundation for how you'll work with Project from here on.

The ABC's of Project Management

Project management is simply the process of managing all the elements of a project, whether it's large or small. Do you need to organize a company holiday party? It's a project. Have you been handed a three-year earth exploration initiative to find oil in Iowa, coordinating subcontractors and government permits and working with a team of 300 people? That's definitely a project.

Understanding what projects, whether large or small, have in common is the basis of understanding what Project can do for you. All projects have

- ✔ An overall goal
- ✔ A project manager
- ✔ Individual tasks to be performed
- ✔ Timing for those tasks to be completed (such as three hours, three days, or three months)
- ✔ Timing relationships between those tasks (for example, you can't begin using a new manufacturing process until you've trained people in the process)
- ✔ Resources (people, equipment, facilities, supplies, and so on) to do the work
- ✔ A budget (the associated costs of people, equipment, facilities, supplies, and so on)

The three T's: Tasks, timing, and dependencies (well, two)

When you understand the goal of your project, you can begin to build the *tasks* needed to get there. A task is pretty much one of those items on your handwritten to-do lists, such as *Write Final Report* or *Apply for Permits.* Tasks are typically organized into *phases* in Project in an outline-like structure, as you can see in the project shown in Figure 1-1.

Task master

A task can be as broad or as detailed as you like. For example, you can create a single task to research your competition, or you can create a project phase that consists of a *summary task* and *subtasks* below it. The summary task might be *Competitive Research* and the subtasks might include *Researching online business databases, Assembling company annual reports,* and *Reviewing competitive product lines.*

A project can have as many tasks and as many phases as you like. You simply use the outlining structure in Project to indent various levels of tasks. The more deeply indented in an outline a task is, the more detailed. One handy thing about this outlining structure is that all the timing and cost data from subtasks within phases is rolled up into summary-level tasks. That means you can view your project at various levels of detail and get automatic tallies of timing and costs if you prefer to simply view the summary-level of tasks.

You'll learn more about how to go about defining and creating tasks in Chapter 4.

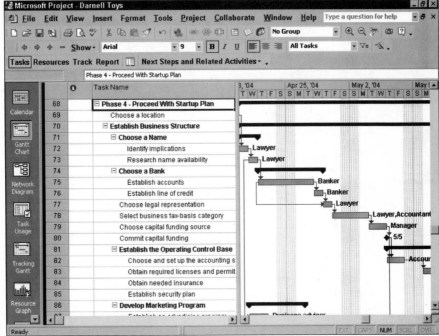

Figure 1-1:
This is the
Gantt Chart
view, the
view you'll
spend the
most time in
when in
Project.

It's all in the timing

They say timing is everything, and that's true with Project tasks, as well. Almost all tasks have timing referred to as duration. A task's *duration* is the amount of time it will take to complete the task.

The only task without a duration is a milestone. A *milestone* is a task of zero duration; in essence it simply marks a moment in time that must be reflected in your Project outline. Typical milestones are the approval of a design or an assembly line startup.

Project doesn't provide magic formulas for duration: Duration is assigned based on your own experience and judgment. Does designing a product package take three days or three weeks? Will obtaining a building permit happen in a day or a month? (Remember, you're dealing with City Hall, so think before you answer!)Project isn't an oracle: You have to provide facts, figures, and educated guesses to build your Project schedule.

Task codependencies

The final piece in the puzzle of how long your project will take is something called dependencies. *Dependencies* are the timing relationships among tasks. If you have a schedule that includes ten tasks that all begin at the same moment in time, your entire project would take as long as the longest task (see Figure 1-2).

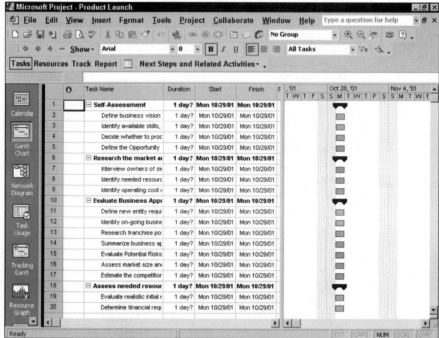

Figure 1-2:
This
schedule
includes
tasks with
timing
but no
depen-
dencies.

After you implement timing relationships, your schedule can stretch out over time like a long rubber band. One task might begin only after another is finished. Another task can start halfway through the preceding task. The second task can only start a week after the first task is over. Only after you've started to assign these relationships can you can begin to see a project's timing related not just to each task's duration but also to the relationship of tasks to each other.

Here are some examples of dependencies:

- You can't begin to use a new piece of equipment until you install it.
- You must wait a week after pouring a concrete foundation so that it can dry before you can begin to build on it.
- You can't start to ship a new drug product until the FDA has approved it.

One other brief note about the timing of tasks: In addition to applying dependencies to tasks, you can apply *constraints*. For example, let's say you don't want to start shipping your new ice-cream flavor until you get the ad for it in your Christmas catalog. So you set a dependency between those two events. But you can also set a constraint that says you must start producing the ice cream no later than November 3. In this case, if you don't make the catalog deadline, the product will still ship on November 3; that task will not be allowed to slip its constraint because of a dependency relationship.

You can find out more about dependencies and constraints in Chapter 6.

Lining up your resources

When people first use Project, some get a bit confused about the topic of resources. Resources aren't just people. A resource could be a piece of equipment you rent or a meeting room you have to pay an hourly fee to use.

There are two kinds of resources: work resources and material resources. *Work resources* are charged by how many hours or days the resource works on a task. *Material resources,* such as supplies or steel, are charged by a per-use cost or by the unit, such as square yard or linear foot or ton.

Some resources, such as people, perform work based on a working calendar. If a person works an 8-hour day, and you assign them to a task that will take 24 hours to complete, that person would have to work three days to complete the task. Someone with a 12-hour day would take only two days. In addition, you can set working and nonworking days for resources, which accommodates variations such as four-day weeks or shift work.

You can set different rates for resources, such as a standard hourly rate and an overtime rate. Project applies the appropriate rate based on each resource's calendar and work assigned.

Several views in Project let you see information about resources and how their assignment to tasks has an impact on project costs. Figure 1-3 is the Resource sheet, which shows columns of information about resources and their costs.

One other important thing you should know about resources: They tend to have conflicts. No, I'm not talking about conference room brawls. These conflicts have to do with assigned resources that become overallocated, based on their available work time. If you assign one poor soul to three tasks that must all happen on the same day, Project has features that do everything but turn on an alarm to warn you of the conflict. Luckily, Project also provides tools that help you resolve those conflicts.

You can also assign *fixed* costs to a task. For example, if your company charges a flat $2000 for a new product package design, no matter how many resources work on it, you could enter a fixed cost of $2000 for the task of package design. For more about resources and costs, see Chapter 7.

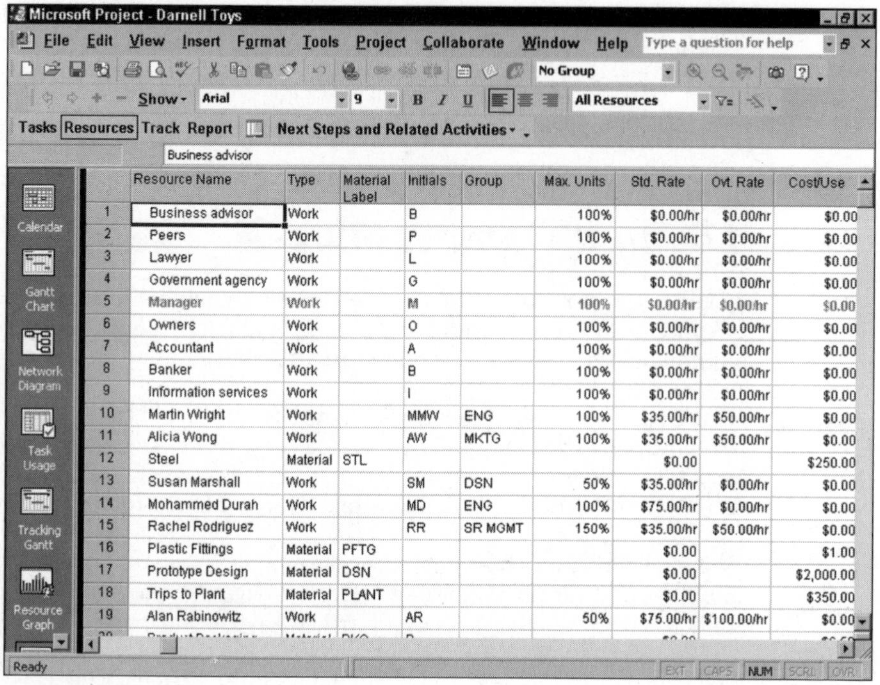

Figure 1-3:
Resources
charged at
a rate per
hour are
the basis of
how Project
tallies costs.

Spreading the news

Up to now, I've been telling you about the type of information you have to put into Project: information about tasks, task dependencies, and resources. But isn't it about time you got something back from Project?

Well, you've finally reached one of the big payoffs for inputting all that information: reporting. After you've entered your information, Project offers a wealth of reporting options to help you view your project and communicate your progress to your project team, clients, and management.

You can generate predesigned reports based on information in your schedule or simply print any of the views that you can display in Project. Figures 1-4 and 1-5 show you just two of the reporting options available in Project.

Planning to keep things on track

Projects aren't frozen in amber like some organizational mosquito: They go through more changes than a politician in a campaign year. That's where Project's capability to make changes to your project data comes in handy.

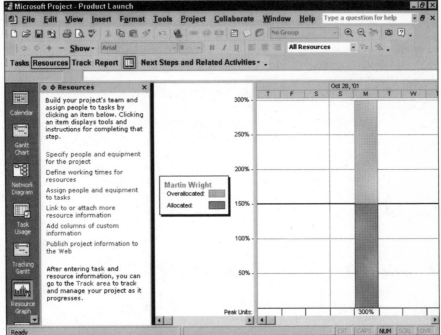

Figure 1-4: Study resource usage with the graphic Resource Graph view.

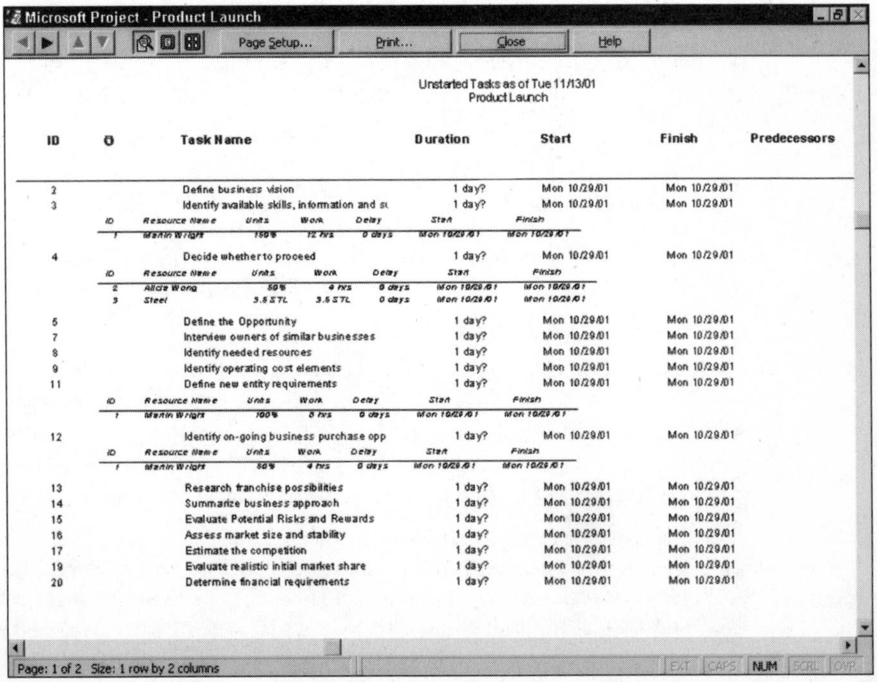

Figure 1-5: The Unstarted Tasks report.

After you've built all your tasks, given them durations and dependencies, and assigned all your resources and costs, you set a baseline. A *baseline* is like a snapshot of your project at the moment when you feel it's ready to go. After you set a baseline, you need to record some activity on your tasks. Then you can compare that actual activity to your baseline.

Tracking activity on your project involves recording the actual timing of tasks and recording the time that resources have put in on those tasks as well as any actual costs you've accrued. You can then display Project views that show you how far off you are at any point in time in terms of timing and costs.

Whether you have good news or bad, you can use reports to show your boss how things are going compared to how you thought they would go. Then, after you peel your boss off the ceiling, you can use a lot more Project tools to make adjustments to get everything back on track.

From To-Do List to Hard Drive

By now you're probably shaking your head and saying, "Boy, handwritten to-do lists look pretty good right now. Beats creating hundreds of tasks, assigning them durations, establishing dependencies among them, creating resources, entering resource calendar and rate information, assigning resources and costs to tasks, entering activity performed on tasks . . ." and so on.

Well, you're right and you're wrong. You do have to enter a lot into Project to get the benefit of its features. However, you can also get a lot out of Project.

Getting up to speed with Project

Take a moment to review some of the wonderful things Project can do for you. This is why you (or your company) bought it and why you're investing the time to read this book.

With Project, you'll enjoy the following benefits:

✔ Project automatically calculates costs and timing for you based on your input. You can quickly recalculate what-if scenarios to solve resource conflicts, get your costs within budget, or meet your final deadline.

✔ Project offers views and reports that make a wealth of information available to you and those you report to with the click of a button. No more running up a report on total costs to-date to meet a last-minute request from your boss. If she wants to know total costs to-date, you can just print your Tracking Gantt view with the Tracking table displayed.

✔ You can use built-in templates to get a head start on your project. Templates are prebuilt plans for typical business projects such as commercial construction, engineering projects, a new product rollout, software development, and an office move.

✔ It's likely that you do similar types of projects all the time. After you create one project, use it as a template for future projects.

✔ You can create resources based on information you've already created in your Outlook address book. You can even create one set of company resources, and give every project manager in the company access to them.

✔ A number of tools in Project employ complex algorithms (that you couldn't even begin to figure out) to do things such as leveling resource assignments to solve resource conflicts, filtering tasks by various criteria, modeling what-if scenarios, and calculating the value of work performed to-date in dollars.

Here's where the Internet comes in

You can also take advantage of all the Internet has to offer by using Project features to collaborate with others. Project allows you to request updates on a task's progress from team members by using e-mail and even publish your project on the Web.

Project offers a companion product called Project Server that enhances workgroup collaboration. If you used Project 2000, you knew Project Server as a built-in feature called Project Central. Now these features have hooks into Project, but you have to buy a separate package. If you do, you can take advantage of an online project center with areas for discussions, tracking progress, exchanging data, and more. Appendix A gives you an overview of this add-on product and its capabilities.

Getting Started

As Shakespeare said, "In delay there lies no plenty." I don't know about you, but I need all the plenty I can get, so it's time to jump in and start using Project.

You have a few choices here. You can use a template to create a project or build one from scratch. In either case, you need to start by telling Project something about your project.

First, enter some project information

When you open a new Project, a Project Information dialog box appears, as shown in Figure 1-6. This is where you enter some basic information about your project.

Figure 1-6:
The Project
Information
dialog box
is used for
some basic
project
settings.

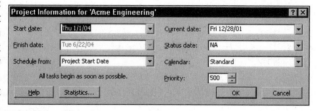

If you want to access this dialog box after you've opened Project, choose Project➪Project Information.

Here's what you can do in this dialog box:

✔ **Set the start date for the project.** If you're not sure when it will start, set the start date about a month or so ahead. Then, when you've built some tasks and have a better handle on the entire length of your project, you can come back here and set a new start date. Project will automatically recalculate all dates when you do.

✔ **Schedule from the start or finish of the project.** Most projects go from the start forward. However, if you have an absolute drop-dead date for the end of your project (for example, if you're organizing an event that will occur on New Year's Day next year), you might want to set the finish date and then work backwards to fit all your tasks in the time allotted. If you change this setting to Project Finish Date, the Finish Date box becomes available.

✔ **Set the current date.** The current date is filled in based on your computer calendar, but you can choose another date if you like.

✔ **Set a status date.** You use a status date when you're tracking. If you set a status date, your computer assumes that any tracking you enter is being tracked as of this date. You can find out more about this in the chapters that deal with tracking (see Chapters 12, 13, and 14).

✔ **Set the working calendar for your project.** You have three choices: Standard, Night Shift, and 24 hour. Your choice should be based on the working habits of your organization. For example, if your company uses resources in three shifts a day, for a total of 24 hours of straight working time, and all those shifts would put in work on your project, choose 24 hour. If you use a day shift and a night shift, choose Standard. Most projects, however, use a standard calendar; this is your typical 8-hour workday.

Calendars can get a little confusing. A project calendar that you set in this dialog box indicates what the usual working day is like in your company, but you can also set up individual calendars for each resource you create. This helps you accommodate both shift workers and nine-to-fivers in the same schedule. See Chapter 3 for more about resource calendars.

✔ **Assign a priority to your project.** This can be useful if you're using the same resources across several projects, for example. With priorities set on all projects, Project tools can automatically reallocate resources based on those priorities.

If you click the Statistics button in this dialog box, you get an overview of your project, as shown in Figure 1-7.

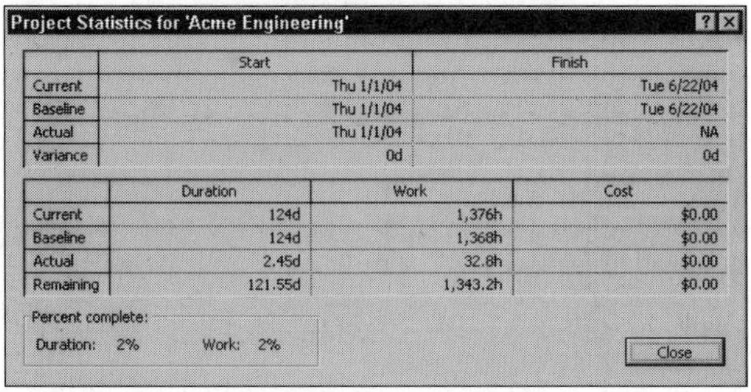

Figure 1-7:
You can review a summary of the information you entered.

Project Statistics for 'Acme Engineering'				? X
	Start		Finish	
Current		Thu 1/1/04		Tue 6/22/04
Baseline		Thu 1/1/04		Tue 6/22/04
Actual		Thu 1/1/04		NA
Variance		0d		0d

	Duration	Work	Cost
Current	124d	1,376h	$0.00
Baseline	124d	1,368h	$0.00
Actual	2.45d	32.8h	$0.00
Remaining	121.55d	1,343.2h	$0.00

Percent complete:
Duration: 2%   Work: 2%

Close

Starting from scratch

When you make settings in the Project Information dialog box and click OK, you are faced with a blank Project schedule, as shown in Figure 1-8. As a writer, I can tell you that nothing is as daunting or inspiring as facing a blank page. This is the canvas on which you'll create your Project plan.

Timescale

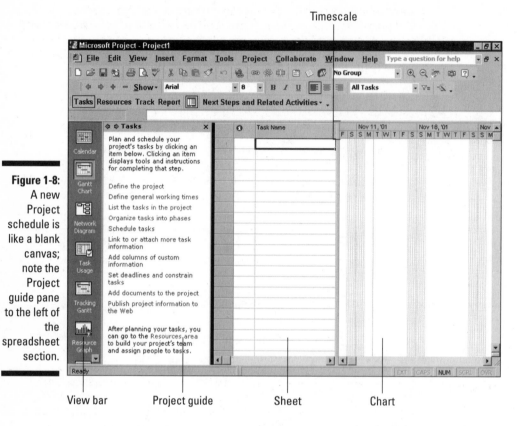

Figure 1-8:
A new
Project
schedule is
like a blank
canvas;
note the
Project
guide pane
to the left of
the
spreadsheet
section.

View bar   Project guide   Sheet   Chart

What you're presented with is the Gantt Chart view. You can discover more about various views in Chapter 2. For now, note the following:

✔ The bar of icons along the left, called the *View bar,* allows you to click and go to different views.

✔ To the right of that is the *Project guide,* an informational area with step-by-step guidance on how to build your project.

✔ In the middle of the view is the *sheet* section. This is a spreadsheet interface that you can use to enter, edit, and view information about your project.

✔ Finally, the *chart* area reflects your task information graphically after you begin to add tasks. *Taskbars* in this area indicate the duration and timing of tasks, as well as progress you record on them. The indications of time increments across the top of the chart area, called the *timescale,* helps you interpret the timing of each taskbar and can be adjusted to show your project in larger or smaller increments of time.

You start building a project by entering tasks. Simply click a cell in the Task Name column and then type the name. You can enter and edit details of a task by double-clicking the task name in the sheet to access the Task Information dialog box (see Figure 1-9) or by entering information directly into various columns, which you can display in many views.

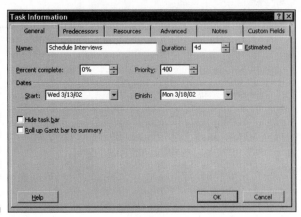

Figure 1-9:
The various tabs in this dialog box hold a wealth of information about a single task in your project.

Using templates

Reinventing the wheel has never been one of my favorite sports, so I'm grateful that Microsoft has provided some convenient project templates. These include projects by type, for example an engineering project or an office move. Templates already have many tasks appropriate to the task type created for you.

After opening a template be sure to check its Project Information (choose Project➪Project Information) to make sure that the Start Date and Calendar options are set as you want.

Figure 1-10 shows the Engineering template. Templates typically contain sample tasks broken into logical phases, with task durations and dependencies in place. The templates from Microsoft often include resources, but you can create your own resources as well as use, edit, or delete the ones provided.

You can open a template from the New Project task pane. To do so, follow these steps:

1. **Choose File➪New.**

   The New Project task pane appears, as shown in Figure 1-11.

2. **Click General Templates.**

   You can also use Templates on My Web Sites or Templates on Microsoft.com to access online templates.

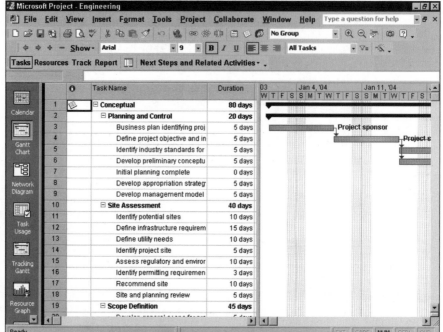

Figure 1-10:
Templates
provide a
great head
start in
building
common
business
projects.

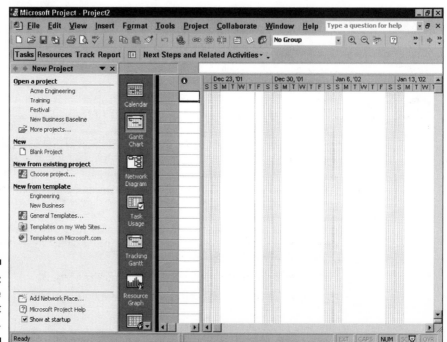

Figure 1-11:
Here's the
New Project
task pane.

3. **Click the Project Templates tab, which is shown in Figure 1-12.**

4. **Click a template to display a preview.**

5. **When you find the template you want to use, click OK.**

    The template opens in Project document format (.MPP). You can then delete tasks, move them around, or add tasks as necessary for your project.

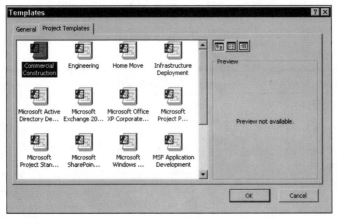

Figure 1-12:
Business and personal templates, such as the Home Move, are included here.

If you modify a template and think that you might use that set of tasks again for future projects, consider saving the file as a custom template before you begin to add specific project details. Just choose File➪Save As, and then select Template in the Save As Type list.

Saving a project for posterity

Saving Project files works just as saving does in most other software you've used. Here's a reminder.

To save a Project file that you haven't saved before, follow these steps:

1. **Choose File➪Save As.**

2. **Use the Save In list to locate the folder where you want to save the file, and then click to select it.**

3. **In the File name text box, type a name for the project.**

4. **Click Save.**

It's a good idea to create a folder for your project where you save not only your Project file but also supporting documents, e-mails, and so on for your project. You can create a new folder from the Save As dialog box by clicking the Create New Folder button.

Getting help from Project

If you can get to work without mishap and turn a computer on, you probably know how to use a help system in software, too. But Table 1-1 offers a rundown of the type of help you'll find in Project 2002.

Table 1-1	Project Help Features
Help Option	*How to Use It*
Microsoft Project Help	Depending on whether you've activated the Office Assistant, this option displays the Assistant or opens the full Help feature with contents, Answer Wizard, and topics listed in an index, along with the What's New listing of Project features.
Show the Office Assistant	Displays the annoying little icon that asks you to enter your question in a natural-language style (that is, a sentence) and offers topics to try to address your questions.
Contents and Index	Displays the same thing as Microsoft Project Help. Go figure.
Reference	Provides reference information such as a comprehensive list of all fields in Project, a glossary, and a table of mouse and keyboard shortcuts.
Getting Started	A side menu for this Help menu option offers a tutorial and project map. The tutorial provides a set of topics explaining Project from the basics of what is project management through creating a plan. The project map is another take on the phases involved in building your project.
What's This?	Click this tool and then click any on-screen element and get a quick definition or description of the item and its function. (This is my favorite help option.)

Help Option	How to Use It
Microsoft Project on the Web	Takes you to Microsoft's Web site on the Project home page.
Office on the Web	Because Project is part of the Office family of products, this link is provided to the Office online Assistance Center.
Detect and Repair	Automatically identifies errors and tries to correct them. Use this if you have serious problems using the software (for example, if the software constantly shuts down and gives you error messages).
Project Guide	The one option not accessed from the Help menu, Project Guide is new in 2002. Project Guide appears when you open a new project. It offers links to step-by-step information on how to build your project.

As you can see, it could take you a year just to learn all the help options in Project. Don't worry — they're there when you need them, and some, such as the Project Guide, even pop up automatically to offer help.

Chapter 2

The Best Laid Plans

*H*omer (not Simpson — the other one) once said, "The evil plan is most harmful to the planner." In the interests of helping you get some good out of your Project plan, it's worth taking a moment to get comfortable with various aspects of it.

The file you create in Project is called a Project plan, or schedule. This plan is like a multidimensional chess game from Star Trek, with a plethora of data about various aspects of your project as well as graphic representations of that information.

To see that information, Project provides more views than the Grand Canyon. These views help you observe the structure of your plan and see the progress in your project. Project also offers many ways to move around and display different information in your views. Navigating Project and displaying and modifying views are the topics you explore in this chapter.

Navigating Around Project

Having a lot of views from which to observe your project information is great, but all those views won't do you any good if you don't know how to get from one to the other, or how to move around a view after you've found it.

Changing views

You can move from one view to another in Project using the view bar or the View menu. The view bar is along the left side of every view. Simply click any view icon there to display that view.

In addition to the eight commonly used views displayed on the view bar are a few dozen other views that you'll need to use as you work through your project. To display views not shown on the view bar, follow these steps:

1. **Click the arrow at the bottom of the view bar to scroll down to the bottom.**

2. **Click the More Views icon.**

   The More Views dialog box appears, as shown in Figure 2-1.

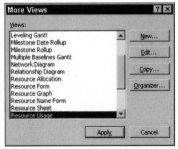

Figure 2-1: Dozens of views are available for display in Project.

3. **Use the scrollbar to locate the view you want.**

4. **Click Apply.**

You can access the More Views dialog box also by choosing View⊄More Views to. In addition, eight of the most commonly used views are available as selections on the View menu.

Scrolling around

The simplest views, such as the Calendar view, have a single pane, with horizontal and vertical scrollbars. Other views, such as the Resource Usage view (see Figure 2-2), have two panes. In that case, each pane has its own horizontal scrollbar but shares the vertical scrollbar, so the panes move up and down at once.

By using the horizontal scrollbars in each pane, you can view additional columns or additional periods of time in any pane with a timescale. Timescale panes cover the life of the project; in longer projects you may be able to scroll through years of time.

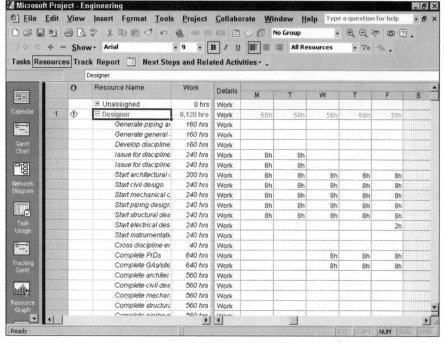

Figure 2-2:
Multiple
panes of
information
maximize
space in
many views.

Use these different methods to work with scrollbars:

✔ **Click the scroll box and drag it until you reach the location in the pane that you want to look at.** When you click and drag the scroll box to move through a timescale display, the date display indicates where you are at any time in your scrolling calendar. Release the mouse button when the date matches the one you want to view.

✔ **Click to the left or right of the horizontal scroll box to move one page at a time.** Note that a *page* in this instance is controlled to some extent by how you have resized a given pane. For example, with a timescale pane and a timescale set to weeks, you move a week at a time. In a sheet pane displaying three columns, you move to the next (or previous) three columns.

✔ **Click the right or left arrow at either end of a scrollbar to move in smaller increments.** With a sheet pane, you move about a half column per click. In a timescale view with weeks displayed, you move about a day at a time.

Go to!

To reach a particular area of your Project plan, you can also use the Go To command on the Edit menu or the Go To Selected Task tool to scroll the timescale to show the taskbar for a selected task. Using the Go To command, you can enter two things in the Go To dialog box to find a task. You can select a date from a calendar, or you can enter a task ID. The task ID is assigned automatically when you create tasks; this number reflects the sequential order of tasks in the plan.

A Project with a View

Views are one way that software designers organize information so that you can get at it in logical ways. Because of the complexity of information in a typical Project plan, many views are available to examine it. If you think of your average word-processed document as being about as complex as a cookie, your average Project plan is a five-tier wedding cake adorned with intricate flowers and garlands in delicate gobs of sugary icing.

In a typical Project plan, you have information about the following:

- ✔ **Resources.** The resource name, type of resource, rate per hour, overtime rate, assignments, department, and cost per use, and more.

- ✔ **Tasks.** The task name, duration, start date, finish date, assigned resources, costs, constraints, dependencies, and so on.

- ✔ **Project timing and progress.** Several types of calendars, project start and finish dates, percent of tasks completed, resource hours spent, baseline information, and critical path information, and more.

- ✔ **Financial information.** Earned value, time and cost variance, projected costs for uncompleted work, and so on.

You can see that finding out how to use the many Project views to enter, edit, look at, and analyze Project data is important. Don't worry that you'll be overwhelmed: After a while, using all those views is . . . well, a piece of cake.

Home base: Gantt Chart view

Gantt Chart view is like a favorite room in your house, the place most people gravitate to. It's the place that appears first when you open a new project. This view, shown in Figure 2-3, is a combination of spreadsheet data and a graphical representation of tasks; it offers a wealth of information in one place.

Taskbar

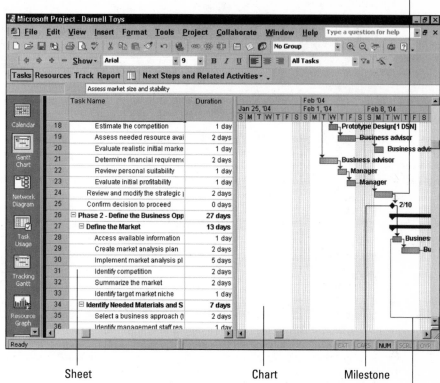

Figure 2-3:
Gantt Chart
view can
display any
combination
of columns
of data that
you want.

Sheet   Chart   Milestone

Dependency link line

Gantt Chart view has two major sections. The area to the left is called the *sheet,*
which is a spreadsheet-like interface with columns of information. To the right
of this view is the *chart.* The chart uses bars, symbols, and lines to represent
each task in your project and the dependency relationships between them.

At the top of the chart area is the *timescale.* This tool is used as a scale
against which you can interpret the timing of the *taskbars.* To see your plan
in greater or lesser timing detail, you can modify the time units used in the
timescale. For example, you can look at your tasks in detail over days or in a
broader overview in months.

Go with the flow: Network Diagram view

Another view that you're likely to use often is the Network Diagram view,
which is shown in Figure 2-4. The organization of information represents the
workflow in your project, with a series of task boxes. The boxes include

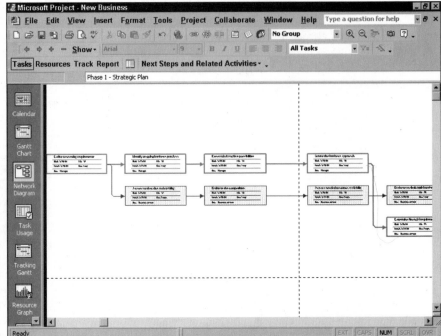

Figure 2-4:
Network
Diagram
view puts
important
task
information
in task
boxes.

dependency lines running among them to reflect their timing relationships. You read this view from left to right, with the earlier tasks on the left flowing into later tasks and subtasks to the right.

Traditionally called a PERT chart, this method of diagramming workflow was developed by the Navy in the 1950s for use in building Polaris submarines.

Network Diagram view has no timescale because the view is used not to see specific timing but to see the general order of tasks in a plan. However, each task box does include specific timing information about each task, such as the start, finish, and duration. You can customize the information in the task boxes, as described later in the "When It Comes to What You See, You're In Charge" section.

Call up Calendar view

Who can think of time without conjuring up a calendar? This familiar view of time is one of the many views offered in Project. The Calendar view, shown in Figure 2-5, shows tasks as boxes that fall across the blocks that represent days in a calendar.

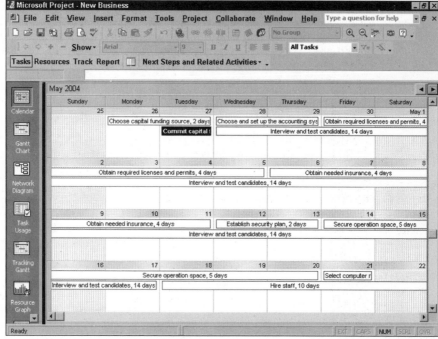

Figure 2-5:
The familiar calendar interface shows you how one task can straddle several days or even weeks.

You can modify Calendar view to display from one to six weeks (or more using a Custom setting in the Zoom dialog box) on the screen at a time. Calendar view also includes a timescale that you can modify to show a seven-day or five-day week and shading to indicate working and nonworking days based on a selected base or resource calendar.

Dozens of views are built into Project. You'll encounter many more as you work through specific elements of Project in this book.

When It Comes to What You See, You're in Charge

Just when you thought you were starting to get a handle on the two dozen or so views available in Project, I'm going to dazzle you with even more possibilities: Every one of those views can be customized to show different information. Now the possible view variations become astronomical.

You can customize every view in Project to show different information; for example you can choose to show different columns of information in spreadsheets, different labels in Network Diagram boxes or taskbars, or different sets of data in graph views. You can modify the size of panes of information, and adjust the timescale.

Why all this flexibility with what you see on screen? At various times in a project, you'll need to focus on different things. Having a problem with costs? Take a look at the Resource Usage view and insert several columns of cost information, such as resource rates and total actual costs. Is your plan taking longer than the Hundred Years' War? You might want to display the Tracking Gantt and look at a bunch of columns with timing and dependency data or examine the project's critical path in the chart pane. Need to display more of the sheet area so that you can read those columns without having to scroll? In this section, you find out how to do all the things you need to do to show a variety of information in each view.

It's a pane

In views that show more than one pane, such as Gantt Chart view with its sheet pane and chart pane, you can reduce or enlarge each pane. This helps you see more information in one area, depending on what your focus is at the time.

Follow these steps to change the size of a pane in a view:

1. **Place your mouse cursor over the edge of a pane.**

2. **When you get a cursor that's a line with two arrows, one pointing left and one pointing right, click and drag to the left or right.**

   Dragging to the left enlarges the pane on the right; dragging to the right enlarges the pane on the left.

3. **Release the mouse button.**

   The panes are resized.

Note that if you display the Project Guide or another task pane such as New Project or Search, Project automatically resizes your panes again to accommodate that pane.

Changing time

I wish I could tell you that Project actually lets you change time and give your project lots more of it, but it doesn't. What it does allow you to do is modify the timescale to display your plan in larger or smaller increments of time.

A timescale consists of a possible total of three tiers, as you can see in Figure 2-6. You can use these to display different increments of time. For example, the top tier could mark off months, the middle tier, weeks, and the bottom tier, days. You can use all three or any combination of these tiers.

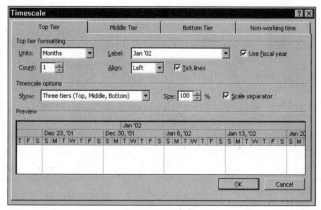

Figure 2-6: The timescale is made up of three tiers so you can view time from several directions.

You can modify the units of time, the style of the label, and the alignment of each tier, and include tick lines to mark the beginning of each increment on the timescale. You also have the option of including or not including nonworking time on the timescale. For example, if you include an indication of nonworking time on a project where weekends are nonworking, Saturdays and Sundays will include a shaded area in the display.

To modify the timescale, follow these steps:

1. **Right-click the timescale in any view that contains one and then click Timescale.**

   The Timescale dialog box shown in Figure 2-6 appears.

2. **Click a tier tab and select a style for Units, Label, and Align.**

3. **Set the Count.**

   For example, if your Units choice is weeks and you change Count to 2, the timescale appears in two-week increments.

4. **If you don't want to display this tier, click the Hide Tier option.**

5. **If you want Project to use fiscal year notation in the timescale, click the Use Fiscal Year option.**

   For example, if your 2003 fiscal year begins July 1, 2002, 2003 is used on all months in the fiscal year.

6. **To show marks at the beginning of each unit of time, click the Tick Lines option.**

7. **Repeat Steps 2 through 6 for each tier you want to modify.**

8. **Click the Non-working time tab.**

9. **In the Draw options, select the one you prefer.**

   Your choices are to have the shaded area for nonworking time appear behind taskbars, appear in front of them, or not appear at all.

10. **In the Color or Pattern list, select different options for the shading format.**

11. **Click the Calendar setting and select a different calendar to base the timescale on.**

   You can find out more about calendar choices in Chapter 3.

12. **Click OK to save your new settings.**

You can use the Size setting on the three tier tabs to shrink the display proportionately to get more information on your screen or the printed page

Displaying different columns

Each spreadsheet view has certain default columns of data that are stored in tables. The Gantt Chart view with the Tracking table displayed, for example, has data related to the progress of tasks. The Resource sheet contains many columns of data about resources that can be useful for entering new resource information. In addition to displaying tables of columns, you can modify any spreadsheet table to display any columns you like.

Follow this procedure to show columns of data:

1. **Right-click the column heading area and then click Insert Column.**

   The Column Definition dialog box appears, as shown in Figure 2-7.

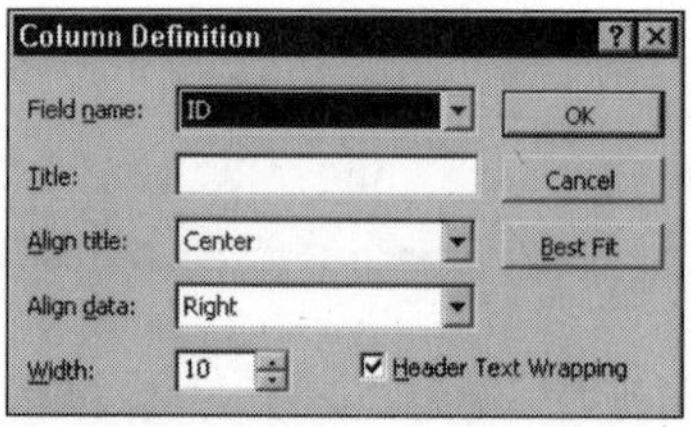

Figure 2-7:
You can select new columns to insert and modify the column alignment and width.

Column Definition	? X
Field name: ID	OK
Title:	Cancel
Align title: Center	Best Fit
Align data: Right	
Width: 10	☑ Header Text Wrapping

2. **In the Field Name list, select the field that contains the information you want to include.**

3. **If you want to enter a different title for the field, type it in the Title box.**

   The title appears in the column heading for this field in this view.

4. **Use the Align Title, Align Data, and Width options to modify the column format.**

5. **Click OK to insert the column.**

To hide a column, right-click its heading and then click Hide Column.

Note that you can also display certain preset tables of sheet data, such as tracking or entering new task information. You do this by simply choosing View⇨Table, and then clicking the table that you want to display.

Modifying the contents of the network diagram box

When you first display the Network Diagram view, you see rectangular boxes, one for each task in your project. You can change the information contained in those boxes.

By default, a typical subtask contains the task name, task ID, start date, finish date, duration, and resource names. For a milestone, you get only the milestone date, milestone name, and task ID number.

Different categories of tasks, such as critical or noncritical, may contain different information, but you can change the information contained by individual box or by category of boxes.

To modify the information included in these boxes, do the following:

1. **Right-click anywhere in the Network Diagram view outside any box, and then click Box Styles.**

   The Box Styles dialog box appears, as shown in Figure 2-8.

2. **In the Style Settings For list, click a category of task.**

3. **To modify the data included in the task boxes, select a different template in the Data Template list.**

   You can choose additional templates and edit templates to include whatever data you like by clicking the More Templates button.

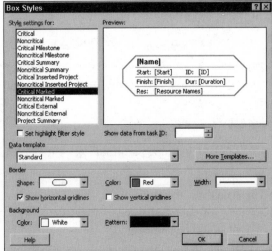

Figure 2-8:
You can use
templates
of data for
Network
Diagram
view task
boxes.

A preview of the data included in the template appears in the
Preview area.

4. Click OK to save the new template.

Chapter 3

Mark It on Your Calendar

Most people live their lives based on clocks and calendars. Think about it: You wake up and your first thoughts are what day is it, what time is it, what's for breakfast, and do you have to go to work that day.

You have a familiar definition for what your typical workday is, whether you're a 9-to-5 kind of person or your particular job calls for you to work from midnight to 8 a.m. You also vary from that routine now and then, putting in a 12-hour marathon in a crunch or slipping away after half a day to go fishing on a nice summer day.

Project calendars are sort of like your life, in that they set some standards for a typical working time and then allow for variation. But unlike you, Project has several types of calendars to account for.

Base, Project, Resource, and Task Calendars — Oh My!

Now bear with me, because I won't kid you: This can be tricky. But understanding how calendars work in Project is essential to mastering the software. Tasks are scheduled and resources are assigned based on the calendar settings you make. The costs accumulated by resource work hours will not be accurate if you haven't understood your calendar settings from the get-go.

How calendars work

When you create tasks and assign resources to work on them, Project has to base that work on some timing standard. So, for example, if you say a task is going to take one day, Project knows a day means 8 hours (or 12 hours, or whatever you set it to) because of the settings you make in calendars. Likewise, let's say you assign a resource to put in two weeks of work on a task in a company that has a standard five-day workweek. If that resource works a four-day week, the two weeks of work put in by that resource will total only eight days.

The nature of a task can have an impact on resource time. A two-week effort-driven task won't be complete until resources have put in two weeks (according to the Project or Task calendar) of effort. More about effort-driven tasks in Chapter 4.

Not everyone in a company works the same schedule, and not every task can be performed in the same eight-hour day. To deal with the variations in schedules that occur in most workforces, Project has three types of calendars: the Project calendar, Resource calendars, and Task calendars. The Project calendar sets the general working times for the project. Task and Resource calendars allow you to specify working and nonworking hours and days to, for example, block out a week of vacation as nonworking for a particular resource.

Project, Resource, and Task calendars can be set to use one of three base calendar templates built into Project. The three base calendars templates are

- ✓ **Standard.** The default. Sets a working day as 8 a.m. to 5 p.m. with an hour for lunch and a five-day, Monday-through-Friday workweek.
- ✓ **24 Hour.** Allows work to go on round the clock every day of the week.
- ✓ **Night Shift.** Sets the working time as 11 p.m. to 8 a.m. with an hour for dinner and a six-day, Monday-through-Saturday workweek. Working times for a Night Shift calendar are shown in Figure 3-1.

You can modify base calendar templates and make new templates based on them. See "Creating Calendar Templates" later in this chapter.

How one calendar relates to another

By default, all calendars in your project are controlled by the Project calendar setting. But here's the tricky part: When you change a Task or Resource calendar, you have to understand which setting takes precedence.

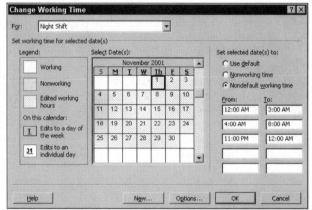

Figure 3-1:
The legend
explains
how
different
hours are
shaded in
the calendar
display.

Here's how it works:

✔ With no other settings made, the base calendar you select for the project when you first create it controls the working time and days of all tasks and resources.

✔ If you use a different base calendar or make changes in the working hours for a resource, those settings take precedence over the Project calendar for that resource when you assign it to a task. Likewise, if you assign a different base calendar for a task, it takes precedence over the Project calendar for that task.

✔ If you've applied a different calendar to a resource and a different calendar for a task that the resource is assigned to, Project uses only common hours to schedule the resource. So, if the Task calendar allows work from 8 a.m. to 5 p.m., and the Resource calendar allows work from 6 a.m. to 2 p.m., the resource will work from 8 a.m. to 2 p.m., the only hours the calendars have in common.

✔ You can set a task to ignore Resource calendar settings by opening the Task Information dialog box and clicking Scheduling Ignores Resource Calendars on the Advanced tab. This setting is not available if the Task Calendar is set to None. You might do this if you know all resources will be required to be involved in a task, such as a quarterly company meeting, regardless of their usual hours.

Calendar options and working times

Just when you thought you were out of the woods, I'm going to throw two more timing elements at you: calendar options and working times. Calendar options are used to change the standards for a working day, week, and year. So, if you set a Project calendar to Standard (by default 8 to 5, five days a week), the Calendar tab of the Options dialog box is where you could designate which five days are working days or modify the working hours to, for example, 9 to 6.

Working time is used to adjust the working time available on a particular date or days. For example, suppose that you make a change to the calendar options so that you have a 32-hour workweek but 8-hour days. You should also check your working time and be sure you've specified three days of the week that are nonworking to jive with the 32-hour week. If you want to set a certain date as nonworking for your project, such as your company offsite meeting day, you can do that with the working time settings.

Calendar options

When you make changes to a Resource or Task calendar, you're simply adjusting the times that a resource is available to work or the time during which a task will occur. You have not changed the standard workday for the project. A day will still be 8 hours long if that's the Project calendar setting, even if you say that a task that takes place on that day will use the 24-hour base calendar.

If you want to change the standard workday to, say, 10 hours instead of 8, you must do so in the Calendar tab of the Options dialog box.

Follow these steps to modify the calendar options:

1. **Choose Tools⇨Options.**

    The Options dialog box appears.

2. **Click the Calendar tab, which is shown in Figure 3-2.**

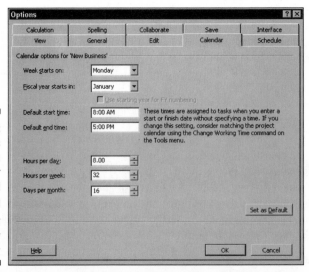

Figure 3-2: This is where you define your typical working day, week, month, and year.

3. **In Week Starts On, select a day from the list.**

4. **To modify the start of your fiscal year, select the month you want in the Fiscal Year Starts In box.**

5. **To change the working hours for a typical day, type new times in the Default Start Time and Default End Time boxes.**

6. **Modify the Hours Per Day, Hours Per Week, and Days Per Month boxes as needed.**

7. **Click OK to save the settings.**

If your company uses these settings for most projects, consider clicking the Set as Default button in the Calendar tab of the Options dialog box to make your settings the default for any new project you create.

Working times

If you want to change the available working hours for a particular day (such as December 24th), you use the working time settings. For example, if you want the day before Christmas to be a half day, you can modify the working time settings for that day; then any resources assigned to a task on this date will put in only a half day of work. You use these settings also to specify global working and nonworking days to match the calendar options settings.

Do this to change working times:

1. **Choose Tools⇨Change Working Time.**

   The Change Working Time dialog box appears, as shown in Figure 3-3.

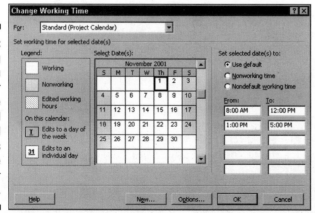

Figure 3-3: The working times you set for your project here should correspond to settings in the calendar options.

2. **In the Select Date(s) section, click the day you want to change.**

   For example, if you want to specify that Friday should be a nonworking day, click the column heading above Friday (labeled *F*) in the calendar to select all Fridays in the project.

3. **Change the From and To times to whatever schedule you like.**

   If you want to set nonconsecutive hours (for example, to build in a lunch break), you have to put two or more sets of numbers here.

4. **If you want to block off a date or a day of the week as nonworking, click the Nonworking Time option.**

5. **Click OK to save your changes.**

Setting the Project Calendar

The first calendar setting you'll encounter is the Project calendar. You set the Project calendar in the Project Information dialog box (see Figure 3-4), which appears when you first start a new project. You can display the dialog box at any time by choosing Project⇨Project Information

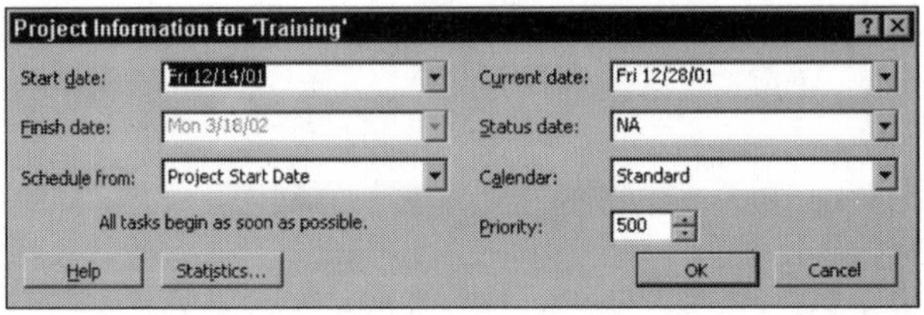

Figure 3-4:
The choice of calendars offered here includes one of three base calendar templates.

Project Information for 'Training'		? ☒
Start date:	Fri 12/14/01 ▼	Current date:	Fri 12/28/01 ▼
Finish date:	Mon 3/18/02 ▼	Status date:	NA ▼
Schedule from:	Project Start Date ▼	Calendar:	Standard ▼
	All tasks begin as soon as possible.	Priority:	500
Help	Statistics...		OK	Cancel

The Project Guide offers a useful Calendar Wizard that can help you make calendar settings when you're new to Project. If it's not already visible, display Project Guide at any time as follows. Choose View⇨Toolbars⇨Project Guide. Then click the Resources button, and then click the Define Working Times for Resources item listed in the Project Guide.

The Calendar setting offers the three base calendar templates: Standard, Night Shift, and 24 Hour. Remember, this is the typical working time for your company; if a few resources on your project will work the night shift but by and large your resources work a standard workday, choose the most commonly used calendar here. You can make changes to specific Resource and Task calendars later.

Modifying Task Calendars

Tasks can be set to use a different calendar template than the Project calendar. Doing so takes precedence over the Project calendar for that task. For example, suppose that you select a Standard calendar for a project and a 24 Hour calendar for a task. If you then specify that the task will have a duration of one day, it will be one 24-hour day.

To set a Task calendar, follow these steps:

1. **Double-click the task name.**

   The Task Information dialog box appears, as shown in Figure 3-5.

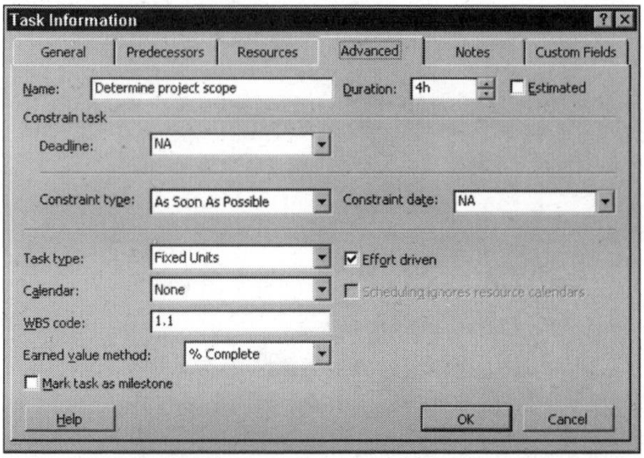

Figure 3-5:
You can apply any calendar template to tasks in your project.

Task Information	? X
General Predecessors Resources **Advanced** Notes Custom Fields	

Name: Determine project scope   Duration: 4h   ☐ Estimated

Constrain task
Deadline: NA

Constraint type: As Soon As Possible   Constraint date: NA

Task type: Fixed Units   ☑ Effort driven
Calendar: None   ☐ Scheduling ignores resource calendars
WBS code: 1.1
Earned value method: % Complete
☐ Mark task as milestone

Help   OK   Cancel

2. **Click the Advanced tab.**

3. **In the Calendar box, select a different base calendar.**

4. **Click OK to save your new calendar setting.**

If a resource assigned to this task has a modified calendar, that resource will work only during the hours that the Task calendar and Resource calendar have in common.

Making Resource Calendar Settings

Even the most resourceful resources have only so many hours in a day to work. When you have to deal with variations in resource schedules, consider modifying the Resource calendars.

Each resource in your project — with the exception of material resources charged not by the time they put in but by the number of units used — can have its own calendar. You can change the base calendar for the resource and set specific dates as working or nonworking.

One word of caution about modifying Resource calendars: Unless a resource truly has a unique working schedule, don't change its calendar. For example, if a resource is working a night shift for a few days during the life of the project but usually works a day shift, don't change its base calendar to night shift. If one person works 10 to 7 because the company allows him to, it's probably not necessary to vary his schedule from the typical 8-to-5 work schedule set in the Project calendar, because he puts in eight hours a day like everyone else. Unless your project deals with the most detailed level of time, where hours and not days are the typical units of measure for tasks, making these types of changes is more work than it's worth.

To modify a resource's calendar settings, follow these steps:

1. **Display a view that includes a resource column, such as the Resource sheet.**

2. **Double-click a resource name.**

   The Resource Information dialog box appears.

3. **Click the Working Time tab, which is shown in Figure 3-6.**

Figure 3-6:
This tab has identical settings to the Change Working Time dialog box, but changes made here affect this resource only.

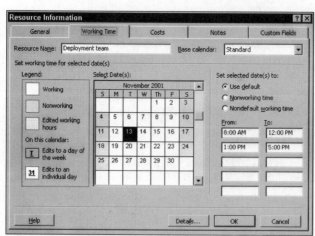

4. **In the Base Calendar box, select a different base calendar: Standard, 24 Hour, or Night Shift.**

5. **In the Select Date(s) calendar, click a date and then click a Set Selected Date(s) To option.**

   You can select several dates or a day column instead of a single date by clicking and dragging.

6. **To change the hours that a resource works, enter new hours in the From and To boxes.**

7. **Click OK to save your settings.**

Can resources work overtime even if their calendar says they're 9-to-5ers? Yes, but you have to tell Project to schedule overtime work. You can also set a different rate to be charged for overtime work for that resource. To find out more about overtime, see Chapter 8.

Creating Calendar Templates

If you've ever wanted to make your own time, here's your chance. Although the base calendar templates probably cover most working situations, you might want to create your own calendar template. For example, if your project involves a telemarketing initiative and most project resources work six hours from 4 p.m. to 10 p.m. (that's when they all call me!), it might be useful to create a new calendar template called Telemarketing.

If you want to save some time (and time is what this is all about), start with an existing calendar template that is closest to your needs. Then modify it as you like, making changes to the working times and calendar options to make sure they're in agreement. (Use the Change Working Time dialog box and the Calendar tab of the Options dialog box.) After you create a new calendar template, it is available for you to apply in all three calendars: Project, Task, and Resource.

Remember, the Project calendar is the basis of your entire project and, as such, should represent the most common working schedule in your project. If only some resources in your project work odd hours, change the Resource calendars, not the Project calendar.

Follow these steps to create a new calendar template:

1. **Choose Tools⇨Change Working Time.**

   The Change Working Time dialog box appears.

2. **Click the New button.**

   The Create New Base Calendar dialog box appears, as shown in Figure 3-7.

Figure 3-7:
Enter
a name
here, even
if you're
basing the
calendar on
an existing
template.

3. **In the Name box, type a name for the new calendar.**

4. **Either click the Create New Base Calendar option or click the Make a Copy Of option and select an existing calendar from the list.**

5. **Click OK to return to the Change Working Time dialog box.**

   Now you'll make changes to the working time for the new calendar template.

6. **Click Options.**

   The Options dialog box appears with the Calendar tab displayed.

7. **Make changes to the start of the week or year, the start and end times for a workday, and the hour or day settings.**

8. **Click OK twice to save the new calendar settings.**

Sharing Copies of Calendars

You can make a calendar available for all projects in two ways. You can set a calendar as the default for all new projects by making that choice in the Change Working Time dialog box. Or you can make calendars from one project available for use in another project. The latter method is especially useful when you want to share calendars with other project managers in your company but don't want to change your own default calendar.

To copy a calendar from one project to another, follow this procedure:

1. **Open the project to which you want to copy a calendar.**

2. **Choose Tools⇨Organizer.**

   The Organizer dialog box appears.

3. **Click the Calendars tab, which is shown in Figure 3-8.**

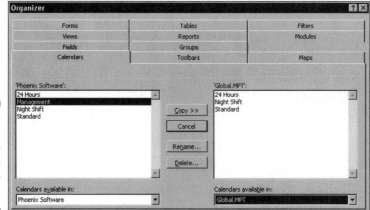

Figure 3-8:
You can
copy your
calendar
to other
projects.

4. **In the Calendars Available In box on the left side, select the Project file that contains the calendar you want to copy.**

5. **In the list on the left, click the calendar you want to copy, and then click the Copy button.**

   The calendar is copied to the current project.

6. **If you'd like to give the calendar a different name, click the Rename button, type a new name in the Rename dialog box, and then click OK.**

7. **Close the Organizer by clicking the close button (the X) in the upper-right corner.**

A few pointers about copying calendars from project to project. First, make sure the name you give the calendar is descriptive so that you can remember its general parameters. Second, if your company has standard calendars, try having one resource create and disseminate them. If ten versions of a management calendar are floating around and you grab the wrong one, it could cause problems. Another way to avoid this is to put the project manager's initials in each calendar template name you create so you know it's the one you created.

Chapter 4

A Tisket, a Task Kit

*T*asks form the to-do list of your project. They incorporate the what, when, who, and where information of your plan. Resources work on a project by getting assigned to tasks. The timing of tasks and the relationships between them form the timing for your project. By tracking the progress on tasks, you can see your project advance over time.

Tasks can be created in a few different ways. You can create them by typing information in the sheet area of the Gantt Chart view (or any other view that displays information in columns) or by using a task information form. You can also import tasks from other programs such as Excel and Outlook.

You'll have to make some choices when you create tasks. You need to consider settings for a task that control its timing, its priority, and certain constraints regarding how it may or may not shift around during the life of your project.

In this chapter, you find out all about tasks and the various settings that give each task its own unique personality.

Your First Task

The first step in creating a task is to identify the individual action items in your project. Then you can create each of those steps as individual tasks in Project.

After you create some tasks, you'll begin to build some structure to your list, creating phases consisting of summary tasks with subtasks below them in an outline structure. For example, you might have a summary task named Obtain Permits with two subtasks, Submit Applications and Pay Fees. You can find out how to organize tasks into outlines in Chapter 5. Here, the focus is on making the settings required to create a task.

What tasks are made up of

Determining all the settings that make up a task's characteristics is a bit more complicated than writing an item on a to-do list. To create a task, you enter not only a task name but also information such as a duration for the task, the task type, constraints for scheduling the task, and the task priority. Some things, such as task priority or task type, can often be left at default settings. Others, such as duration, require some input from you.

Pretty much everything in this list except the task name involves how the task timing is controlled. Several of these settings work in combination, with Project performing complex algorithms to set the timing of the task according to the value of each setting. Other elements, such as the deadline, don't determine timing but rather cause Project to display a symbol in the Indicator column to alert you to a timing issue.

You can also specify a unique task calendar in the Task Information dialog box; calendars are covered in Chapter 3.

Let there be tasks

On the simplest level, you can create a task by entering a name for it. You can fill in the details of duration, task type, and so on at the same time or later.

You can enter task names in a Gantt Chart view sheet pane, in a Task Information dialog box, or by importing them from Excel or Outlook.

Putting tasks in a column

For long projects, many people find that entering all task names in the sheet pane of the Gantt Chart view is the quickest and easiest way to go. You can simply enter one task name in the Task Name column, press the down arrow on your keyboard to move to the next blank row and enter another task, and so on.

Follow these simple steps to enter a task in the Gantt Chart view:

1. **In the Task Name column, click a blank cell.**

2. **Type a task name.**

   You can edit what you type by clicking in the entry box above the sheet and typing or using the Delete or Backspace key to clear characters (see Figure 4-1).

3. **Press the down arrow on your keyboard to move to the next cell in the column and type the next task name.**

4. **Repeat Step 3 until you've entered all task names.**

You can also display whatever columns you like in the Gantt Chart view to enter additional task information, such as duration, task type, start dates, and finish dates. To display additional columns, simply right-click any column heading, click Insert Column, and select the column to display from the Field Name list.

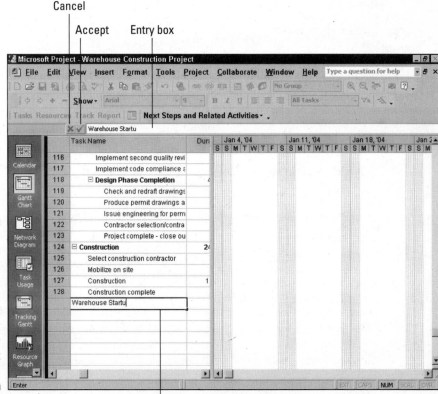

Figure 4-1:
Use the
X and
checkmark
buttons to
the left of
the entry
field to clear
or accept
your entry.

Naming your tasks in a dialog box

If you're a dialog box kind of person, consider using the Task Information dialog box to enter task information. The series of tabs in the Task Information dialog box contain all the information there is to know about a task.

Use these steps to create your task with the dialog box:

1. **In the Task Name column, double-click a blank cell.**

   The Task Information dialog box appears, as shown in Figure 4-2.

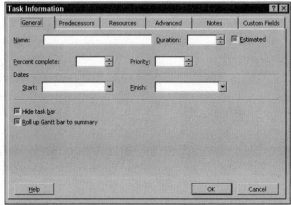

Figure 4-2:
The General and Advanced tabs of this dialog box contain various timing settings for the task.

2. **In the Name field, type a task name.**
3. **Click OK to save the new task.**

   The task name now appears in the Gantt Chart view.

4. **Press the down arrow key to move to the next cell.**
5. **Repeat Steps 1 through 4 to add the next task.**

As you name tasks, note that it can be useful to try to keep task names in a project both descriptive and unique. However, if you can't make all the names unique (for example, you have three tasks called Hire Staff), you can use the automatically assigned task number or the WBS code to identify tasks; these numbers are always unique for each task.

Getting your tasks from Outlook

Like rabbits breeding, it seems that what starts as a series of simple to-do tasks in Outlook often becomes a full-fledged project with hundreds of tasks. When that happens, you'll be glad to know that Microsoft has provided an easy-to-use import feature to take the tasks you created in Outlook and put them into Project.

Although Project has an import-mapping feature that allows you to map fields in a file created in another application to fields in Project to import data, it can be a tedious process. The Import Outlook Tasks feature is essentially an import map that's preset to work with Outlook task fields.

Follow these steps to import Outlook tasks into Project:

1. **Open the plan you want to insert tasks into, or open a new project (choose File⇨New).**

2. **Choose Tools⇨Import Outlook Tasks.**

   The Import Outlook Tasks dialog box appears, as shown in Figure 4-3.

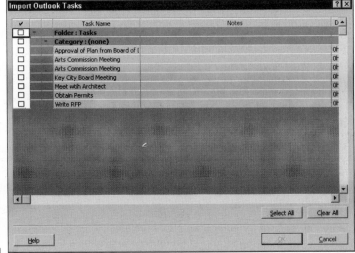

Figure 4-3:
Task name, notes, and duration entered in Outlook all come along for the ride.

3. **Click the options for the tasks you want to import, or click Select All to import all Outlook tasks.**

4. **Click OK.**

   The tasks are imported and appear at the end of your list of tasks.

By default, Outlook keeps tasks in a Tasks folder. Clicking the check box for the Folder: Tasks item is another way to select all tasks in Outlook.

When you import tasks from Outlook, the task name, duration, and any task notes are brought over. If a task in Outlook has no duration, Project creates the task with an estimated one-day time frame.

Importing an Excel task list

I am a firm believer that you should make things easy on yourself. If you like to noodle around with your task list for a project in Excel, you shouldn't have to retype everything into Project to build a Project plan. For that reason, Microsoft has provided an Excel Task List template. This template, located in the Microsoft Office template folder, can be opened from Excel.

The template provides four Excel worksheets, as shown in Figure 4-4, in which you can enter tasks, resources, and resource assignments, and then export that data from Excel to Project.

Follow these steps to use this template:

1. **In Excel, open the template, called Microsoft Project Plan Import Explore Template.**

2. **Fill in information about Tasks, Resources, and Assignments on the appropriate tab, and then save the file.**

3. **Open Project and choose File➪Open.**

   The Open dialog box appears.

4. **Locate the Excel Project Template file you just saved and then click Open.**

   The Import Wizard appears.

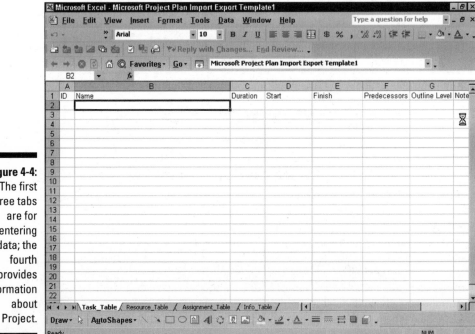

Figure 4-4:
The first three tabs are for entering data; the fourth provides information about Project.

5. **Click Next to begin the wizard.**

6. **Choose the second option, Project Excel Template, for the format of the data you're importing. Then click Next.**

7. **On the next Wizard screen, choose the method for importing the file.**

   You can import the file As a New Project, to Append the Data to the Active Project, or to Merge the Data into the Active Project. If you choose the third option, you have to create a merge key that delineates how the data should merge with existing tasks.

8. **Click Finish.**

   The project appears with whatever tasks, resources, and assignment information you entered in a project plan format.

Linking to tasks that live somewhere else

You can insert hyperlinks in a project outline; doing so allows you to quickly open the other project by clicking the hyperlink. The link text is placed in the Indicator column.

Inserting a hyperlink creates a task that you can use to represent the timing or costs of another project or subproject in your plan. However, you'll have to enter timing and cost information yourself — it doesn't get brought over from the hyperlinked project.

To insert a hyperlink to another Project file in your project, follow these steps:

1. **Click to select the blank task name cell where you'd like the hyperlinked task to appear.**

2. **Choose Insert⇨Hyperlink.**

   The Insert Hyperlink dialog box appears, as shown in Figure 4-5.

Figure 4-5: You can link to a document, an e-mail address, or a Web page.

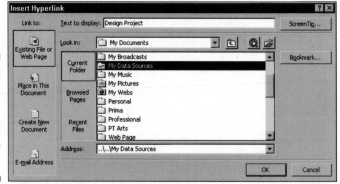

3. **In the Text to Display box, type a name for the hyperlinked file.**

   Make sure this text explains to readers of your plan what information is being summarized.

4. **In the Link To area, click the Existing File or Web Page option.**

5. **In the Look In list, locate and click the file to which you want to insert a hyperlink.**

6. **Click OK.**

   The link text is inserted and a hyperlink symbol appears in the indicator field. You can simply click that link symbol to open the other file.

Inserting one project into another

You can also insert an entire subproject into a Project file. This is a useful method when various project team members manage different phases of a larger project. The capability to assemble subprojects in one place allows you to create a master schedule from which you can view the entire project.

Follow these steps to insert another Project file into your plan:

1. **In the Gantt Chart view, click the task in your task list above which you want the other project to be inserted.**

2. **Choose Insert⇨Project.**

   The Insert Project dialog box appears, as shown in Figure 4-6.

3. **In the Look In list, locate the file that you want to insert and click it to select it.**

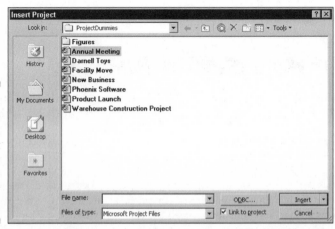

Figure 4-6:
You can insert a link to a project so that any changes appear in both.

4. **If you want to link to the other file so that any updates to it are reflected in the copy of the project you're inserting, click the Link to Project option.**

5. **Click Insert to insert the file.**

   The inserted project appears above the task you had selected when you began the insert process.

Note that the inserted project's highest level task appears at the level of the task you had selected when you inserted the project, with all other tasks falling below it in outline order. If you need to, use the Indent and Outdent tools on the Formatting toolbar (arrows pointing to the left and right, respectively) to place the inserted tasks at the appropriate level in your project.

You're in It for the Duration

In projects, as in life, timing is everything. Timing in your projects starts with the durations you assign to tasks. Although Project helps you see the impact that timing of your tasks has on the overall length of your plan, it can't tell you how much time each task will take: That's up to you.

Estimating the duration of tasks isn't always easy; it has to be based on your experience with similar tasks and your knowledge of the specifics of your project.

If you often do projects with similar tasks, consider saving a copy of your schedule as a template that you can use in future, thereby saving yourself the effort of re-estimating durations every time you start a project. Find out about saving templates in Chapter 18.

There's more than one kind of task

Before you begin to enter task durations, you need to be aware of three task types. These types have an effect on how Project schedules the work of a task.

Essentially, your choice of type determines which element of the task will not vary when you make changes to the task:

- ✔ **Fixed Duration task.** A task that takes a set amount of time to complete, no matter how many resources you add to the mix. For example, a test on a substance that requires that you leave the test running for 24 hours has a fixed duration even if you add twenty scientists to oversee the test.

✔ **Fixed Units task.** The default task type. With this task type, when you assign resources to a task with a certain number of units (hours of work expressed as a percentage of their working day), their assignments won't change even if you change the duration of the task, even though the work amount for the task does change.

✔ **Fixed Work task.** The number of resource hours assigned to the task determines its length. If you set the duration of a Fixed Work task at, say, 40 hours, and assign two resources to work 20 hours each (simultaneously), the task will be completed in 20 hours. If you take away one of those resources, the single resource must put in 40 hours to complete the task.

Understanding how the choice of task type causes your task timing or resource assignments to fluctuate is an important part of creating an efficient project.

Follow these steps to set the task type:

1. **Double-click a task.**

   The Task Information dialog box appears.

2. **Click the Advanced tab, if necessary, to display it (see Figure 4-7).**

3. **In the Task Type list, click one of the three choices.**

4. **Click OK.**

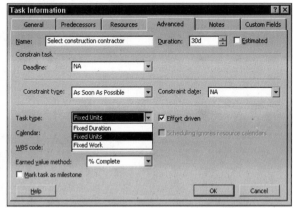

Figure 4-7:
The Task
Type list
has three
choices.

You can also display the Type column in a Gantt sheet and make this setting there.

Tasks that take time

Most tasks in a project have a duration, whether it's ten minutes or a year or something in between. Deciding how finely to break down your tasks can affect how efficiently you track progress on those tasks: Tasks that wander on for a year are usually too broad, and tasks that take ten minutes too narrow. But whatever your best guess at task duration, Project can accommodate you.

If your project is to run a one-day event, getting to the level of ten-minute tasks might make sense. In most projects, however, you will probably find that such finely detailed timing doesn't make sense because it defeats the point of all the tracking and reporting features of Project (unless you have people tracking their progress on a minute-by-minute basis!). On the flip side, creating a 12-month-long task suggests that you might be defining your project too broadly to track all that can happen in a year efficiently.

As with all task information, you can enter duration in the Task Information dialog box or in a Gantt Chart sheet. Follow these steps to enter a duration through the dialog box:

1. **Double-click a task to display the Task Information dialog box.**

2. **If necessary, click the General tab to display it.**

3. **In the Duration box, use the spinner arrows to increase or decrease the duration.**

4. **If the current duration units aren't appropriate (for example, days when you want hours), type a new duration in the Duration box.**

   You can use the following abbreviations for various units of time: *m* for minutes, *h* for hours, *d* for days, *w* for weeks, and *mo* for months.

   Note that changing the start and finish dates of a task does not change the duration.

5. **Click OK to accept the duration setting.**

If you are not sure about the timing of a particular task and want to alert people to your lack of certainty, click the Estimated check box (in the General tab) when you enter the duration.

Milestones

I mentioned in the preceding section that almost all tasks have durations; the exception is a milestone. Milestones are tasks with no duration (they're the ones I like to be assigned to most). In fact, they are less of a task than the marking of a moment in time. Examples of milestones are the approval of a prototype (though the deliberations to make that decision may have taken months) or the completion of a phase of tests.

Some people include tasks such as *Design Complete* or *Testing Complete* at the end of each phase of their project. They can then create timing relationships to the moment of completion, for example, allowing production of a drug to proceed after the testing is over. Such milestones also alert you and your team members to a moment of progress in your project that can help to keep the team motivated.

Note that new tasks are created with an estimated duration of one day, unless you enter a duration. To create a milestone, you indicate that the task has a zero duration. The quickest way to do that is to simply type 0 in the Duration column of the Gantt Chart view or to click the Advanced tab and click the Mark Task As Milestone check box. When you do, the milestone is designated in the Gantt Chart with a black diamond shape rather than a task bar.

Like a bad penny: Recurring tasks

Some tasks occur again and again in projects. For example, attending a monthly project debriefing or generating a quarterly project report is considered a recurring task.

No one wants to create a task for the monthly debriefing in a project that will take a year to complete. Instead, you can designate the recurrence, and Project creates the twelve tasks for you.

Here's how you create a recurring task:

1. **Choose Insert⇨Recurring Task.**

   The Recurring Task Information dialog box appears, as shown in Figure 4-8.

2. **In the Task Name box, type a name for the task.**

Figure 4-8: By completing this information, Project creates multiple occurrences of a task automatically.

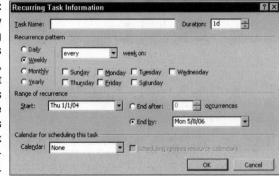

3. **In the Duration box, click the up or down arrows to set a duration, or type a duration, such as** 10d **for 10 days.**

4. **Select a recurrence pattern by clicking the Daily, Weekly, Monthly, or Yearly option.**

   What you select here provides different options for the rest of the recurrence pattern.

5. **Depending on the selections offered to you, make choices for the rest of the pattern.**

   For example, if you selected the Weekly option, you must choose a Week On setting, such as Every Other Week on Wednesday, or Every 5th Week on a Friday. Or if you selected Monthly, you must set which day of every month the task will recur.

6. **In the Range of Recurrence area, type a Start date. Then click and fill in either the End After or End By option.**

   For example, you might start on January 1 and end after 12 occurrences to create a task that occurs every month for a year.

7. **Click OK to save the recurring task.**

If your choice causes a task to fall on a nonworking day (for example, if you choose to meet on the 8th day of every month and the 8th is a Sunday in one of those months), a dialog box appears asking you how to handle this. You can choose not to create the task, or you can let Project adjust the day to the next working day in that time period.

To assign resources to a recurring task, you can use the resource column in the Gantt Chart view. (The Recurring Task Information dialog box doesn't have a Resources tab.)

Getting Started

When most people start using Project, one of the first things they try to do is enter a start date for every task in the project. After all, you always include due dates when you write up a to-do list. So why not, right? Wrong. In fact, one of the great strengths of project management software is its capability to schedule tasks for you based on a sometimes complex combinations of factors such as dependencies between tasks and task constraints. By allowing Project to determine the start date of a task, you take full advantage of its capabilities.

If you enter a task duration and don't enter a start date for the task, by default that task starts as soon as possible after the project start date you set in the Project Information dialog box, based on any dependencies you have set up between tasks.

Typically, if you want to change a task's start date, you look for something in the project that would dictate a different start date; for example, if you don't want construction to begin until you've obtained permits, link the permits task to the construction task in such a way that construction can't start before the end of the permit task.

Certain tasks, however, must start on a specific date. Examples include a holiday, an annual meeting, or the start of the fishing season.

Project sets the finish date of a task based on when it starts. But once again, if a task must finish on a certain date, you can set a finish date and let Project determine the start date.

Entering the Task Start date

Setting a start date or a finish date for a task applies a kind of constraint on it that may override dependency relationships or other timing factors. Task constraints, discussed in the "Constraints You Can Live With" section later in this chapter, are the preferred way to force a task to start or end on a certain day. But if you've determined that a particular task must begin or end on a set date, no matter what, you can enter a specific start or finish date — and setting the start or finish date is simple.

To enter a start or finish date for a task, simply follow these steps:

1. **Double-click a task.**

   The Task Information dialog box appears.

2. **Click the General tab if it's not already displayed.**

3. **Click the Start or Finish box.**

   A calendar appears.

4. **Click a date to select it, or use the forward or backward arrow to move to a different month and select a date.**

5. **Click OK.**

Note that setting a start date is not quite as strong a factor in how Project determines timing as applying the Must Start On constraint. You can find out more about how constraints work in the "Constraints You Can Live With" section.

Take a break: Splitting tasks

Sometimes you have tasks that start but then have to be put on hold before they can start again later — for example, a work shutdown due to labor negotiations. In that case, you can use a Project feature to split a task so that a second or third portion starts at a later date, with no activity in between. You can place as many splits in a task as you like.

Use these steps to split a task:

1. **Click the Split Task button on the Standard toolbar.**

   A box appears, as shown in Figure 4-9.

2. **Click the task at the date where you want to split the task, and then drag until the box contains the date where you want the task to begin again.**

3. **Release the mouse button.**

   The task is split.

You can rejoin a split task by placing your mouse over the taskbar until the move cursor appears, and then clicking the split taskbar and dragging it back to join with the other portion of the taskbar.

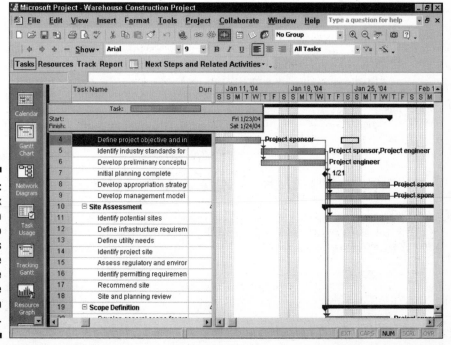

Figure 4-9: This box provides a readout to guide you as you set the start date for the continuation of the task.

Don't use the split task approach to put an artificial hold on a task until some other task is complete. For example, suppose that you start testing a product but then have to wait for final approval before finalizing the test results. In that case, you should create a testing task, a final approval milestone, and a finalize test results task and create dependency relationships among them. That way, if one task runs late, your final task will shift along with it, rather than being set in stone as a split task can be.

It's Such an Effort: Effort-Driven Tasks

When you hear the word *effort* in Project you can think *work*. When you create a task, by default it is effort-driven, which means that if you adjust resource assignments, the duration might change but the number of hours of effort (work) you need to put in to complete the task stays the same. When you add or delete a resource assignment on an effort-driven task, work is spread around equally among resources.

So, here's how an effort-driven task works. Let's say you have a two-day task to set up a computer network in a new office. With one resource assigned to it, working 8 hours a day, it will take 16 hours to complete (two 8-hour days). If you assign a second resource, the task will no longer take two days because the hours of effort required will be completed more quickly by the two people working simultaneously.

Effort Driven is a simple check box choice on the Advanced tab of the Task Information dialog box (see Figure 4-7). Click this check box to activate or clear the Effort driven selection. What happens when you clear this setting? Well, the same task that you set to run two days will take two days no matter how much effort resources put in. In other words, adding resources will not cause the task to be completed sooner. An example of a task that would not be effort driven is attending a daylong seminar. No matter how many people attend or how many people present, the seminar takes one day to complete.

Constraints You Can Live With

A constraint is something you're forced to live with, such as dandruff or noisy neighbors. You have to live with constraints in Project as well, but Project *constraints* consist of a timing condition that controls a task.

How constraints work

When you create a task, the As Soon As Possible constraint is selected by default. In other words, the task starts as soon as the project starts, assuming there are no dependency relationships with other tasks that would delay its starting.

Task start and finish dates work with dependencies, the task type, the effort-driven setting, and constraints to set the timing of each task. However, in performing calculations to try to save you time in a project that's running late, constraints are the most sacred timing setting for Project. For example, if you set a constraint that a task Must Finish On a certain date, Project will shift around almost any other task in a schedule in recalculating timing before it suggests that that task might finish on another date. Because of this, use constraints only when there is an absolute need to force a task's timing.

Table 4-1 lists all the constraints and an explanation of their effects on your task's timing.

Table 4-1	Task Constraints
Constraint	*Effect*
As Soon As Possible	The default setting; the task starts as early in the schedule as possible based on dependencies and the project start date.
As Late As Possible	The task occurs as late as possible in your schedule, based on dependencies and the project finish date.
Finish No Earlier Than	The end of the task will not occur any earlier than the date you specify.
Finish No Later Than	The end of the task will not occur any later than the date you specify.
Must Finish On	Sets an absolute date for when the task will finish.
Must Start On	Sets an absolute date for when the task must start.
Start No Earlier Than	The task will not start any earlier than the date you specify.
Start No Later Than	The task will not start any later than the date you specify.

Establishing constraints

You can set only one constraint for a task. Setting a constraint involves selecting the type of constraint you want in the Task Information dialog box. Some constraints work together with a date you choose. For example, if you want a task to Start No Later Than, you need to select a date by which a task must start. Other settings such as As Soon As Possible work off a different date — in this case, the start date you set for the whole project.

To set a task constraint, follow these steps:

1. **Double-click a task.**

   The Task Information dialog box appears.

2. **Click the Advanced tab.**

3. **In the Constraint Type list, click a constraint to select it.**

4. **If the constraint requires a date, select one in the Constraint Date list.**

5. **Click OK to save the settings.**

Setting a deadline

I don't know about you, but sometimes I think deadlines were made to be overlooked. Project agrees, because strictly speaking, deadlines aren't constraints (although you'll find the setting for the deadline in the Constrain Task area of the Task Information dialog box's Advanced tab). Deadlines aren't constraints because they don't force the timing of your tasks in any sense. If you set a deadline, it simply causes Project to display a symbol in the Indicator column, alerting you that the deadline has passed so that you can panic (I mean take action) appropriately.

To set at deadline, follow these steps:

1. **Double-click a task.**

   The Task Information dialog box appears.

2. **Click the Advanced Tab.**

3. **In the Deadline list, click a date.**

   If necessary, use the forward or backward arrow to move to a different month.

4. **Click OK to save the deadline setting.**

Taking a Task Note

In spite of the wealth of information that you can enter about a task and its timing, not everything can be said with settings. That's why every task includes an area to enter notes. You might use this feature, for example, to enter some background information about changes in timing or other changes that occur during the schedule or to list vendor contact information relevant to the task.

To enter task notes:

1. **Double-click a task.**

   The Task Information dialog box appears.

2. **Click the Notes tab (see Figure 4-10).**

Figure 4-10:
Enter
contact
information,
notes about
resources,
or other
useful
information
about
the task.

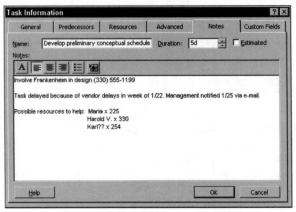

3. **In the Notes area, type any information you like.**

4. **Format the note.**

   Use the buttons at the top of the Notes area to change the font, to left align, center, or right align the text, or to format the text as a bulleted list.

5. **Click OK to save the settings.**

Saving Your Project

Now that you have some tasks in your project, don't lose 'em! Save your project on a regular basis.

You save a Project file using the same process you've used hundreds of times to save files in other software applications, with one exception: If you have not yet set a baseline when you save a Project file, every time you save it, Project asks you whether you want to save it with or without a baseline. You can find out more about baselines in Chapter 12, but to help you out with this decision, I'll give you a sneak preview.

A *baseline* is a saved version of your project plan against which you can track actual progress when the project gets going. It's like a photograph of your best-guess plan that's saved right along with the data you update as your project proceeds. You can save multiple baselines throughout the life of your project. If you haven't set a baseline and you save a Project file, a dialog box is displayed. If you don't want to save a baseline at that point, say no; otherwise, you can choose to save the baseline then and there.

To save a Project file, do this:

1. **Choose File⇨Save.**

   The Save As dialog box appears, as shown in Figure 4-11.

2. **In the Save In list, locate the folder in which you want to save the file.**

3. **In the File Name box, type a name.**

4. **Click Save.**

Figure 4-11:
If you've used other software products, you've probably seen this dialog box many times before.

If you want to save changes to a previously saved Project file using a different file name, choose File⇨Save As and provide a new file name in the Save As dialog box.

Chapter 5

Getting Your Outline in Line

In This Chapter

▶ Understanding the task/subtask structure

▶ Including a project summary task

▶ Promoting and demoting tasks

▶ Displaying and hiding outline levels

▶ Working with WBS codes

*C*ertain things bring order to the universe: clocks, stop signs, and outlines, to name just a few. Whereas clocks bring order to time and stop signs bring order to rush hour, outlines bring order to information by imposing a hierarchy on it. One idea, or topic, or category of information is broken down by an outline into smaller units with some logical sequence.

Project uses an outline structure to organize tasks in your project. The software also offers tools and functionality to help you build, reorganize, and view the outline structure. Learning how to create an outline is something you did back in Mrs. Plotkin's fourth-grade English class, but showing you how to use an outline to organize the many tasks in a project is my job. Welcome to outlining, 101.

Mamma and Papa Tasks and Little Baby Subtasks

If you take a look at a project outline such as the one in Figure 5-1, you'll see that it organizes tasks into levels; each level represents a phase of your project. A task that has other tasks indented below it in this outline structure is what's often referred to as a *parent*, or *summary, task*. The tasks indented below it are referred to as *child tasks*, or *subtasks*. Summary tasks are indicated in bold in your Project outline. You can tell when a summary task has a family of subtasks clinging to its skirts: When subtasks are hidden, the summary task displays a little plus sign symbol next to it. When you click the plus sign, the task expands to show its whole clan of subtasks.

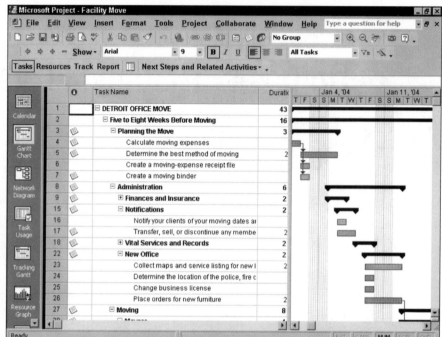

Figure 5-1:
A project
outline is a
collection
of subtasks
nested
within other
tasks.

You can build several of these little families of tasks, representing project phases in your outline. Think of a project outline as being like those little wooden nesting dolls, with each successive doll representing a deeper level of detail. The highest-level task is the outer doll, the biggest of the bunch. The next doll in the group is a little smaller, just as the next level of tasks in an outline reflects a little smaller level of detail, and so on, right down to the littlest baby doll. The largest task in a project might be Build New Plant, and the smallest detailed task might be Empty Dumpster, with a whole lot of tasks in between.

And here's an important concept you need to understand: All the information about a family of tasks (a phase of your project) is rolled up into its highest-level summary task. Therefore, any task with subtasks has no timing information of its own: It gets its total duration from the sum of its parts.

You *can* assign resources and costs to a summary task — for example, assigning a project manager for that phase of tasks. But that task will also include the total of the costs of any tasks below it.

This roll-up functionality is cumulative: The lowest level task rolls up to its parent, which may roll up into another summary task, which rolls up into a project summary task, for example. Any task with tasks below it gets is information from its subtasks, no matter how deeply nested it may be in the hierarchy.

How many levels can you go?

There's really no limit to the number of levels of tasks you can create in an outline (except perhaps how much memory you have in your computer to accommodate a monster schedule!). But remember, at some point, you have to deal with assigning timing and resources to each of these tasks and tracking their progress. Too much detail can make for a project plan that's difficult to update.

Also, if you find that you're building in three or four or five levels of detail throughout your plan,

consider the fact that you might really be building several projects at once. Too many levels suggests that a few of these project phases might be more manageable if you broke them off and made them projects on their own with their own project managers. Unless you want maintaining your Project plan to become a project itself, don't overdo the level of detail in your outline.

The structure of phases in an outline is also useful when you need to reorganize an outline: When you move a summary task, all its subtasks come right along for the ride!

The One-and-Only Project Summary Task

It's a good idea to create what I call a *project summary task;* this task represents the highest level of information, and is often simply the title of the project, such as New Product Rollout or Space Shuttle Launch. A project summary task is created when every task in the project falls under it in the outline, indented to become subordinate to it, as in Figure 5-2. Just as there is only one captain on a ship, there can only be one task that summarizes all other tasks in each project.

When you think about it, an upper-level headline in an outline is the sum of its parts: It reflects the umbrella concept for all the items below it. The project summary task takes this a step further; this task roll ups all the actual data from other tasks into one line item. So, the project summary task duration reflects the duration of the entire project. The project summary task total cost reflects the total of costs for the entire project.

Now, not everyone uses project summary tasks. At the highest level of your outline, you can simply create tasks that represent major project phases — with subphases and subtasks below them — and not create one task that is higher in the order than all others. But my advice is to always have a project summary task, for two reasons:

✔ You get the ability to quickly view totals for the project at a glance in the columns of data in the Gantt Chart view and other views.

✔ You can place a link to your summary task in another project, so that all the data for that project is reflected in the other project. For example, if you create five schedules for new product launches in your company, you can easily create a master schedule for all company product launches by linking to the summary tasks in each of the projects. Neat, huh?

You can simply create a summary task yourself as you build your project, or you can use a Project feature to generate one automatically at any time — even after you've built all the phases of your project. To do this, follow these steps:

1. **Choose Tools⇨Options.**

   The Options dialog box appears.

2. **Click the View tab to display it.**

3. **Click the Show Project Summary Task option.**

4. **Click OK to insert the upper-level task.**

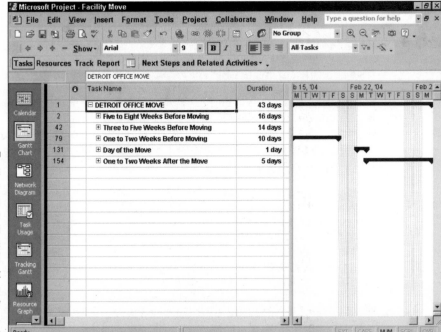

Figure 5-2:
The highest-level task in the outline with all tasks indented below it is the summary task.

I'm Gonna Get Me Some Structure

Now that you understand how outlines work in Project, you're no doubt anxious to start building your own. But project outlines take a little upfront thought. You have to understand two important things about your project to build a logical project outline: your goal, and the scope of the project.

The *goal* seems somewhat obvious: what do you want to achieve at the completion of your project? Is your goal to manage an entire space shuttle mission? Then you need as many tasks as it takes to get from here to splashdown. But if your goal is only to launch the space shuttle your focus is narrower and the level of detail of certain tasks will probably be different.

The *scope* is a little more specific: Do you want to build a new warehouse from scratch, outfit it with equipment and furniture, and deal with moving people into their offices by December 1 for a budget of $20 million? Or is the scope of your project to hook up the computer network by November 1 for a budget of $50,000? Understanding what your overall deliverables are helps you further define where to start and where to stop your project.

Look around your own office: you'll be surprised to find that many projects that go off track never had a clear goal to begin with. In fact, inputting project data into project management software is a waste of time if you don't know what your mission is. To paraphrase Lewis Carroll, if you don't know what your goal is, any set of tasks will get you there.

To define a goal and scope for your project, answer these questions:

For a goal:

- What will be different when my project is complete?
- What will my project achieve? Will a building be built, a workforce trained, or a space shuttle launched?

For the scope:

- What will my project cost?
- How many people will be involved?
- On whom does my project have an impact: my workgroup, my division, my company, or my clients?
- What deadlines does my project have?

Everything but the kitchen sink: What to include

Once you understand your project goals and the scope of work to be done, you can begin to think about what your outline should contain. For example, here is the first of three approaches to an outline of tasks for planning a company party:

I. Send out invitations

II. Reserve Conference Room B

III. Order food

Perhaps a little more detail would be helpful:

I. Company Christmas Party

   A. Invitations

      1. Design invitations

      2. Mail invitations

   B. Location

      1. Reserve Conference Room B

      2. Order extra chairs

      3. Decorate space

   C. Food

      1. Hire caterer

      2. Clean up

Or, what about the really detailed approach:

I. Company Events

   A. Company Christmas Party

      1. Planning

         a) Set party date

         b) Invitations

         c) Design

         d) Send out

         e) Budget

        f) Research costs

        g) Create budget

        h) Obtain budget approval

    2. Location and Furniture

        a) Location

           (1) Reserve Conference Room B

           (2) Arrange for carpet cleaning

           (3) Pick decoration theme

           (4) Decorate space

        b) Furniture

           (1) Order extra chairs

           (2) Arrange for serving table

    3. Food

        a) Research caterers

        b) Set food budget

        c) Hire caterer

        d) Provide kitchen access to caterers

        e) Assign clean up committee

        f) Clean up

  B. Halloween Party

    1. Etc. . . .

Which one of these outlines is best for this project? That depends on how complex these arrangements are and how narrowly you define the project. Are you planning the entire year of company events, or only one party? How many people will perform the tasks, and over what period of time? Will one person research, budget, and hire the caterers in a single hour? If so, a single task, *Hire Caterer,* might be enough. Will one person research, another set the budget, and another do the hiring of the caterer, and might these tasks be separated by days or even weeks of time? If so, having several tasks might be the way to go.

If one task must happen before another can start, you may have to break the tasks down to reflect the causality between certain events. For example, if you can't begin a new manufacturing process before people have been trained, it's probably not prudent to lump training and the implementation of the new process into a single task.

The important thing to remember is that too little detail might let some tasks slip through the cracks, and too much detail might cause your project team to be inefficient, spending more time reporting their progress and breaking down their activities than they do working. Understand the scope of your project and the relationship of each task as you create your project outline.

Building the outline

People approach building a project outline in different ways. Some create all the tasks they can think of in whatever order, and then promote and demote tasks to different levels and move them around to the right order.

Others create upper-level tasks first, and then go back and fill in detail below each. Still others work one phase at a time, creating one upper-level task and filling in every possible task underneath it. Then they go on to the next phase and create every task under that, and so on.

The approach you use depends to some extent on how you think. Some people think chronologically, and others group like information. You will eventually have to deal with all levels of structure in your final outline, but which you tackle first is up to you.

All the Right Moves

You discover how to create tasks in Chapter 4. In this section, you move those tasks around to create the outline structure. If you've used any word-processing outlining feature, this will be pretty easy stuff. If you haven't, it's still easy!

The outdent and indent shuffle

Outdenting and identing are the functions you use to move tasks to higher or lower levels of detail in your outline. In some software programs, this is referred to as demoting and promoting.

- ✔ **Outdenting** a task moves it up a level in the outline (literally shifting it to the left in the outline). The concept behind outdenting is that a task is now at a higher level of detail (in other words, less detailed).

- ✔ **Indenting** a task moves it down a level in the outline (literally indenting the task to the right in the outline) and putting it at a deeper level of detail.

You use tools on the Formatting toolbar (see Figure 5-3) to indent and outdent tasks in a project outline. The Outdent tool looks like a left-facing arrow; the Indent tool looks like a right-facing arrow. You can outdent and indent tasks from any view, even the Network Diagram view. However, it's a lot trickier to see the effect in the Network Diagram view, and I recommend the Gantt Chart for manipulating tasks in an outline structure.

If you've used an outlining feature in other software, you'll be tempted to press Tab to demote a task and Shift+Tab to promote a task in an outline. Don't: It won't cause disaster, but it will only move your cursor from one column to the other. In the Network Diagram view, it will move the cursor from field to field in a single task box.

To promote or demote a task, follow these steps:

1. **Click a task in a columnar view to select it.**

   An example of a columnar view is the Gantt Chart view.

2. **Click the Promote or Demote button according to what action you want to take.**

Promote task

Demote task

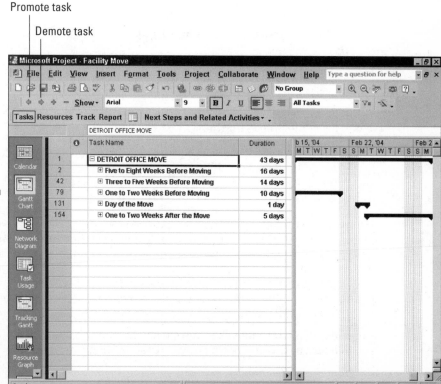

Figure 5-3: These tools can be pressed as many times as you like to move a task up or down levels of a multiphase outline.

Moving tasks

When you enter tasks in a project outline, odds are you'll need to move those tasks around at some point. You can move subtasks to other phases of the outline by simply clicking and dragging them.

You should understand that moving a task can change its outline level. A task retains its level in the outline when you move it to follow a task at the same level. If you move a lower-level task to a section of tasks at a higher level — for example, move a third-level task to a section of second-level tasks — the task will take on the level of the task preceding it. This is also true when you take a higher-level task and move it to follow a lower-level task. However, the exception to this is when you move a lower-level task to follow a summary task. If you move, say, a second-level task to immediately follow a summary task, it will stay at the second level (not take on the preceding summary task level).

Moving is a drag

The quickest way to move a task in an outline is to use the click and drag method. To move a task with this method, follow these steps:

1. **Display a columnar view, such as the Gantt Chart.**

2. **Select a task by clicking its task ID number.**

3. **Drag the task where you want it to appear in the outline.**

   A gray line appears, indicating the new task position, as shown in Figure 5-4.

4. **When the gray line is located where you want to insert the task, release the mouse button.**

   The task appears in its new location. If you want the task to be at a different level of the outline you can now indent or outdent it as you wish.

If you want to move more than one task at a time, click and drag to select multiple task IDs, and then drag them to a new location. Note that you can also use the Shift+click and Ctrl+click selection methods to select multiple tasks in a Project outline. However, only selected contiguous tasks (using Shift+click) can be moved in an outline.

Cut!

Clicking and dragging is fine in most cases, but in very large projects — projects with a few hundred or more tasks — it can be like dragging a peanut to Tibet: It's not the difficulty; it's the distance you have to travel.

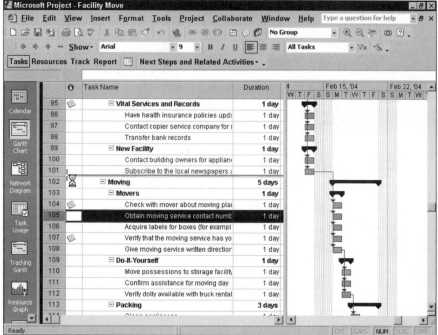

Figure 5-4:
This gray
line shows
you where
the task will
appear if
you release
the mouse
button.

In a larger outline, simply use the cut-and-paste method as follows:

1. **Select a task by clicking its task ID number.**

2. **Click the Cut Task tool on the Standard toolbar.**

   The task is removed from its current location and placed on the
   Windows clipboard.

3. **Scroll to display the location where you want the task to appear.**

4. **Click the task after which you want to insert the task.**

5. **Click the Paste tool.**

If you want to insert a copy of a task in a project outline, you can use the
preceding steps but click Copy Task instead of Cut Task.

Now You See It, Now You Don't

Since caveman days (or whenever the first fourth-grade teacher taught
the first set of kids how to outline their book reports), outlines have allowed
you to focus on different levels of detail. Outlines do this on paper by
essentially ordering information so that you can more easily look at the level
of information you need and ignore the rest.

With the invention of computer outlining, the capability to focus on only certain portions of an outline comes into its own. That's because you can easily open and close an outline to show or hide different levels of information or different sections of your outline. The project outline in Figure 5-5, for example, is open to show details of just one phase of the project.

What does that capability mean to you? It means you can hide all but the upper level of tasks in a project to give your manager an overview of progress. It means you can close every phase of your project except the one currently in progress so that your team can focus on those tasks in a status meeting. It means you can close most of your outline so that jumping to a late phase of a very large schedule doesn't involve more scrolling than a Baroque fireplace.

A task with all tasks displayed has a minus sign. A task with hidden subtasks has a plus sign symbol to its left. To display or hide different levels of information in your outline, do the following.

When a task (a summary task or any other task) has a minus sign next to it, you can click it and do one of three things:

- ✔ Click the minus sign to hide all subtasks.
- ✔ Click the Hide Subtasks button on the Formatting toolbar to hide all subtasks.
- ✔ Click the Show button on the Formatting toolbar and then click the level of detail you'd like to leave open in the entire outline; click Outline Level 1 for only the highest level of detail in the outline.

If you don't want to see plus and minus outlining symbols, you can remove them from all views by deselecting the Show Outline Symbols option on the View tab of the Options dialog box.

When a summary task has a plus sign next to it, you can click it and do one of three things:

- ✔ Click the plus sign to display one level of subtasks.
- ✔ Click the Show Subtasks button on the Formatting toolbar to display one level of subtasks.
- ✔ Click the Show button on the Formatting toolbar (see Figure 5-6) and click the level of the outline you want to reveal for the entire outline.

To quickly reveal all subtasks in a project, click the Show button and then click All Subtasks.

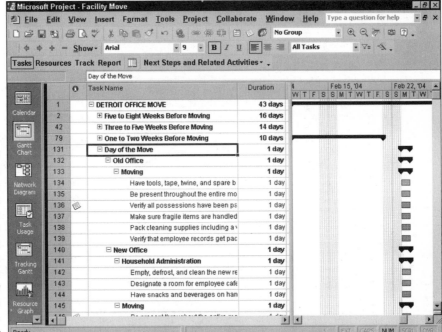

Figure 5-5:
The minus symbol next to this summary task indicates that all the tasks below it are displayed.

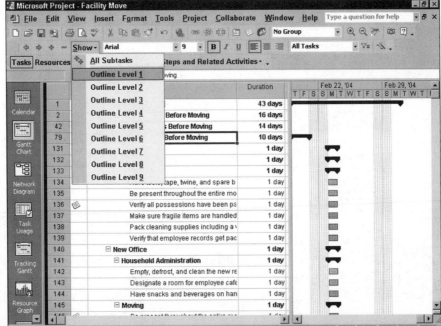

Figure 5-6:
Choose whatever level of detail you'd like to see from this drop-down list.

Cracking the WBS Code

Some codes are used for disguising things (think Mata Hari). In Project, however, codes are used to make it easier to identify elements of a project. These codes, which are called *work breakdown structure, or WBS,* codes, can be generated automatically to give a unique identity to each task in your project by its order in the project outline.

For example, the fourth task in the third phase of a project would have a code similar to this: 1.3.4. This code helps you identify all tasks that belong to Phase One, no matter at what level of the outline they may lie, as shown in Figure 5-7. Quite simply, assigning a WBS code to an outline helps you to identify the location of individual tasks in the outline so that people can find and reference them easily. This is similar to the way page numbers in a book help you go right to a specific page.

The United States government often requires the use of such a code, so companies doing business with them will find this automatic application of a WBS code useful.

A standard WBS code uses numbers for each level of the code. You can also create custom codes that provide a few options for how the code is defined.

Figure 5-7:
With larger projects this code can get quite lengthy!

	WBS	Task Name	Duration	Start
126	1.3.2.4.3	Plan meals that will use up the food	1 day	Thu 2/19/04
127	1.3.2.4.4	Empty, defrost, and clean refrigerato	2 days	Thu 2/19/04
128	1.3.2.4.5	Prepare a survival kit for move day	1 day	Thu 2/19/04
129	1.3.2.4.6	Prepare management survival kit	1 day	Thu 2/19/04
130	1.3.2.4.7	Plan employees' survival kit	2 days	Thu 2/19/04
131	1.4	⊟ Day of the Move	1 day	Mon 2/23/04
132	1.4.1	⊟ Old Office	1 day	Mon 2/23/04
133	1.4.1.1	⊟ Moving	1 day	Mon 2/23/04
134	1.4.1.1.1	Have tools, tape, twine, and spare b	1 day	Mon 2/23/04
135	1.4.1.1.2	Be present throughout the entire mo	1 day	Mon 2/23/04
136	1.4.1.1.3	Verify all possessions have been pa	1 day	Mon 2/23/04
137	1.4.1.1.4	Make sure fragile items are handled	1 day	Mon 2/23/04
138	1.4.1.1.5	Pack cleaning supplies including a v	1 day	Mon 2/23/04
139	1.4.1.1.6	Verify that employee records get pac	1 day	Mon 2/23/04
140	1.4.2	⊟ New Office	1 day	Mon 2/23/04
141	1.4.2.1	⊟ Household Administration	1 day	Mon 2/23/04
142	1.4.2.1.1	Empty, defrost, and clean the new re	1 day	Mon 2/23/04
143	1.4.2.1.2	Designate a room for employee cafe	1 day	Mon 2/23/04
144	1.4.2.1.3	Have snacks and beverages on han	1 day	Mon 2/23/04

Display a WBS code

Here's the good new: You don't really have to create a WBS code per se because the very structure of your outline creates the code. All you have to do is display it. To do that, follow these steps:

1. **Click the Gantt Chart icon in the View bar.**

   The Gantt Chart view appears.

2. **Right-click anywhere in the column headings and then click Insert Column.**

   The Column Definition dialog box appears, as shown in Figure 5-8.

Figure 5-8:
You can use
this dialog
box to set
options
such as
column
width and
alignment,
as well.

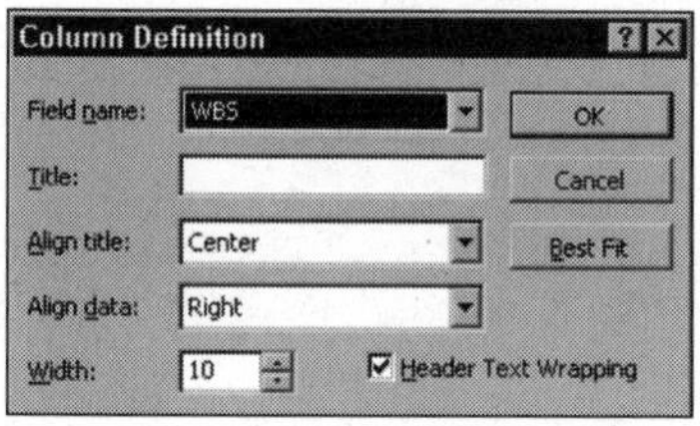

3. **Click the arrow on the Field Name box and then select WBS.**

   Use the scrollbar if necessary to locate that field name.

4. **Click OK.**

   The WBS column is displayed. If you add a task, or move, promote, or demote a task in your project outline, the WBS code is updated automatically.

Customize it

Now, many times the off-the-rack WBS code works just fine for projects. But for those times when you want to make changes, Project allows you to modify the code to use a prefix — say the name of your project, a client ID, or your department number — and to vary the use of numerals or letters to indicate the various levels of your code structure. An example of a customized code is shown in Figure 5-9.

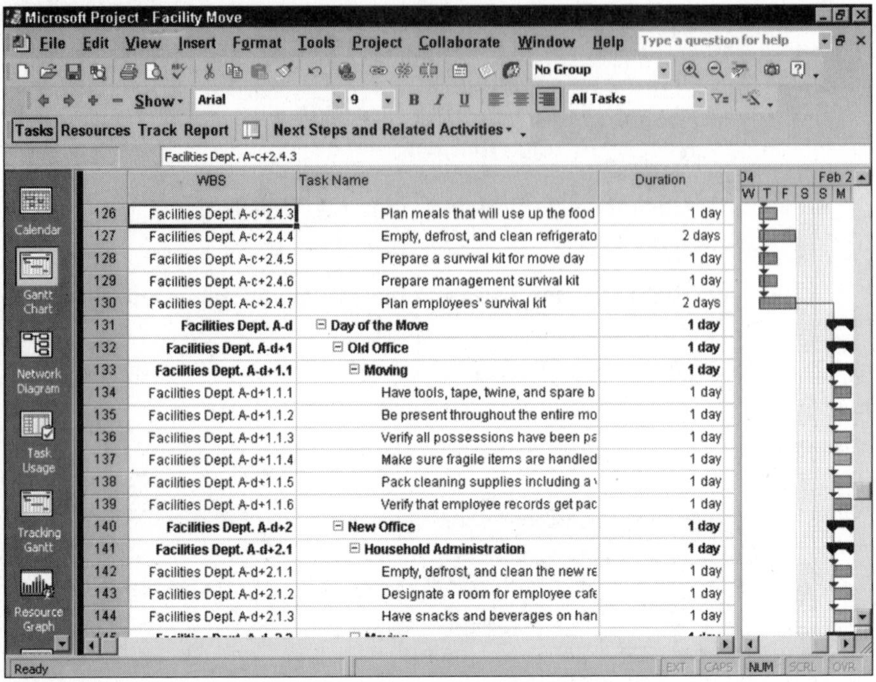

Figure 5-9:
Customized
WBS codes
can help
you identify
your tasks
by
categories
such as
division,
client, or
company.

The elements used to make up the code are called *code masks*. You can specify the following choices for WBS code masks:

- ✔ **Numbers (ordered)** uses a numerical code.

- ✔ **Uppercase Letters (ordered)** uses letter codes (such as A, B, C to correspond to the first, second, and third phases of a project) with uppercase formatting.

- ✔ **Lowercase Letters (ordered)** also uses letters, but with lowercase formatting.

- ✔ **Characters (unordered)** is used for combinations of letters and numbers. This choice generates an asterisk; you can replace the asterisk with whatever characters you like in a columnar view.

To customize a WBS code, follow these steps:

1. **Choose Project➪WBS➪Define Code.**

   The WBS Code Definition dialog box appears, as shown in Figure 5-10.

2. **In the Project Code Prefix box, type a prefix.**

3. **Click at the top of the Sequence column, and then select a mask for the first level.**

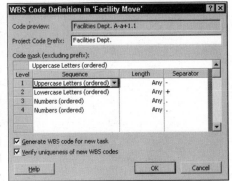

Figure 5-10:
Note that
Project
offers a
Code
preview
field so you
can see
what your
changes will
do as you
make them.

4. **Click the Length column, and then select a length for the mask sequence that corresponds to the number of tasks you expect to have at that level.**

   Each number represents a single character. If you choose 4, for example, your first task at this level is numbered 0001. If you aren't sure, leave the default choice of Any to allow for any length.

5. **Click under the Separator column, and then click a choice of separator.**

   The choices are a period, a hyphen, a plus sign, or a forward slash.

6. **To define WBS code elements for additional levels of your outline, repeat Steps 3 through 5.**

7. **When you're finished, click OK to save the new code.**

The essential point of a WBS code is to provide unique identifiers for each task in your project. The WBS Code Definition dialog box does offer an option to Verify uniqueness of new WBS codes that is active by default. If you turn this option off, you won't be alerted if, for example, you insert a subproject that contains duplicate WBS numbers.

If you don't want Project to automatically add a custom WBS code when you insert new tasks, clear the Generate WBS Code for New Task option in the WBS Code Definition dialog box (Project⇨WBS⇨Define Code). If at a later point you want to renumber all tasks to accommodate new tasks, subprojects you've inserted, and changes, choose Project⇨WBS⇨Renumber. This can be useful if you want to try what-if scenarios but don't want all your tasks to change.

Chapter 6

Timing Is Everything

*I*magine this: If you create a hundred tasks, leave their default constraints so they start As Soon As Possible, and have no dependencies, all those tasks will start on the project start date and occur simultaneously. The project of a hundred tasks will take exactly as long as the longest task.

But wander back over here to reality for a moment. When was the last time every task in your project could be performed at the same time? When did you last have enough resources to even begin to make that feasible? When did you ever have a set of tasks where not a single task had to be completed before another could start? Imagine if you poured a building's foundation before you got the building permit. Or what if you tried to train your employees to use a new piece of equipment before the equipment even arrived?

Tasks in a project don't all start at the same time. To reflect that in a Project plan, you have to build in a timing logic. That logic consists of dependency links between tasks. *Dependencies* are timing relationships between tasks that are caused either by the nature of the tasks (you can't build the house frame until the concrete foundation is dry; otherwise, the building will sink) or lack of available resources (you can't have your operations manager attend two plant inspections simultaneously).

Becoming Codependent

In Chapter 4, I mention that you shouldn't set task start dates very often. That's because projects are fluid — they change and grow faster than bad guys come at you in the average computer game. If you build in a timing logic, rather than assigning certain dates to tasks, Project can reflect changes by adjusting your project based on that logic.

So, if the task of getting materials in-house is delayed by a week, the dependent task of starting the manufacturing process automatically moves out a week. You can then note the change when tracking activity in your plan, and Project will make adjustments accordingly. The alternative to this is going in and changing the start date of just about every task in your schedule every time a task is running late — you don't even want to think about doing that!

When tasks depend on each other

As with human relationships, every dependency relationship involves roles. Every task is either a *predecessor* or a *successor.* There will be a predecessor and successor pair even if the timing of the two tasks overlaps or they are set to happen concurrently.

Figure 6-1 shows how the task bars in the Gantt Chart view graphically depict the predecessors and successors in dependency relationships between tasks. Notice how taskbars represent the relationship when a task starts after or during the life of another task. Notice also the lines drawn between tasks, indicating dependency links.

Here's some important advice about dependencies, so listen up: You can have more than one dependency link to a task, but don't overdo it. Many people who are new to Project make the mistake of building every logical timing relationship that exists. If things change and they have to delete or change dependencies (for example, to shorten a schedule), a more convoluted web of dependencies can create a nightmare.

For example, both obtaining a permit and pouring a foundation for a building have to be completed before you can start framing the building. However, a link from framing to the foundation task is sufficient to establish the correct timing, assuming you have a link from the foundation task to the permit task.

Dependency types

You can establish four types of dependency links: finish-to-start, start-to-finish, start-to-start, and finish-to-finish. Using these types efficiently can mean the difference between a project that finishes on time and one that is still going on long after you retire.

Predecessor   Successor

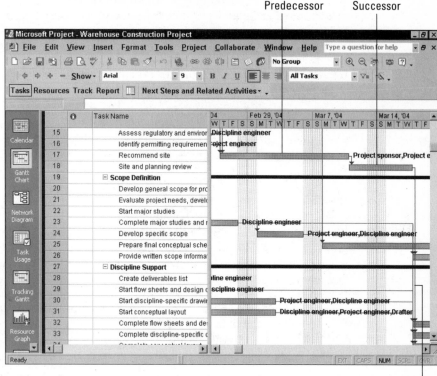

Dependency link line

Figure 6-1:
In this view,
dependency
relationships
are shown
by the lines
between
taskbars.

In Chapter 4, I cover task constraints and priorities. These settings work in concert with dependencies to determine the ultimate timing of tasks in your project.

Here's how the four dependency types work:

- **Finish-to-start.** A finish-to-start dependency is the most common type of dependency link. In this relationship, the predecessor task must be completed before the successor task can start. When you create a dependency, the default setting is finish-to-start.

  An example of a finish-to-start dependency is when the *Print Invitations* task must be completed before you can begin the *Send Out Invitations* task. Figure 6-2 shows two tasks with the finish-to-start relationship indicated by a successor taskbar that starts where the predecessor taskbar leaves off.

- **Start-to-finish.** In a start-to-finish dependency, you can finish the successor task only after the predecessor task has started. If the predecessor is delayed, the successor task can't finish.

Suppose that you're planning the building of a new cruise ship. You might start selling tickets for the ship's maiden voyage while the ship is being built, but you don't want to stop selling tickets until the ship is ready to leave. So, the predecessor is *Ship Ready for First Voyage* (a milestone) and the successor task is *Sell Tickets for Maiden Voyage*. If the ship is not ready, you can keep selling tickets. When the ship is ready to go, the ticket windows closes, and that task can finish. Bon voyage!

✔ **Start-to-start.** Start-to-start does what it says: Two tasks must start simultaneously. For example, you might want to insure that a new blockbuster movie you're producing is released to theaters the same day that the new action figures are available in fast-food chains.

Figure 6-3 shows such a start-to-start relationship between two tasks.

✔ **Finish-to-finish.** Finish-to-finish has nothing to do with warm relations between citizens of Finland. Finish-to-finish — you guessed it — means that two tasks must finish at the same time.

Suppose that you're preparing the annual report for your adventure travel company. You have to obtain photographs of travel destinations and have the brochure copy typeset. You have to have both items in hand before you can forward the report to the printer. If you set a finish-to-finish dependency between these two, you allow both tasks the most time to be completed (Why have the photos sitting around for four weeks when the copy isn't ready?)

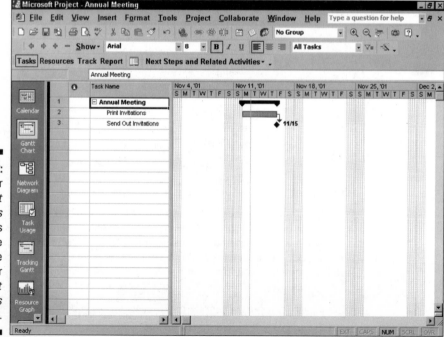

Figure 6-2:
The taskbar for the *Print Invitations* task ends where the milestone symbol for *Send Out Invitations* begins.

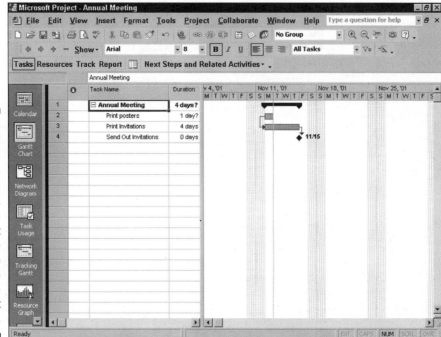

Figure 6-3:
Because
you're
sending the
posters and
invitations
to the
printer at
the same
time, these
tasks have
a start-
to-start
relationship.

Allowing for Murphy's Law: Lag and lead time

Now that you understand the four types of dependency links, it's time to show you how dependencies can get a little more complex. You can use lag time or lead time to get your timing relationships even more finely tuned.

Lag time occurs when you add time to the start or finish of a predecessor task; lag time causes a gap in timing. *Lead time* is when you subtract time from the start or finish of the predecessor; lead time causes an overlap between two tasks.

Here are some examples:

✔ Suppose that you set up a start-to-start dependency relationship between the *Begin Print Media Advertising* predecessor task and the *Begin TV and Radio Advertising* successor in a project to launch a new toy product to the market. With a simple start-to-start relationship, both will start at the same time. However, what if you want the TV and radio ads to come out a week after the print ads begin? In that case, you'd want to build in a week of lag time to the start-to-start relationship where *Begin Print Media Advertising* is the predecessor and *Begin TV and Radio Advertising* is the successor.

✔ In a project to train a new set of volunteer docents to give tours of an historic mansion, you create a finish-to-start relationship between the *Locating Recruits* and *Training Recruits* tasks. However, to save time in your project, you decide to incorporate two days of lead time — that is, allow the training of the earliest hires to start before all the recruits are hired. In that case, you essentially deduct time from the finish-to-start relationship that allows you to start training two days before the finish of the hiring predecessor.

Building in lag time between two tasks is one way to add slack to a project. *Slack* is extra time you plan as insurance against the first task running a bit late. Find out more about slack in Chapter 10.

Making the Connection

Just as falling in love is easy after you find the right person, making dependency relationships is simple. You simply create a dependency, make settings to select the dependency type, and build in any lag or lead time. What's important is that you understand how each type of dependency affects your plan when your project goes live and you start to record actual activity on tasks.

Adding the missing link

When you create a dependency, it is by default a finish-to-start relationship — one task must finish before another can start. If that's just the kind of dependency you want, that's all there is to it. If not, after you create this link, you can edit it to change the dependency type or to build in lag or lead time.

To establish a simple finish-to-start link with you mouse, follow these steps:

1. **Display the Gantt Chart view, making sure that the two tasks you want to link are visible.**

2. **Click the predecessor task and drag your mouse to the successor task.**

   As you drag, a box appears, as shown in Figure 6-4 and your cursor changes to the shape of a sideways 8.

3. **When the readout indicates the task number that you want to link to, release your mouse button.**

You can establish the finish-to-start relationship also by clicking the predecessor and dragging to link to the successor task.

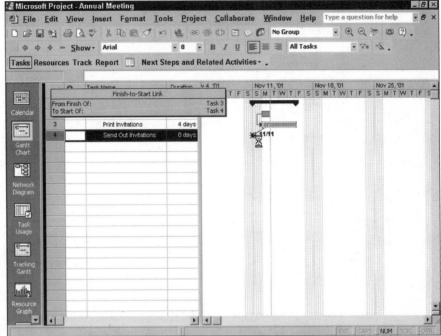

Figure 6-4:
This box lets
you know
when your
cursor is
resting over
the task to
which you
want to link.

To establish a link in a Task Information dialog box, follow these steps:

1. **Double-click the successor task.**

   The Task Information dialog box appears.

2. **Click the Predecessors tab, which is shown in Figure 6-5.**

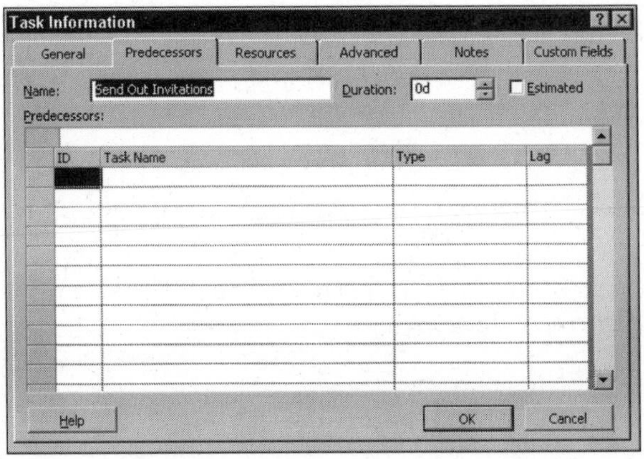

Figure 6-5:
You can
build as
many
dependency
relationships
here as
you like.

3. **Click the ID box and type a task ID number of the Predecessor task.**

4. **Press Tab.**

   The task name and the default finish-to-start dependency type with 0 lag time are entered automatically.

5. **Click the Type box to display the dependency types, and then click the appropriate one for your dependency.**

6. **If you want to add lag or lead time, click the Lag box and use the spinner arrows.**

   Click up to a positive number for lag time or down to a negative number for lead time.

7. **Repeat Steps 3 through 6 to establish additional dependency relationships.**

8. **When you're finished, click OK to save the dependencies.**

The Gantt chart displays your dependencies with lines and arrows, as shown in the project displayed in Figure 6-6.

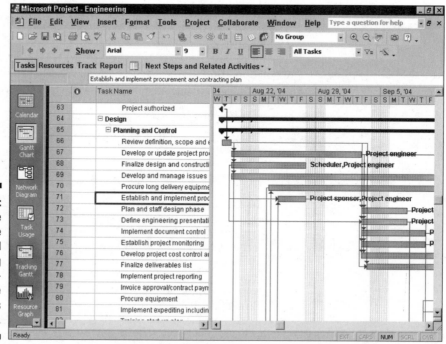

Figure 6-6:
The more complex the project and its timing relation- ships, the more lines you'll see.

Most dependency links are between tasks that are reasonably close to each other in the Project outline. However, if you have to link tasks that won't fit on a single screen of information, the click-and-drag method can be tricky. In that case, use the successor Task Information dialog box to create the relationship by entering the predecessor task ID number.

Extending your reach with external dependencies

No person is an island — and no project exists in a vacuum. Many times, another project you're managing or another project going on somewhere else in your organization will affect your project. Perhaps resources or facilities are shared or perhaps the timing of tasks in other projects affects the timing of tasks in yours. For example, if your project is to plan the opening of a new store, you may have to create a dependency from your *Begin Move-In* task to the *Final Building Inspection Complete* task in someone else's construction project.

To deal with this, you can create a hyperlinked task in your project that represents the other project or a task in it. Enter a start date and duration for the task. You can then create dependencies between that task and other tasks in your project that will reflect the external timing. Use the hyperlink to quickly go to the other project at any time to update timing information. See Chapter 4 for information about hyperlinking tasks and entering the start date and duration.

You can also insert an entire project and include a link to it so that updates to the other file are reflected in your plan automatically. See Chapter 4 to read more about hyperlinked tasks and inserted projects.

Things change: Deleting dependencies

Just when you think you can depend on someone, you sometimes find that dependency wasn't in the cards. That can be true with Project dependencies as well. When you need to get rid of a dependency, you can undo what you did either in the Gantt chart or in the Task Information dialog box.

In the Gantt chart, follow these steps:

1. **Select the two tasks whose dependency you want to delete.**

   For two adjacent tasks, you can click and drag their ID numbers. For nonadjacent tasks, click one task, press and hold the Ctrl key, and then click a nonadjacent task.

2. **Click the Unlink Tasks button on the Standard toolbar.**

Be careful when you use this method: If you click only one task and then click the Unlink Tasks button. All dependency relationships for that task are removed.

To remove dependency relationships in the Task Information dialog box, do this:

1. **Double-click a successor task name.**

   The Task Information dialog box appears.

2. **Click the Predecessors tab to display it**

3. **Click the Type box for the dependency that you want to delete.**

   A list of dependency types appears, as shown in Figure 6-7.

4. **Click None.**

5. **Click OK to save the change.**

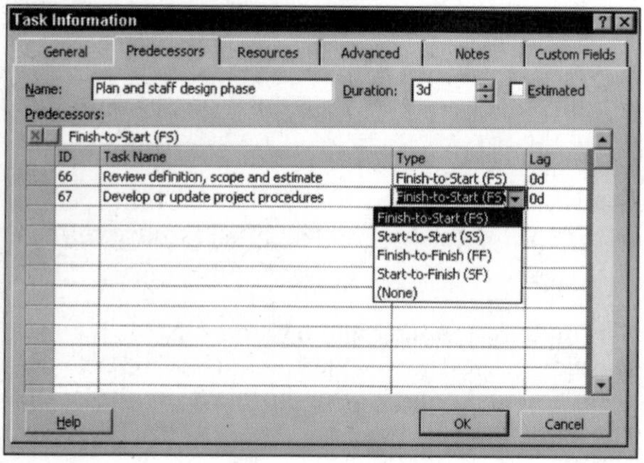

Figure 6-7:
This tab can be used to both create and delete dependency links.

The dependency line on the Gantt chart is gone, and the next time you open that Task Information dialog box, the dependency will be gone.

Just Look At What You Did!

Project provides several ways to view dependencies in your project. The method you choose will probably relate to how you visualize data, so there's no right or wrong here!

You've already seen the dependency link lines that appear in the Gantt chart (refer to Figure 6-6). Another great way to see the flow of dependencies is in the

Network Diagram. This workflow view uses similar lines and arrows to reveal dependency relationships, but it allows you to get a different perspective on them.

Figure 6-8 shows the Network Diagram view of an engineering project. Notice that each task has a node containing its vital statistics. Between nodes are lines revealing dependency relationships among tasks. Although you can't see it in black and white, by default any task dependency links on the critical path are in red and noncritical tasks are in blue. (*Critical path tasks* are tasks that have no slack: They can't be delayed without delaying the entire project.)

A neat trick in Network Diagram view is to edit the layout to show link labels. (Right-click outside any task nodes, click Layout, and then click the Show Link Labels check box.) A code, such as FS for finish-to-start, is displayed to explain the type of dependency represented by each dependency line.

You can also display columns that itemize successors or predecessors for each task by task ID number in any view with a sheet area, such as Gantt Chart view. Figure 6-9 shows Gantt Chart view for the same engineering project with successor and predecessor columns displayed. These columns also include a notation of the type of dependency (other than the default finish-to-start) and any lead or lag time using percentages. For example, 71SS+50% is a start-to-start link to task 71, with lag time set so that the successor begins halfway through the predecessor task.

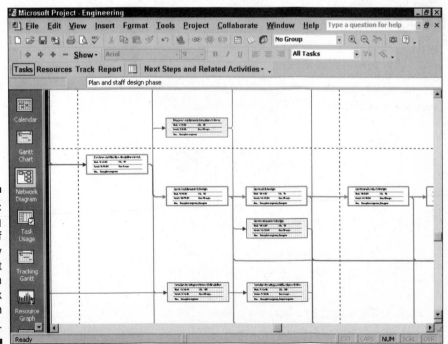

Figure 6-8:
Following the flow of dependency lines is a bit easier in Network Diagram view.

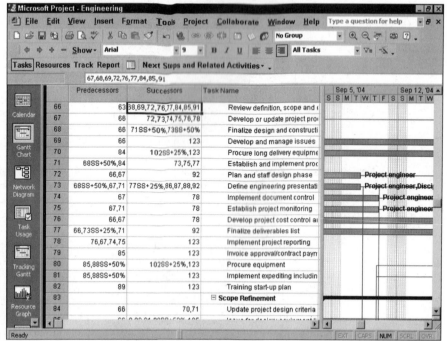

Figure 6-9:
Of course,
you have to
know which
task number
is which to
use the
information
in these
columns!

Note that you can also edit the contents of Network Diagram nodes to include predecessor and successor data.

Part II
People Who Need People

The 5th Wave — By Rich Tennant

"We can monitor our entire operation from one central location. We know what the 'Wax Lips' people are doing; we know what the 'Whoopee Cushion' people are doing; we know what the 'Fly-in-the-Ice Cube' people are doing. But we don't know what the 'Plastic Vomit' people are doing. We don't want to know what the 'Plastic Vomit' people are doing."

In this part . . .

Projects don't occur in a vacuum. Most involve scads of people, equipment, facilities, and materials. These are called *resources* in Project, and you hear all about resources in this part.

First you gain an understanding of the different types of resources you can create and how they relate to costs in your project. You explore not only how you represent the people who work on your tasks in Project, but also how you add fixed costs such as a consulting fee and the difference between a work and material resource.

After you know how to create various kinds of resources, you can start to assign them to tasks and see how your costs — and worktime conflicts — grow.

Chapter 7

Using Your Natural Resources

In This Chapter

▶ Understanding work and material resources

▶ Creating resources to get your project done

▶ Using resource groups and shared resources

▶ Dealing with resource calendar settings

*P*rojects are like giant water coolers — that is, they're gathering places for people. Projects also utilize equipment and materials. Those people, equipment, and materials are your project resources.

Unlike water coolers (you can take an analogy only so far), resources are also how Project tallies up costs in your plan. Assign a resource to work for ten hours on a task, give that resource an hourly rate of $20, and you've just added a $200 cost to your project. Create a resource called cement, give it a unit cost of $200, and assign 10 units (for example, 10 tons of cement), and you've added a whopping $2000 to the bottom line.

Using resources wisely in Project doesn't involve only assigning them a cost. It's a delicate art of combining the right resource, with the right skills, and assigning that resource to put in the right amount of time or units on tasks. And you have to do this all without overbooking anyone at any point in your schedule.

Because they affect timing and costs, resources are a big deal in Project. Resources are so important that many tools are available to help you create them, make settings for how and when they'll work, assign them to tasks, manage costs, and manipulate their workload. The first step in working with resources is to create them and enter certain information about them. That's what this chapter is all about.

Resources: People, Places, and Things

Many people hear the word *resources* and think of people. Well, people are a big part of Project resources, but they're not the whole story. Resources can also be equipment that you rent or buy and materials such as paper clips or scrap iron. You can even create resources that represent facilities you have to rent by the hour, such as a laboratory or a meeting space. You could create a resource named Plant Visit and assign it a unit cost of $400 — the average cost for a trip to your plant, including airfare, hotel, and rental car.

Here are some typical and not-so-typical project resources:

- Engineers
- Trade show booth
- Office supplies
- Hotel ballroom
- Administrative assistants
- Rocket fuel
- Speaker fees
- Furniture
- Computer software
- Printing services
- Prototype design

You get the picture. Resources can be practically anything or anyone that you use to complete your Project.

Becoming Resource-full

After you create and organize the tasks in your project, the next typical step is to create resources. You can also borrow resources that have been created by others and assign them to your project. But before you starting creating resources willy-nilly, it's important that you understand how they affect your project.

Understanding resources

The key to understanding resources is to realize that resources in Project equal costs. If you want to account for costs in your project — such as a person putting in hours working on a task or computers you have to buy or rent — you must create resources and assign them to a task. When you do, you can see the resulting costs in the Cost column of the Gantt Chart spreadsheet, as shown in Figure 7-1.

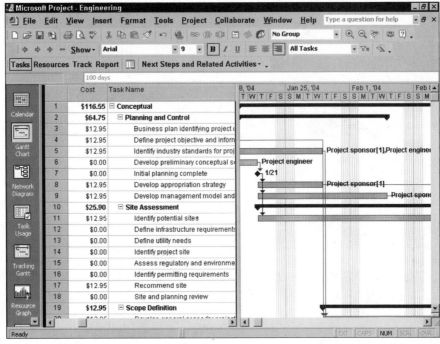

Figure 7-1:
Tasks with assigned resources show the associated total costs in the Cost column.

One other way to add costs to a project is to use a fixed cost. Fixed costs are not assigned through resources. Instead, they are applied directly to individual tasks. For more on fixed costs, see Chapter 8.

If a cost is not task specific — such as a flat $10,000 consulting fee to a firm that's advising you on an overall project — you can create and assign a resource with that cost to the summary task for the entire project.

After you create resources that Project uses to tally costs in a project, you'll need to manage the workflow for any resource that has limited time availability in your project. You create resources that are available so many hours a day and so many days a week. When you assign those resources to your project, you can use various views, reports, and tools to see whether any resource is overbooked at any point during your project. You can also see whether people are sitting around twiddling their thumbs when they might be available to help out on another task. You can even account for resources that work on multiple projects across your organization and make sure they're being utilized efficiently. Views such as the Resource Usage view shown in Figure 7-2 help you visualize resource working time in your project.

Finally, it's important to understand that the number of resources you assign to work on a task will usually have an effect on the duration of that task. In others words, if you have a certain amount of work to perform but few people to do it, a typical task will take longer to finish than if you had scads of folks.

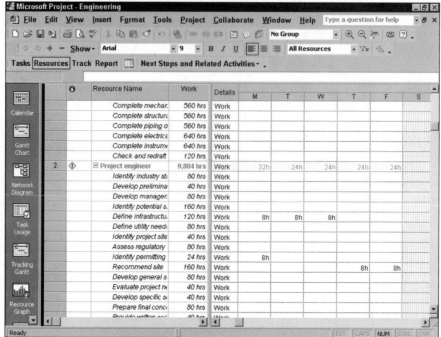

Figure 7-2:
You can see
total hours
on the
project by
resource
and an
itemization
of the hours
assigned
task-by-task
for that
resource.

The task type determines whether or not a task's duration will change based on the number of resources assigned to it. Take a look at Chapter 4 for more about task types.

Resource types: Work and material

Although people and things come in all shapes and sizes, to Project there are only two types of resources: work resources and material resources.

- **Work resources** are typically (but not always) people. Their costs are associated with the amount of work time they put in, usually at an hourly rate. Work resources are assigned to tasks based on a Working Time calendar (see Figure 7-3), where you specify their working and nonworking hours.

- **Material resources** can have an hourly rate or a unit cost, and they have an unlimited working time. This type of resource has no calendar, and you make no settings for working and nonworking time.

A typical work resource is a person working eight hours a day at a standard rate of $20 an hour and an overtime rate of $30. Another example of a work resource is a meeting facility available only eight hours a day at an hourly rate. Even though it's not a person, the meeting facility would probably be created as a working resource because it has limited "working" hours.

The three kinds of calendars are Project, Task, and Resource. Calendars, their settings, and how those settings interact are discussed at some length in Chapter 3.

A typical material resource is any material — such as steel, rubber, and paper or books, chairs, and shoes — assigned to a task with an associated unit cost. A resource called *Books* with a unit price of $12.95 assigned to a task called *Computer Training* at ten units will accrue a cost of $129.50 to the task. Another example of a material cost is anyone performing a service for a fee where working time is not an issue. A speaker who presents at a conference for a fee of $1000 but whose working calendar and time are not your concerns might be created as a material resource with a unit cost of $1000.

Figure 7-3:
You can select one of three base calendars and then modify specific working hours.

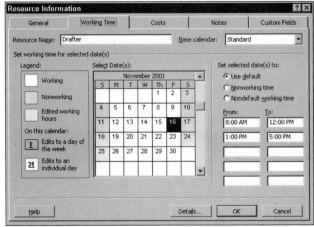

How resources affect task timing

For a fixed-unit or fixed-work task type, the addition or removal of resources assigned to the task will have an impact on the time it takes to complete the task. In essence, the old saying that "two heads are better than one" might be modified to "two heads are faster than one."

Here's an example: Suppose that one person is assigned to the *Dig Ditch* task, which should take four hours of effort. Two people assigned to the *Dig Ditch* task will finish the job in two hours because two hours are being worked by each resource simultaneously, which achieves four hours of effort in half the time.

One BIG word of warning here: Assigning additional people to tasks doesn't always cut work time down geometrically, though that's the way Project calculates it. When you have more people, you have meetings, memos, duplicated effort, conflicts, and so on. If you add more resources to a task, you might consider upping the amount of effort required to complete that task to account for inevitable workgroup inefficiencies.

Estimating resource requirements

You usually know how many material resources it takes to complete a task: In most cases, you can calculate the number of pounds, tons, meters, and so on with a standard formula. But how do you know how much effort it will take on the part of work resources to complete the tasks in your project?

As with many aspects of information you put into a Project plan, this judgment rests to a great degree on your own experience with similar tasks and resources. But remember these guidelines:

- ✔ **Skill counts.** A less skilled or experienced resource is likely to take more time to finish something.

- ✔ **History repeats itself.** Look at previous projects and tasks. If you've tracked people's time, you can probably see how much effort was required to complete various types of tasks.

- ✔ **Ask and you shall receive.** Ask the resources themselves how long they think it will take. Then add 10 percent to that time to cover yourself!

The Birth of a Resource

When a person is born, someone fills out a birth certificate with his or her name, parents' name, date of birth, and so on. Creating a resource in Project involves filling out a form, too. On the Resource Information form, you enter information such as the resource name, rate per hour or cost per use, and availability. You can also enter optional information such as the work group the resource belongs to or the resource's e-mail address.

You can create a resource as a single person or thing, as a generic resource (that is, a skill set with no person attached), and even as a group of several resources that work together.

One at a time

On the simplest level, you create a resource — whether it's a person, a piece of equipment, or a material — as a single entity. In this case, you're thinking of a particular person, or meeting room, or piece of equipment. You create the resource by entering information in the Resource Information dialog box.

Another method for entering resource information is to display the Resource Sheet view and enter information in the columns included there. This is often a faster way to create several resources at once.

When you create a resource, you must at a minimum type the Resource Name, but you can also include as much information as you want. Some people prefer to create all the resources first and deal with contact and cost information at a later stage.

To create a resource, follow these steps:

1. **Click the Resource Sheet view in the View bar.**

   You can also display any view with a sheet, right-click a column heading, click Insert Column, and then click the Resource Name column to display it.

2. **Double-click a blank Resource Name cell.**

   The Resource Information dialog box appears, as shown in Figure 7-4.

3. **In the Resource Name box, type a name.**

4. **In the Type box, click Work or Material.**

   The settings available to you differ slightly based on this choice.

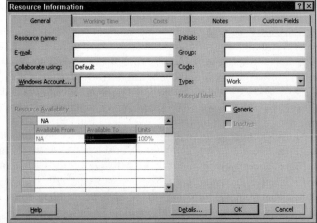

Figure 7-4: These five tabs can hold a wealth of information about any resource.

5. **In the Initials box, type an abbreviation or initials for the resource.**

   If you don't enter anything here, the first letter of the resource name is inserted when you save the resource.

6. **Continue to enter any information you want to include for the resource.**

   That information might include an e-mail address, the group (a department, division, or workgroup, for example), Material Label (for example, pounds for food coloring or tons for steel), or Code (such as a cost-center code). Note that a material resource won't have the E-mail box available, and a work resource won't have the Material Label box available.

   If you enter information in the Group box, you can then use filters, sort features, and the Group feature to look at sets of resources. See Chapter 11 for more about filtering and working with groups.

7. **Click OK to save the new resource.**

If you use Project Server (a companion product to Project used for online collaboration) a Collaborate Using box appears in place of the Workgroup box. You can use this box and the Windows Account option in the Resource Information dialog box to specify how you'll communicate with the team.

Getting generic

In the planning stages of a project, you'll often find that all your resources aren't assembled. Sometimes even well into the project, you don't know what resource you'll be using; you know only that you need a resource with a certain skill set to complete upcoming tasks. In that case, you might be better off creating some resources as generic resources.

If you want to create a generic resource, you should give it a name that describes its skill, such as Engineer, or Designer, or even Meeting Space (as opposed to a specific resource named Conference Room B). Then, in the Resource Information dialog box, be sure to select the Generic check box.

The usefulness of the generic setting is limited. Although you can display a Yes/No column titled *Generic* to identify these resources, you can't filter resources by this characteristic. No formula takes the Generic setting into account in recalculating your schedule based on resource availability. However, many people find this setting useful in long-range planning and in situations where they aren't responsible for specific resource assignment (for example, assigning a temporary worker to a task when the specific worker will be chosen by the temp agency).

Resources that hang out together

Although you'll probably have little use for chain gangs in your project, they exemplify the principle of a resource that represents multiple resources. Rather than assigning people one by one to some tasks, you'll want to assign a group of people who typically work together. Being able to make one assignment of such a *consolidated resource* rather than several separate resources and assignments can be a timesaver in larger projects.

Here's an example of a consolidated resource: Suppose that you are managing a project to get a new Web site up and running. You have four Web designers of equal skill at your disposal, so you create a resource named Web Designers. You can assign Web Designers to a task at 100%, and have all four designers working at once. Or you can assign the Web Designer resource to work on a task at 50%, thereby assigning two resources to it.

There is no special setting to designate a multiple resource: however, you might want to include some indication of the number of resources in the resource name. For example, you could name your designer resource *Four Web Designers* (if you know the Web design group consists of four people) or *Web Design Group.* What really defines this type of resource is the maximum assignment units; 400% would indicate four resources in the group.

Sharing Resources

Many organizations have lots of projects going on at the same time. Some, such as a project to organize an office move, will be the only project of its type happening in a company. Others, such a building design project in an architectural firm, will happen simultaneously with several other similar projects and draw on many of the same resources, such as architects and draftspeople.

When an organization has projects of a similar nature going on at the same time, it's often useful to create centralized resources. This can save you time because you don't have to create resources when they already exist. It can also help to track resources across projects.

Another timesaving Project feature allows you to pull existing resources from a company address book or your own address book in Outlook.

In the swim: Drawing on resource pools

If you use Project throughout your company, it can be beneficial to create a centralized repository of common resources and allow project managers to assign those resources to their various projects. This collection of enterprise resources is called a *resource pool.* By using a resource pool, you can get a more realistic idea of how busy resources are across all projects at any point in time.

Both individual resources and consolidated resources can be created in a blank project as a resource pool, and saved to an accessible location on your company server. Then, any project manager can call on those resources for his or her own projects; those projects are then referred to as *sharer files* because they share resources with the resource pool. For example, if you have a pool of maintenance people that everyone in your manufacturing company assigns to projects, create a project called *Resource Pools* and then create all your enterprise resources in this project. Or you could create a resource called *CEO* and let all the people managing projects that require the CEO's involvement assign him or her from that central location. Then use the resource-sharing tools in Project to assign these resources to your plan.

When anyone makes resource assignments in a sharer file, that information is also saved in the resource pool file. Then, anyone can use that file to look at resource allocations across all projects in the organization.

To access a resource that's available to your entire organization, follow this procedure:

1. **Choose Tools⇨Resource Sharing⇨Share Resources.**

   The Share Resources dialog box appears, as shown in Figure 7-5.

2. **Specify the resources for the project.**

   If you want to specify that a project will use only its own resources (the default), click the Use Own Resources option. If you want to share resources, click the Use Resources option and then select a project in the From list.

3. **Specify what Project should do when a conflicting resource setting, such as the resource base calendar, exists.**

   If your project's setting will take precedence, click the Sharer Takes Precedence option. If you want the pool setting to rule, click Pool Takes Precedence.

4. **Click OK to complete the process.**

   All resources in the specified resource pool are added to your own project's resource list, ready to be assigned to tasks.

After you've added a shared resource to your project, you can update shared resource information. You would want to do this in case the person who maintains those shared resources has made a change, such as upping the resource's rate per hour. To do this, choose Tools⇨Resource Sharing ⇨ Refresh Resource Pool.

Figure 7-5:
When many
people pull
on the same
resources in
a company,
sharing
resources
becomes a
good idea.

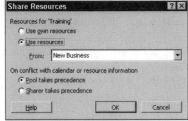

If you combine separate projects into one master project at any point, Project allows you to have duplicated resources. If you link the combined projects and then delete a duplicate resource in the master project, it's deleted in the subproject as well.

Importing resources from Outlook

If you're like me, you've spent months or years building up your list of e-mail contacts in Outlook. You might as well have a way to leverage all that work: Project supplies this in its capability to pull resources from Outlook.

Drowning in the resource pool

Drawing resources from resource pools saves you time because you don't have to recreate those resources again and again. However, should you track your resource's time in the resource pool file to see whether the resource is overbooked? Most projects in the real world use resources who are not solely dedicated to a single project. New users of Project often get confused because almost every person working on their projects puts in time on other work, from general communication with co-workers and clients to efforts put in on other projects. Should they build resource pools to account for time shared among several projects at one time?

Generally speaking, it would be chaos to try to track every minute of all your resources' days

to see whether they're working 100% or 50% on your tasks or are being shared among multiple projects. Ask yourself this question: when this resource works on a task in your project, "Will he or she put his entire focus on that task at that time?" If so, you may not need to fool around with tracking shared resources across many projects. Especially on shorter tasks, not trying to micromanage the efforts of your resources outside of your own project usually works just fine. If, on the other hand, you have resources who work only half time or split their time between two projects routinely, consider using shared resource tools to keep track of those resources across projects.

When you insert one or more Outlook resources in your project, they're added to your project list, taking the resource name and e-mail address as they exist in the Outlook address book. The default first-letter initial and work type is also preassigned. You can then add any details you like to the resource.

To insert resources from your Outlook address book, follow these steps:

1. **Choose Insert⇨New Resource From⇨Address Book.**

   The Choose Profile dialog box appears.

2. **Select Outlook.**

   The Resources dialog box appears, as shown in Figure 7-6.

3. **Specify a name.**

   You can type a name in the Type Name or Select from List box, or you can click a contact name in the Name list.

4. **Click Add to place the selected name in the Resources list.**

5. **Repeat Steps 2 and 3 to add all the resource names that you want to import to your project.**

6. **When you're finished, click OK.**

Figure 7-6:
If you use Outlook as your e-mail client, Microsoft makes it easy to use contacts you've stored there as resources in your project.

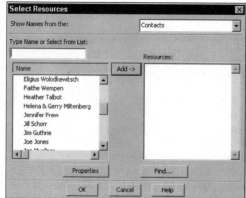

The names now appear in your project resource list, ready for you to add additional information.

If you use Project Server, you can access a feature called Team Builder through the Tools menu of Project. This allows you to choose resources from among various projects and your enterprise resource pools to build a project team.

Say, When Do These Guys Work?

Chapter 3 is all about calendars, including Project, Task, and Resource calendars. Now that you're working with resources, it's worth a closer look at how Resource calendars work.

First, there's a base calendar that can be Standard, Night Shift, or 24 Hour. (You can also create custom calendars.) Standard is a typical 9-to-5 day and five-day week. Night Shift is an 8-hour day scheduled between midnight and 8 a.m. in a six-day week. And the 24 Hour base calendar is just what it says: 24 hours, seven days a week.

After you specify a base Resource calendar, you can specify working hours, such as 9 to 12 and 1 to 5 for a standard eight-hour day or 8 to 12 and 1 to 4 for a variation on that eight-hour day. Finally, you can select specific days when a resource is not available (for example, when someone will be on vacation, at an off-site seminar, or busy with another commitment) and mark them as nonworking.

Avoid micromanaging nonworking time for your resources — it could leave you no time to manage anything. For example, if someone is taking half a day to go to a doctor's appointment, it's probably not necessary to block a day off. But if a resource is taking a two-week vacation or a three-month sabbatical, it's probably useful to modify the resource's working time calendar.

To make all these settings, you can use the Working Time tab of the Resource Information dialog box, which is shown in Figure 7-7.

Figure 7-7:
The legend on the left explains how nonworking and working days appear.

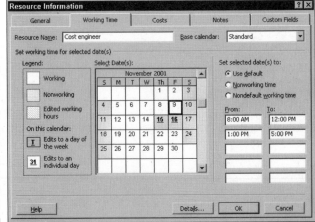

To make changes to a resource's calendar, follow these steps:

1. **Display the Resource sheet.**

2. **Double-click a resource name.**

   The Resource Information dialog box appears.

3. **In the Base Calendar box, select a base calendar.**

4. **If the default base calendar hours don't match your organization's, click the From and To boxes and type new times.**

   Note that to build in a break or lunch hour, you must enter two sets of numbers.

5. **If you want to mark any days as nonworking, click them in the Select Date(s) calendar, and then click the Nonworking Time option.**

   To display other months or years, drag the scrollbar box.

6. **Click OK when you're finished.**

To find out more about calendars or to create a custom Resource calendar, see Chapter 3.

Chapter 8

What's All This Gonna Cost?

There's no such thing as a free lunch — and if you use Project to track costs, there's no such thing as a free resource. That's because Project uses resources working on tasks as a way of calculating most of the costs on your project.

When you create a resource, you specify a work resource rate (by default, this rate is tallied up per hour) or a material resource per use cost. You can also create *fixed costs* — that is, a set cost for a task that isn't calculated using a per use or hourly rate, such as a trade show fee.

Some other factors come into play as well, such as how many hours a day a resource is available to work and any overtime rates. At the end of the day, all these settings come together to put you over — or under — budget.

In this chapter, you explore the relationship between resources and costs, and find out how to set resource standard and overtime rates, create fixed costs, and set the availability of resources on individual tasks in your project.

Mary, Mary, How Do Your Costs Accrue?

Project accounts for costs on your various tasks with a combination of costs per hour, costs per unit, and fixed costs. Before you begin to flesh out cost information about resources, you have to understand how these calculations work.

You'll have two main pictures of the budget in your project: one at the moment you freeze your original plan (called a *baseline plan*) and the ongoing picture of actual costs that comes from the actual activity and material usage you record as your project moves along. You record a certain amount of work effort on tasks, and tasks with resources assigned to them then run up costs based on the effort expended or units of materials used.

It all adds up

The best way to understand how costs add up in your project is to look at an example. John Smith (that's not his real name) is managing a project involving the building of a new gourmet ice cream packaging plant. John has created a task called *Install Ice Cream Mixers*. Here are the costs John anticipates for that task:

- About ten person hours of effort to do the installation

- A fixed cost of $500 paid to the mixer manufacturer to oversee the installation and train workers on the machine

- Twenty pounds of ice cream to test the mixers

The ten hours of effort will be expended by work resources. The total cost for the ten hours is a calculation: 10 times the resource rate. If the resource rate is $20, this cost totals $200. If two resources work on the task, one at a rate of $20 and one at a rate of $30, by default, Project will split the ten hours of effort between them, so the resulting cost is $250.

The fixed cost of $500 for a fee to the manufacturer is not assigned through a resource. Instead, you enter it in a Fixed Cost field for the task. This cost won't change based on the number of resources nor the time involved.

Finally, the cost for twenty pounds of ice cream (any flavor you like) is calculated as 20 times the unit cost of the ice cream. If the unit cost is $2, this cost would be $40.

And that's how costs are assigned and add up on your projects.

You can create and assign resources that have no associated costs — for example, if you want your boss to be available to review status reports, but your company doesn't require that your boss be charged to your project. You can simply use those resource assignments to remind you about the need for your boss's involvement on that day or at that time.

When will this hit the bottom line?

In business, you rarely get to choose when you'll pay your own bills.
In Project, however, you can choose when your costs will hit your budget.

Both resources and fixed costs can be set to accrue at the start or end of the task they're associated with or to be prorated throughout the life of the task. So, if a three-month-long task begins April 1, a $90 fixed cost could be added to your actual costs to date on day 1, on day 90, or at a dollar a day until the end of the task.

This isn't exactly a reflection of how you have to pay for costs, because let's face it: Most bills come due 30 days after they hit your desk. It's more a factor of when you want that cost to show up for the purposes of tracking costs and reporting on your project.

It's Pay Day!

Most projects involve a combination of cost types: fixed, work, and material. You'll have to do your homework before you can enter the information at the task or resource level. You have to find out the fixed costs as well as the hourly or unit rates for all your resources.

During the planning stages, it may not be possible to anticipate exactly what a particular cost will be or know every resource's rates. If you have to, build the resource or fixed cost with your best estimate. Then at least some cost will be reflected in your plan, and you can go back to enter more accurate information as soon as you know it.

Use the estimated check box in any task to which you assign estimated fixed or resource costs so you can easily go back to those tasks and make updates as your plan progresses.

There's no avoiding fixed costs

Maybe it's that huge fee for a consulting company your boss insisted you use, even though you knew their report wouldn't tell you a thing you didn't already know. Or perhaps it's the $2000 for a laptop computer you talked your boss into getting you so you could manage your project when you're on the road. Whatever it is, it's a cost that won't change no matter how many hours the task goes on or how many people work on the task. It has no unit cost or rate per hour. It's what's called a *fixed cost*.

You can enter fixed costs for tasks by using the Fixed Cost column in the Gantt Chart sheet. The easiest way to display this is to use the Cost table. Tables are variations on column combinations that make entering certain information easier. Follow these steps to enter a fixed cost for a task:

1. **Display the project in Gantt Chart view.**
2. **Choose View⇨Table⇨Cost.**

   The table of columns appears, as shown in Figure 8-1.
3. **Click the Fixed Cost column for the task to which you want to assign the cost, and then enter the amount.**

That's all there is to it, but because you can enter only one fixed-cost amount for a task, you should also enter a task note where you can itemize fixed costs if you have more than one. Note also that the default fixed-cost accrual method is prorated; if you prefer to have your fixed costs hit your budget at the start or end of a task, use the Fixed Cost Accrual column in this table to select another option.

When resources get paid per hour

To represent most people involved in your project, you create work resources and charge them to your project at an hourly rate. You enter the estimate of how many hours they'll work on each task that they're assigned to, and Project totals their estimated costs in your plan. When you track actual effort expended on tasks, a calculation of actual effort times the hourly rate returns actual costs. By comparing estimated costs and actual costs, you get an ongoing picture of whether or not your project is on track.

To set resource rates per hour, follow these steps:

1. **Display the Resource Sheet view.**
2. **Click the Std. Rate column for the resource to which you want to assign a cost.**
3. **Type a dollar amount.**

   If you're entering a rate for a unit other than hours, type a slash (/) and then the unit (for example, *minute* or *month*).
4. **Press Enter and the entry is saved.**

Note that you can also make cost-rate entries in the Resource Information dialog box. The Costs tab of this dialog box, which is shown in Figure 8-2, offers a Standard Rate, an Overtime Rate, and a Per Use Cost.

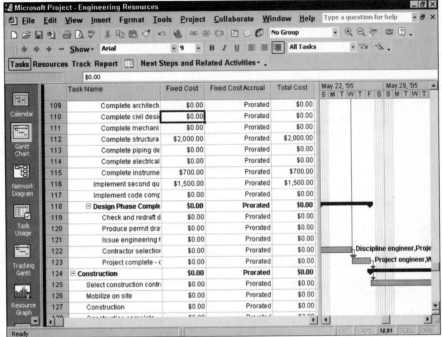

Figure 8-1:
You can
insert the
Fixed Cost
column in
any sheet,
but the Cost
table is
ready for
you to use.

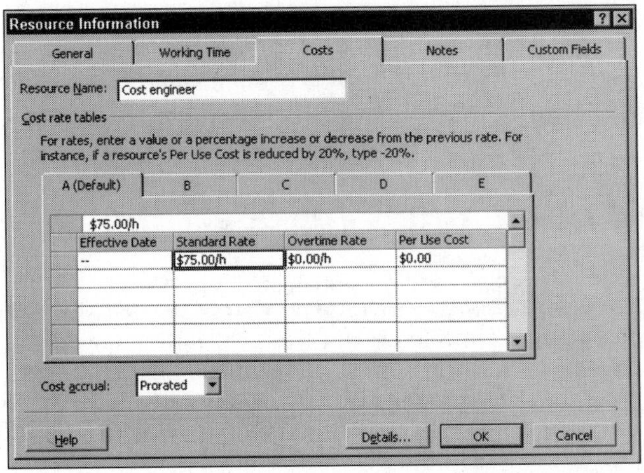

Figure 8-2:
You can set
several sets
of rates for
a resource.

In addition, five tabs labeled A through E allow you to enter different rates for
the resource. By using the Effective Date column, a resource could work for
several months at one rate and then start working at a different rate on a
preset date. This helps you account for periodic raises or seasonal shifts in
rates (for example, paying a premium for construction resources in months
with better weather when they are more in demand).

If you use ten gallons at $2 a gallon . . .

This one may feel like your high school algebra class. So many gallons of water in a bathtub with a leak. . . . Well, unless your project is to raise the Titanic, no leaks are involved, but there is a pretty straightforward calculation when you use cost per use.

Technically speaking, you can have a cost per use for either a work or material resource. You could, for example, have a consultant who costs $500 per use (that is, each time you use him to consult on a task, you get hit with a $500 fee). More commonly, you use a cost per use for a material resource such as rubber or milk, assign a cost for a single unit (per yard, or ton, or gallon, for example), and assign so many units to each task. The cost is tallied by the number of units times the cost per use.

To assign a cost per use, follow these steps:

1. **Display the Resource Sheet view.**

2. **Click the Cost/Use column for the resource you want to set, and then type an amount for the per-use cost.**

3. **Click the Material Label column for that resource, and then type a unit name (such as gallon).**

4. **Press Enter to accept your entry.**

Note that you can use the Resource Information dialog box also to enter up to five per-use costs with effective dates to account for fluctuations in unit cost over the life of your project.

Making allowances for overtime

Overtime is a fact of life: It's great for people who earn it and hard on the project manager with a budget. If you have resources that shift into earning overdrive after so many working hours, you can enter an overtime rate for them. Overtime kicks in when their calendar indicates that their regular day is over. So, a resource with a standard 8-hour-day calendar who puts in 10 hours on a one-day task will be charged by Project with 8 hours at the standard rate and 2 hours at the overtime rate.

To enter an overtime rate for a resource, follow this procedure:

1. **Display the Resource Sheet view.**

2. **Click the Ovt. Rate column for the resource.**

3. **Type an amount.**

4. **Press Enter.**

   The entry is saved.

It's an Availability Thing

Of the Project features dealing with resources, a big chunk is used to spot resource overallocation. *Overallocation* is a calculation involving the resource's calendar and availability.

So, consider Monica Melendez, an engineer who works a standard, 8-hour day based on her calendar. Monica is assigned to the *Write Final Report* task at 50% of her availability and to the *Create Design Specs* task — which occurs at the same time as the report task — at 100% of her availability. Monica is now working at 150% of her availability, or 12 hours per day. Poor Monica is overbooked.

By default, a resource is assigned to a task at 100% availability, but you can modify that if you know someone will be busy with several tasks and is likely to put in only part of their time over the course of a task.

Setting availability

Availability is easier to estimate for some than for others. A manager isn't likely to give an entire day over to any single task because he has to deal with all the people who report to him, sign authorizations, go to meetings concerning various projects, work on budgets, and so on. With a production worker, it might be simpler to pin down availability to a single task: If one manufacturing job is going through the line for three days and that person is working on the line all that time, it's closer to the mark to say that he or she is working on that task full time.

One big mistake that new users of Project make is to micro-think availability. Of course, no one actually spends eight hours every day on a single task in one project. People spend part of their days reading e-mail about company holidays, chatting with co-workers, and answering phone calls about non-project-related stuff. A resource might spend seven hours on a task one day but only three the next. Don't get hung up on a day-by-day resource schedule in estimating availability. If *over the life of a task* the person is pretty much devoted to it, 100% availability is a good setting. If that person will put in only, say, five days of work on a ten-day task, whether they work four hours a day for ten days or five full days at any point, that's 50% availability.

Remember, the availability setting is there to help you spot overbooking of a resource that might work on multiple tasks at the same time in a project schedule.

To set resource availability, follow these steps:

1. **Display the Resource Sheet view.**

2. **Double-click a resource.**

   The General tab of the Resource Information dialog box appears, as shown in Figure 8-3.

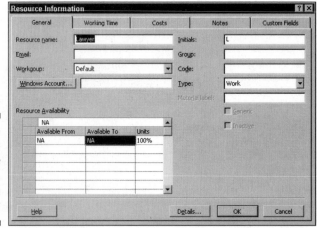

Figure 8-3:
You can
enter any
number you
like in the
Units box.

3. **In the Units column (in the Resource Availability area), click the arrows to raise or lower the availability in 50% increments or type a number.**

   For example, type 33 for a resource available a third of the time, or 400% for a pool of four resources all available full time. The most common entry here is 100% for a single resource working full time on the task.

4. **Click OK to save the setting.**

When a resource comes and goes

In addition to being available only a certain percentage of the time on any task, a resource may be available for only a certain period of time during the life of the task. Another scenario might be a resource that is available half time for the first few days of the task and then full time for the rest of the task. In that case, you enter a date range in the Available From and Available To columns of the Resource Availability area in the Resource Information dialog box (see Figure 8-3) to specify varying availability.

Adding It Up: How Your Settings Affect Your Budget

In Chapter 9, you explore assigning resources to tasks. But to help round out this discussion of costs, you should know that in addition to a resource cost per hour or use and a resource base calendar and availability, you will assign resources to tasks at certain percentages. All these factors work together in calculating the cost of the resource when assigned to tasks.

Don't worry about the calculations — Project does those for you. That's the beauty of this: After you make settings for your resources, Project does the work of tallying and showing total costs to you in views such as the Cost table of the Gantt Chart view shown in Figure 8-4.

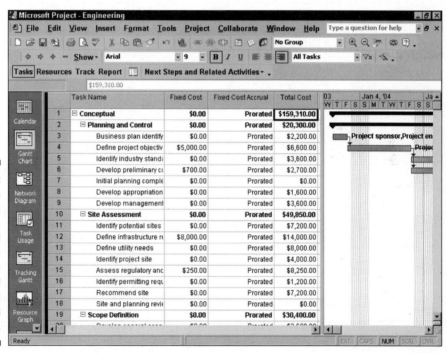

Figure 8-4: Total costs at the summary-task level give you a quick idea of your total budget and costs in this table.

For example, suppose that you want to assign a mechanic to a task. Here are the specifics:

Base calendar: Night Shift (eight hours, six days a week, between midnight and 8 a.m.)

Cost per hour: $20

Overtime cost: $30

Availability: 100%

Assigned to a two-day task: 50%

What is the cost of this resource? Here's how it works: two days at half time availability based on an eight-hour calendar is a total of eight hours (four hours each day). The resource incurs no overtime, so the cost is 8 times $20, or $160.

Change one setting for the same resource, and see what you get:

Assigned to a two-day task: 150%

Now the resource is working 12 hours a day (150% of 8 hours) over two days. With 16 total hours at the standard rate ($20) and 8 hours of overtime ($30), this person will cost $560.

Chapter 9

Your Assignment, Should You Choose to Accept It

In This Chapter

▶ Understanding how assigning resources affects task timing

▶ Making resource assignments

▶ Checking resource availability

▶ Notifying team members of their assignments

*Y*ou might have entered a cost per hour or per use for every resource in your project, but they won't cost you a thing until you assign them to tasks.

When you do begin making assignments, several interesting things happen. Not only will your budget start to swell, but also some of your tasks may actually change duration. You may also start to see evidence of people who are overbooked on several tasks that happen around the same time. Understanding how those results occur is key to making intelligent assignments.

But your work won't be over even when everything about your assignments looks hunky-dory. That's when you have to communicate the assignments to everyone and make sure they agree to take them on. If they don't, it's back to the assignment drawing board.

In fact, assigning resources is something of an ongoing process throughout your project. As usual, Project provides the tools to help you manage this entire process relatively painlessly.

You'd Be Surprised What Assignments Can Do to Your Timing

The three task types (which are described in Chapter 4) are fixed units, fixed work, and fixed duration. Each defines the relationship between a task's duration, the work required to complete the task, and resource assignments.

Your selection of task type in combination with a setting called effort-driven has an impact on the timing of your tasks relative to your resource assignments.

Pinning down your type

Essentially, task types specify what will remain constant in a task when you add or remove work resources to it after making the initial resource assignment. Although this whole work and duration and resource assignment percentage calculation can be complicated, it's important that you understand it if you want Project to accurately determine task durations in your plan based on resource assignments.

The default task type is fixed units. With a fixed-units task, the task duration you enter and the resource effort assigned to that task jointly determine the timing of the task. With this task type, the assignment units you specify for your resources won't change even if the number of hours required to complete the task shrinks or grows.

With a fixed-units task, if you increase the duration of Task A from two to three days, your resources will continue to work on it at the assigned units for the specified duration; Project will increase the Work amount accordingly. When you add or take away resources, Project will change the task duration accordingly, based on the assignment units you specify.

The fixed-work task type, on the other hand, takes a specified number of work units to be completed. A one-day task requires eight hours to be completed (assuming a Standard calendar). This type of task changes duration based on the number of resource units you assign.

With a fixed-work task, resource assignments may change based on a work change. For example, suppose Task A takes four days to complete when one person is assigned; with a fixed-work task the same task takes only two days when two people are assigned. Project will not modify the hours of work required to complete the task, but will modify resource assignment units to complete that work within the specified timeframe. So, if you up the duration of Task A, resource assignment units shrink in response. If you reduce the time to complete Task A, resource assignments increase to complete the unchanged amount of work hours in less time.

A fixed-duration task will not vary its length no matter what resource assignments you make.

With a fixed-duration task, Task A will take four days. If you assign additional resources or remove resources, the task will still take four days, but the resource assignment units will change.

Figure 9-1 shows the same task with the three different types. Each task was created with a four-day duration and one resource at 100%. Then an additional resource was added at 100%. Note the resulting change — or lack of change — with each type. The fixed-duration task didn't change duration but did reduce resource assignments. The fixed-units task kept resource assignments constant at 100%, and reduced the task duration. Fixed work was accomplished faster, but the work (4 days times 8 hours a day for a total of 24) stayed constant.

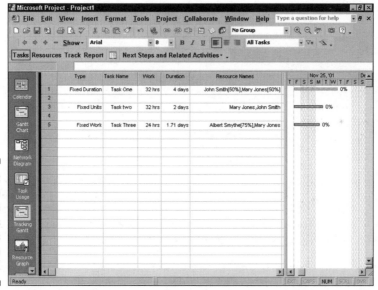

Figure 9-1:
Select the task type that reflects what is variable on your task.

When effort is in the driver's seat

Project's complex calculation of work, task duration, and assignment units involves not only task types but also the effort-driven setting. (In Figure 9-1, the effort-driven setting is active for all tasks.)

With the *effort-driven* setting active, if you add resources to a task, Project distributes the specified work equally among them and may change the task duration based on the total resource effort, depending on the task type.

With all three task types, effort-driven is on by default. You can turn the effort-driven setting on or off if you choose the fixed-duration or fixed-units task type. With the fixed-work task type selected, the effort-driven setting is turned on automatically and can't be turned off.

Follow these steps to change the settings for an effort-driven task:

1. **Double-click a task.**

   The Task Information dialog box appears.

2. **Click the Advanced tab, which is shown in Figure 9-2.**

3. **To turn off the effort-driven setting, click the Effort-Driven check box to remove the check mark.**

   The effort-driven setting is on by default.

4. **Click OK to save the new setting.**

Suppose task calendars prevail?

One other setting on the Advanced tab of the Task Information dialog box, Scheduling Ignores Resource Calendars, has an effect on how resources are scheduled when you make task assignments. You can instruct Project to let the Task calendar override any Resource calendar setting for resources assigned to it. Then, if a task is set to use the Standard calendar and a resource assigned to it uses a Night Shift calendar, that resource will work standard hours on that task.

Use this setting, for example, if someone who normally works the night shift will be called on to attend a two-day seminar taking place during standard working hours.

Finding the Right Resource

Sometimes there's no one in the world who can perform a certain task like Albert, and you'll get Albert to do that job if it kills you. But other times, any number of people could handle the work.

If any Tom, Dick, or Mary with a certain skill level or a certain rate per hour will do, you can use Project features to find the right resource and make sure he or she has enough time to take on just one more task.

Needed: One good resource willing to work

You've probably used the Find feature in other software to find a word or phrase or number. That's child's play: Project's Find feature can find you a backhoe, a corporate jet, or an entire person! You can use Project's Find feature to look for resources with certain rates or in a certain workgroup. You can search for resources by their initials, their maximum assignment units, their standard or overtime rate, and so on.

For example, you might need to find a resource whose standard rate is less than $50. Or you might want to find someone who can put in extra work on a task, so you search for any resource whose maximum units are greater than 100%. (In other words, the resource can put in a longer than usual day before he or she is considered overallocated.) Perhaps you need to find a material resource that is a chemical measured in gallons, but you can't remember the exact chemical name. In that case, you can search for resources whose material label includes the word *gallons*.

Follow these steps to find resources in Project:

1. **Choose Edit⇨Find.**

   The Find dialog box appears, as shown in Figure 9-3.

2. **In the Find What box, type the text you want to find.**

   For example, you would type 50 if you want to search for a resource with a standard rate of $50 or less, or laboratory if you want to find a resource whose material label contains that word.

3. **In the Look In Field list, click the name of the field you want to search in.**

   For example, to search for resources that have a maximum unit assignment percentage of more than 100%, click the Max Units field here.

Figure 9-3:
Searching
is a
combination
of looking
for some
element in a
particular
field that
meets a
certain
criterion.

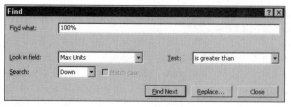

Figure 9-3:
Searching
is a
combination
of looking
for some
element in a
particular
field that
meets a
certain
criterion.

4. **In the Test box, select a criterion.**

   For maximum units of more than 100%, for example, this choice would
   be Is Greater Than.

5. **If you prefer to search backwards from your current location instead
   of forward, click Up in the Search box.**

6. **If you want to match the case of the text, click the Match Case check box.**

7. **To begin the search, click Find Next.**

8. **Continue to click Find Next until you find the instance you're
   looking for.**

You can use the Find feature also to find and replace an entry. For example, if
your Design Services department changes its name to Multimedia Production,
you can search the Group field for the words *Design Services,* click the Replace
button, and type the words *Multimedia Production,* as shown in Figure 9-4.
Then click the Replace button to replace each instance one by one, or click
the Replace All button to replace every instance in that field in your project.

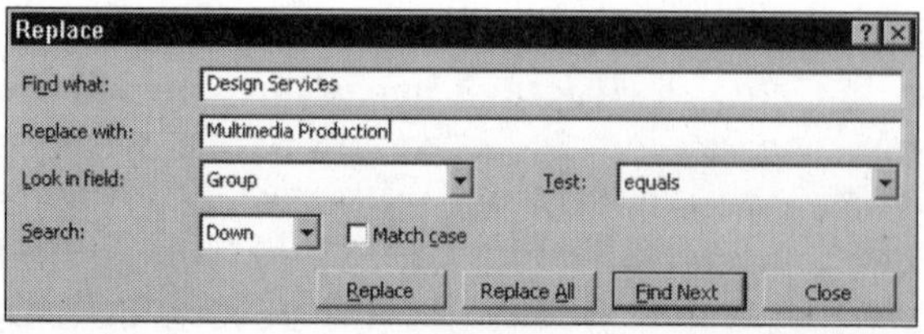

Figure 9-4:
The Replace
feature
offers a fast
way to
change
every
instance of
some text in
your project
field by field.

Custom fields: It's a skill

When assigning resources, you'll often need to take a person's skills into account. If a person with less skill or experience could work on a particular task (and save you money because they have a lower rate per hour), wouldn't it be nice to be able to find such resources easily?

Well, Project doesn't include a Skill field, but it does allow you to add fields of your own. You can use these fields for anything, but one great use of them is to code your resources by skill level. You can use a rating system such as A, B, C or use terms such as Exp for an experienced worker and Beg for a beginning-level worker.

Here's how to add a custom field:

1. **Display the Resource Sheet.**
2. **Choose View⇨Table⇨Entry.**
3. **Right-click a column heading and select Insert Column.**

   The column will be inserted to the left of the column you clicked.

4. **In the Field name box, select one of the custom fields, designated as Text 1 through Text 30.**
5. **In the Title box, type a name for the field.**
6. **Click OK to insert the column.**

Now you can enter whatever you like in this column for each resource in your project. Then you can search for specific entries in that field using the Find feature, or turn on a filter to display only resources with a certain skill level in that field. (Read more about filters in Chapter 10.)

 Some organizations designate custom fields for certain kinds of information. If you have a Project administrator who is in charge of these enterprise-wide standards, check with him or her before you choose a custom field to designate skill level.

A Useful Assignation

If you understand how task types and effort-driven scheduling can affect your tasks' timing, you've fought 95 percent of the battle in assigning resources. The rest is just the software equivalent of paperwork.

First, you have to create resources before you can assign them. (If you haven't, wander to Chapters 7 and 8 for a refresher course.) After you create resources, they are available to select from a list in each Task Information dialog box. Then, all you have to do is specify the resource assignment units. These differ slightly between work resources and material resources, however, so read on.

Assigning work and material resources

Work resources, which are typically people, are assigned to a task using a percentage, for example 100%, 50%, or 150%. When you assign a resource at a percentage, the assignment is based on the Resource calendar. A resource with a Standard calendar will put in 8 hours a day if you assign it at 100% assignment units. A resource with a 24-hour calendar will work a grueling 24 hours a day at 100% and 12 hours at 50%.

A material resource is assigned in units, such as gallons, consulting sessions, yards, or tons. When you assign a material resource to a task, you designate how many units of that resource will go to that task.

Note that material resource units are part of the entire work-unit-duration calculation that can cause work resources assignments to change task durations.

To assign a work or material resource to a task, follow these steps:

1. **Click a task to select it.**

2. **Click the Assign Resources button on the Standard toolbar.**

   The Assign Resources dialog box appears, as shown in Figure 9-5.

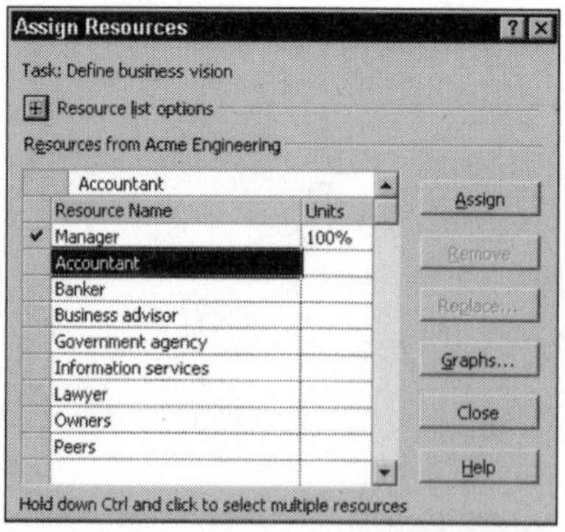

Figure 9-5:
Every
resource
you've
created is
shown in
this list.

3. **Click a resource to select it, and then click the Assign button.**

   A check mark appears next to the assigned resource in the Resource Name column.

4. **Click the Units column for the resource you just assigned.**

   If it's a work resource, the default assignment of 100% appears. If it's a material resource, the default is one unit.

5. **Specify a percentage of assignment units for the resource.**

   Click the spinner arrows in the box to increase or decrease the setting. For a work resource, change the percentage units in 50% increments by clicking the arrows, or type a percentage. For a material resource, use the spinner arrows in the Unit column to increase or decrease the unit assignment, or type a unit number.

6. **Repeat Steps 3 to 5 to add all resources.**

7. **If you want to replace one resource with another, click an assigned resource (indicated with a check mark), click Replace, select another name on the list, set its units, and click OK.**

8. **Click the close button in the top-right corner of the dialog box to save all the assignments.**

You can assign resources also on the Resources tab of any Task Information dialog box.

Getting the contour that's right for you

When you make a work resource assignment, Project spreads the work out evenly over the life of the task. However, you can modify the level of work that goes on during the life of the task, called a work *contour*, so that more work takes place near the beginning, middle, or end of the task.

For example, if you know that the people on a task to install a new computer network will have to spend some time upfront studying the manuals and reviewing the schematics for the wiring before they can begin to make measurable progress on the installation, you might use a late peak contour. Or if you know that people are likely to put in a lot of work upfront on a survey, and then sit back and wait for the results to come in, you might choose an early peak contour.

Using a different contour on a particular resource's task assignment could free up that resource to work on a second task that occurs during the life of the first task. This can help you resolve a resource conflict.

The contour you select will have slightly different effects depending on the task type. Trust me: Most project managers don't even want to try to understand this complex equation. Simply try a different contour and see whether it solves your problem and doesn't make too dramatic a change to your task duration or other resource assignments.

To set a task's contour, follow these steps:

1. **Display the Task Usage view.**

   This view shows resource assignments by task.

2. **Double-click a resource.**

   The Assignment Information dialog box appears, as shown in Figure 9-6.

Figure 9-6:
This is a
handy
summary
of all
assignment
information
for a
resource
on a task.

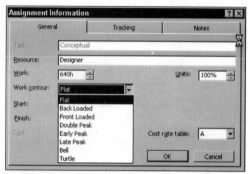

3. **In the Work Contour box, select one of the preset patterns.**

4. **Click OK to save the setting.**

   A symbol for the contour pattern is displayed in the Indicator column for the resource.

If none of these patterns fits your situation, you can manually modify a resource's work by changing the number of hours the resource puts in day by day on a task in the Task Usage view. But be sure your modifications still add up to the number of hours you want, or you could inadvertently change the resource's assignment.

Communicating an Assignment to Your Team

Now that you've worked out all your resource assignments on paper, it's time to see whether your ideas will work for your resource's schedules.

Of course, you should check to see who is available for your project. But in the time it takes to work out your plan and make assignments, things can change. So, before you commit yourself to a final plan, make sure your resources are committed to you.

If you use the Project Server product with Project, you can use collaborative tools to publish assignments to the server, where people can review them and accept or decline. For more on Project Server, read Appendix A.

You can send your entire project plan to resources as an e-mail attachment or just send selected tasks. You can also generate a resource assignment report and send that to people so that they can review their assignments in detail.

It's in the e-mail

E-mail can be a project manager's best friend. You can use it to communicate throughout the life of your project and to send your project plan for review at various stages. One of those stages is the point at which you want your resources to commit to their task assignments.

You can send your project as an e-mail attachment or as a schedule note, which is an e-mail with only updated tasks attached. You also have the choice of sending an entire plan or just selected tasks.

To send a project as an e-mail attachment, follow these steps:

1. **Choose File⇨Send To⇨Mail Recipient (as Attachment).**

   An e-mail form is displayed.

2. **Fill in a subject and your e-mail message.**

3. **Click Send to send the message.**

If you want to send a schedule note, follow these steps:

1. **Choose File⇨Send To⇨ Mail Recipient (as Schedule Note).**

   The dialog box in Figure 9-7 appears.

Figure 9-7:
Use this dialog box to specify who will receive your note.

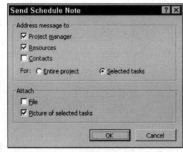

2. **Choose any intended recipients of the message from among Project Manager, Resources, and Contacts.**

3. **Click either Entire Project or Selected Tasks to specify what to include in the schedule note.**

4. **In the Attach area, choose what to attach to the e-mail message.**

   If you click the File option, the entire file will be attached. If you instead click the Picture of Selected Tasks option, Project will attach a bitmap picture of the selected tasks in the view you had active when you started the Send procedure.

5. **Click OK.**

   An e-mail form is displayed.

6. **Fill in a subject and your e-mail message.**

7. **Click Send to send the message.**

To help you track e-mails to resources on your project, set your e-mail program to provide return receipts when messages are received or read.

Report your findings

Remember the days when you read a report on paper, instead of on your computer screen? Those days aren't gone — in lots of situations, a printed report is your best bet for communicating about your project.

You can use several assignment reports to inform resources of their assignments on projects. The four assignment report types provide the following information:

- ✔ **Who Does What report.** Provides a list of tasks organized by resource with total work hours, number of days delay from the original schedule, and start and finish dates. It also reflects a total number of work hours for a resource on all tasks in the project.

- ✔ **Who Does What When report.** Shows a calendar listing of tasks organized by time period with resource assignment totals.

- ✔ **To Do List report.** Generated for a single resource (not all resources as with the other report types) week by week in a project. It lists the task names, durations, start and finish dates, and predecessor tasks by task number.

- ✔ **Overallocated Resources report.** Shows resource assignments for resources who are overbooked on tasks during the project, and includes total hours, unit assignments, total hours of work on each task, and any delay from the original schedule.

Follow these steps to generate an assignment report:

1. **Choose View⇨Reports.**

2. **Click Assignments, and then click Select.**

   The Assignment Reports dialog box appears, as shown in Figure 9-8.

3. **Click one of the four reports.**

4. **Click Select.**

   A preview of the report appears. Figure 9-9 shows a sample Who Does What report.

5. **If you need to modify the Page Setup, click Page Setup.**

   For example, you might want to modify the margins or set the document to print landscape or portrait.

6. **To print the report, click Print.**

If you want to print to a fax machine or a file, change your printer choice in the Print dialog box.

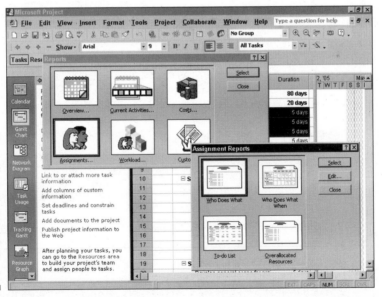

Figure 9-8:
Assignment
reports
deal with
resource
assign-
ments to
individual
tasks.

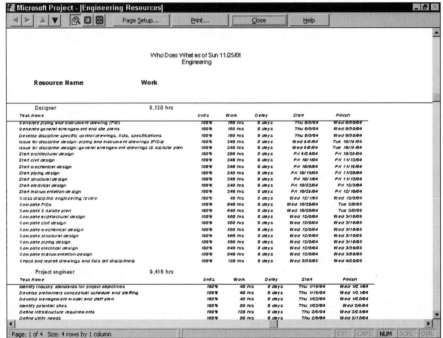

Figure 9-9:
A wealth of
assignment
information
can be
contained in
these
reports.

Part III
Well, It Looks Good on Paper

The 5th Wave   By Rich Tennant

"Why, of course. I'd be very interested in seeing this new milestone in the project."

In this part . . .

After you've built all the tasks in a project and assigned resources to carry them out, you're not finished. Almost every project starts out with a set of challenges that you must solve before you can finalize your plan. These harken back to the familiar project parameters of time, money, and overworked resources.

Project offers a plethora of tools to help you spot and solve timing relationships between tasks that don't work and people who are working 24-hour days (not a good thing). You can also call on different sets of information about your schedule and budget and try a few automated solution tools to save time and money.

This is also the part where you get your project plan looking good before you hand it in to your boss and sign off on all the commitments you'll spend the next part of your life fulfilling.

Chapter 10

Fine-Tuning Your Plan

• •

In This Chapter

▶ Using filters to view timing and resource issues

▶ Adding slack to your tasks to plan for change

▶ Making adjustments to shorten your schedule

▶ Reigning in your costs

▶ Resolving resource conflicts

• •

As they say, the best laid schemes of mice and project managers oft go awry, and your plans are no different. When you've taken your best shot at laying out your project plan, created every task, and assigned every resource, and you think you're ready to start your project, think again.

A close look at almost any plan will reveal some issues that you should resolve before you begin working on your first task. These might include a schedule that ends a month after your deadline, resources that are working 36-hour days, or a budget that exceeds the national debt.

But even if you don't see any glaring problems in the areas of time, workload, or money, you should do a few things to make sure that your project is as realistic as possible before you commit to it. So take a moment to give your project the once over.

Everything Filters to the Bottom Line

A first step in making sure that your plan is solid is simply looking at it from a few different perspectives. It's like turning around in front of the mirror to see your outfit from every angle before you go out on a date. Filters and grouping are two Project features that help you get that kind of perspective.

Two major problem areas that filters and grouping can help you examine at this stage are *overallocated resources* — that is, resources working more than the number of hours you specified — and tasks that are on the critical path. The *critical path* consists of the series of tasks in your project that must happen on time for the project to meet its final deadline. Any task that has *slack* — that is, any length of time that it could be delayed without delaying the entire project's timing — is not on the critical path. If your project has little in the way of slack, any delays that occur are likely to derail your project.

Predesigned filters

Filters are to Project what a magnifying glass was to Sherlock Holmes. They let you examine various aspects of your plan to spot clues about problems, such as overallocated resources. You can set a filter to highlight tasks or resources that meet certain criteria or to remove any tasks or resources from view that don't meet such criteria.

Project provides predesigned filters that you can simply turn on for tasks or resources, using criteria such as

- ✔ Tasks with a cost greater than a specified amount
- ✔ Tasks on the critical path
- ✔ Tasks that occur within a certain date range
- ✔ Milestone tasks
- ✔ Tasks that use resources in a resource group
- ✔ Tasks with overallocated resources

Several filters, such as Slipping Assignments and Work Overbudget, help you spot problems after you've finalized your plan and are tracking actual progress. See Chapter 13 for more about tracking.

You can access filters in a couple of ways. When you use the Filter button, you choose from a list of predesigned filters. The filters act to remove any tasks from view that don't meet specified criteria.

To turn on such filters from the Formatting toolbar, follow these steps:

1. **Display a resource view (such as Resource Sheet view) to filter for resources or a task view (such as Gantt Chart view) to filter for tasks.**

2. **Click the Filter list on the Formatting toolbar, and then click a criterion.**

   The Filter list is a drop-down list; when no filter is applied, All Tasks or All Resources appear in the list. If you choose a filter that requires input, you'll see a dialog box such as the one in Figure 10-1. Otherwise, the filter is applied and removes from view any resources or tasks that don't match your criteria.

3. **If a dialog box is displayed, fill in the information and then click OK.**

   The filter is applied.

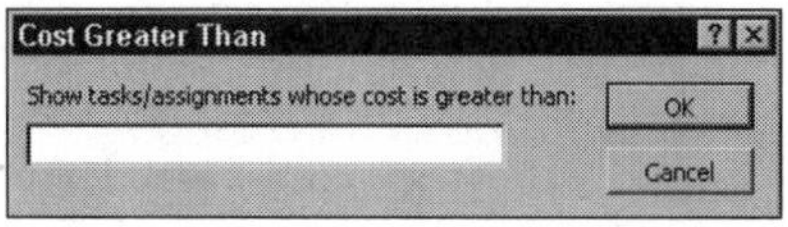

Figure 10-1:
Some filters
require
additional
input.

To redisplay all tasks or resources, click Filter on the Formatting toolbar and then click either All Resources or All Tasks (depending on whether a Resource or Task filter is currently applied).

You can also use the AutoFilter button on the Formatting toolbar to turn on an AutoFilter feature. When you click the AutoFilter button, arrows appear at the head of columns in the currently displayed sheet. Click the arrow for the Task Name column, for example, and the name of every task in your project is listed. Click a task name, and all tasks but that task and any parent tasks for it are removed from view. You can also choose a Custom setting from each of these menus (see Figure 10-2) to customize AutoFilter with certain criteria.

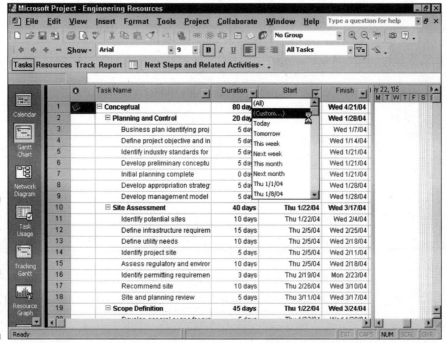

Figure 10-2:
AutoFilter
choices are
specific to
each field of
information
in your
sheet.

Follow these steps to activate and use AutoFilter:

1. **Display the view that contains the fields (columns) you want to filter.**

2. **Click the AutoFilter button.**

   Arrows appear at the top of each column.

3. **Click the arrow on the column that you want to filter.**

4. **Click the criterion you want for your filter.**

   For example, if you are filtering for task duration, in the Duration column you can choose >1 day, >1 week, or any number of days such as 5 days or 100 days. All tasks or resources that don't meet your criteria disappear.

If you want to highlight each item that meets filter criteria rather than remove nonmatching items from view, choose Project⇨Filtered For⇨ More Filters. Click the filter you want, and then click Highlight.

Do-it-yourself filters

You don't have to use predesigned filters: You can get creative and design your own filters. To define a new filter, you specify a field name, a test, and a value.

For example, the following filters for any task on the critical path:

   Critical (field name) Equals (test) Yes (value)

You can also include additional qualifiers to the filter. The following filters for tasks that are both on the critical path and have a baseline cost of more than $5000:

   Critical (field name) **Equals** (test) **Yes** (value)

   and

   Baseline Cost (field name) **Is Greater Than** (test) **5000** (value)

Here's how to build your own filter definition:

1. **Choose Project⇨Filtered For⇨More Filters.**

   The More Filters dialog box appears, as shown in Figure 10-3.

Figure 10-3:
This dialog
box lists all
available
filters —
both pre-
designed
and custom.

2. **Click either the Task or Resource option to specify which list of filters you want the new filter to be included in.**

3. **Click New.**

   The Filter Definition dialog box appears.

4. **In the Name box, type a name for the filter.**

5. **Click the first line of the Field Name column, and then click the arrow that appears to display the list of choices, as shown in Figure 10-4.**

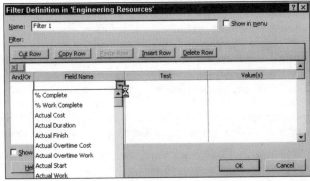

Figure 10-4:
It's a good
idea to give
your new
filter a
name that
describes
what it
does.

6. **Click a field name to select it.**

7. **Repeat Steps 5 and 6 for the Test and Value(s) columns.**

8. **If you want to enter a qualifier, such as a dollar amount, click the entry box above the column headings and type the amount at the end of the filter definition.**

   For example, if you choose Cost for the field name and Equals for the test, you might enter the number $5000 at the end of the definition in the entry box.

9. **If you want to add another condition, choose And or Or from the And/Or column, and then make choices for the Field Name, Test, and Value(s) boxes.**

   Note that you can cut and paste rows of settings you've made to rearrange them in the list, or use the Copy Row or Delete Row button to perform those actions for filters with several lines of criteria.

10. **If you want the new filter to be shown in the list when you click the Filter box on the Formatting toolbar, click the Show in Menu check box.**

11. **Click OK to save the new filter, and then click Apply to apply the filter to your plan.**

You can click the Organizer button in the More Filters dialog box to copy filters you've created in one Project file to another file.

Looking at things in groups

Remember those groups you used to hang out with in high school? (I'm sure you were part of the cool group!) Groups helped you see the underlying order of your adolescent hierarchy. Project groups things, too. The Group feature essentially allows you to organize information by certain criteria. For example, you can use the Group feature if you want to see resources organized by work group, or you might organize tasks by their duration, shortest to longest.

Like filters, groups can be predefined or created as custom groups.

Follow these steps to apply a predefined group structure to your project:

1. **Display either a resource view (such as Resource Sheet view) to group resources, or a task view (such as Gantt Chart view) to group tasks.**

2. **On the Standard toolbar, click the Group By list, and then click a criterion.**

   The information is organized according to your selection. See Figure 10-5 for an example.

To redisplay all tasks or resources in their original order, click the arrow in the Group box on the toolbar to display the list, and then click No Group. (When no Group is applied, the Group box displays No Group.)

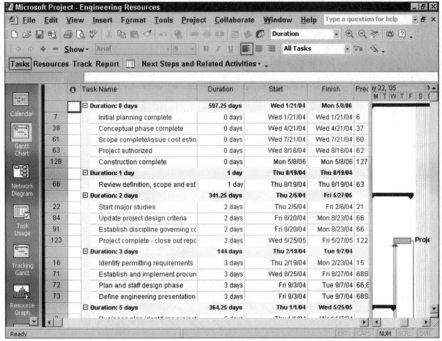

Figure 10-5:
Organizing
tasks by
duration
provides
this view of
your project.

Devising your own groups

Custom groups include three elements: a field name, a field type, and an order. For example, you might create a group that shows the field name (such as Baseline Work) and a field type (such as Tasks, Resources, or Assignments) in order (Descending or Ascending). A group that shows Baseline Work for Tasks in Descending order, for example, would show you tasks in order from the tasks with the most work hours to the least. Other settings control the format of the group's appearance.

Follow these steps to create a custom group:

1. **Choose Project⇨Group By⇨More Groups.**

    The More Groups dialog box appears, as shown in Figure 10-6.

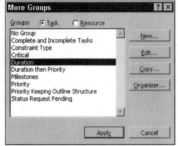

Figure 10-6:
This dialog
box is
organized
by task- or
resource-
oriented
groups.

2. **Click either Task or Resource to specify in which list of groups you want the new group to be included.**

3. **Click New.**

   The Group Definition dialog box appears, as shown in Figure 10-7.

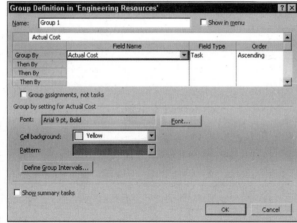

Figure 10-7:
Use your
own groups
to organize
data.

4. **In the Name box, type a name for the group.**

5. **Click the first line of the Field Name column, click the arrow that appears to display the list of choices, and then click a field name to select it.**

6. **Repeat Step 5 for the Field Type and Order columns.**

   Note that if you want the Field Type option of grouping by assignment rather than by resource or task, you must first select the Group Assignments Not Tasks check box to make that field available to you. Otherwise the Field Type of Task or Resource appears by default.

7. **If you want to add another sorting criteria, click a row titled Then By, and make choices for the Field Name, Field Type, and Order columns.**

8. **If you want the new group to be shown in the list when you click the Group box on the Formatting toolbar, select the Show in Menu check box.**

9. **Depending on the field name you've chosen, you can make settings for the font, cell background, and pattern to format your group.**

   For example, the font and color of each duration group heading in Figure 10-5 was determined by making choices from these three lists.

10. **Click OK to save the new group, and then click Apply to apply the group to your plan.**

If you want to make changes to an existing predefined group, apply the group and then choose Project⇨Group By⇨Customize Group By. This takes you to the Customize Group By dialog box for that group. This dialog box is identical to the Group Definition dialog box and allows you to edit all those settings for an existing group.

It's About Time

We've all had this experience: Your boss asks you to commit to getting a project finished by a certain date. Your palms sweat, you get a sick feeling in the pit of your stomach, you add a week onto the deadline the boss suggests to cover yourself, and then you promise to deliver the impossible. You hope you can do it. You want to do it. But can you do it?

Project allows you to feel much more confident about committing to a time-frame because you can see how long all your tasks will take to complete. Before you go to your boss and make any promises, make sure you're comfortable with two things: the total time it takes to complete the project and the critical path.

The timing data for your project summary task tells you how long the entire project will take. Just display the Gantt Chart view and look at the Duration, Start, and Finish columns. If your finish date doesn't work, you'll have to go back and modify some tasks.

You should also make sure that there's room for error. You can use filters and groups to identify the critical path in, for example, the Gantt Chart view or Network Diagram view. If you judge that too many tasks are on the critical path, it's wise to add some slack to plan for inevitable delays.

Giving yourself some slack

How many tasks should be on the critical path in your project and how many should have some slack — that is, some time for delay without delaying the entire project? It's not a science. Ideally, every task in your project should have slack because things can come up that you never expected. If you add slack to each and every task, however, your project is probably going to go on into the next millennium. Figure 10-8 shows a more typical scenario, with a mix of noncritical and critical tasks.

Some tasks have slack naturally because they occur during the life of a longer task with which share a dependency. The shorter task could actually be delayed until the end of the longer task without delaying the project.

Think about this example: You can start installing the plumbing and electrical elements of a new office building as soon as the framing inspection is complete. The plumbing takes two weeks and the electrical work takes one week. The next task, mechanical inspection, can't happen until both the plumbing and electrical tasks are finished. The shorter of the two, electrical, has a week of slack because nothing will happen until the dependent task, plumbing, is finished (see Figure 10-9). However, if electrical runs one week late, it then becomes critical.

Noncritical tasks

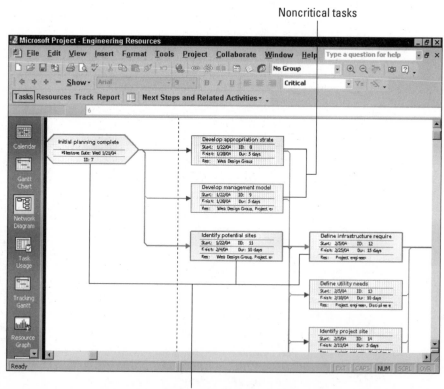

Figure 10-8:
Follow the critical path in Network Diagram view.

Critical tasks

Figure 10-9:
Taskbars
will help
you visualize
slack
available to
tasks that
are not on
the critical
path of your
project.

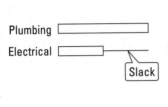

These natural cases of slack occur in any project. But in many cases, you have to build in slack. Slack can be added in a few ways.

First, you can simply inflate task durations: Add two days to the duration of all the tasks in your project, or go in and examine each task to figure out the risk of delay and pad each duration accordingly. This method is a little problematic, however, because when changes occur, you may have to go into many tasks and adjust durations to deal with a schedule that's ahead or behind. You also have to keep track of exactly how much slack you built into each task.

The second method of building in slack is the one I like best. You build one task or several tasks that occur throughout your project — say, one at the end of each phase of the project, as shown in Figure 10-10. Now, you don't call this task *Slack,* because even the dumbest boss will catch on eventually and make you get rid of your slack to hit an impossible deadline. You can call slack tasks *Engineering Analysis,* or *Debriefing,* or *CYA Meeting.* Then, give the task a duration that provides slack for the other tasks in that phase. For example, at the end of a two-month phase of designing a new product package, you might add a task called *Design Debriefing* and make it one week long. Then, you simply create a dependency between that task and the last task in the phase.

As things slide in your project (and they will, trust me), you'll spot it because the slack task is suddenly ending later than the date you'd wanted the phase to end. You can change the duration of the slack task, reflecting the fact that your slack is being used up. The duration of that task will give you a good indication of how much more time you have before the entire phase will run late.

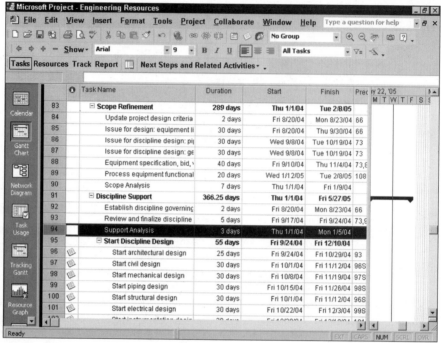

Figure 10-10:
Each phase of this project ends with an Analysis task that actually represents slack.

Doing it in less time

If you do your homework and add slack to tasks, you're making your plan realistic, but the price you pay is that you're adding time to your project. What happens when your project finish date just won't cut it with the powers-that-be? That's when you have to try a few tactics to chop your timing down to size.

Check your dependencies

The timing of your plan is determined to a great extent by the timing relationships you build among tasks, that is, by dependencies. So ask yourself, did I build all my dependencies in the best way I could? Perhaps you didn't start one task until another was completely finished, but you could actually start the second task two days before the end of its predecessor. Building in that kind of overlap will save you time.

Here's an example: You created a finish-to-start relationship for the *Do Research and Write Speech* task, such that you could not start writing the speech until your research was finished. But is that true? Couldn't you do a first draft of the speech starting three-fourths of the way through the research?

Over the life of a project with hundreds of tasks, adding that kind of overlap to even a few dozen tasks could save you a month of time or more!

You can take a refresher course in creating and changing dependencies in Chapter 6.

We could use some help here!

Another reason for timing is the availability of resources. Here are a few things to look for:

- ✔ Maybe you delayed the start of a task because a resource wasn't available. But could some other resource do the work? If so, switch resources and let the task start sooner.

- ✔ Project calculates the duration of some tasks (fixed work and fixed units with effort-driven scheduling) based on the number of resources available to do the work. If you add resources to those tasks, Project will shorten their duration.

- ✔ If you assign a more skilled resource to some tasks, you might be able to shorten the task durations because the skilled person will finish things more quickly.

Chapter 9 covers the mechanics of making and changing resource assignments.

Cut to the chase: Deleting some tasks and slashing slack

When all else fails, it's time to cut corners. Can you skip some tasks, such as that final quality check, the one that occurs after the other three already built in? Or should you pull back on some of the slack you've allowed yourself?

Never, I repeat, NEVER get rid of all the slack in your schedule. Otherwise, it will come back and haunt you like the Ghost of Christmas Past. Just tell your boss I said so.

Could you get some other project to handle some of your tasks for you with different sets of resources? If your buddy has a project that involves writing specs for a new product, could you convince him to also write the user's manual, which was your responsibility in designing product packaging? It's worth a shot.

Getting It for Less

When you've assigned all your resources to tasks and set all your fixed costs, it's time for sticker shock. Project will tally all those costs and show you the project's budget. But what if those numbers just won't work? Here are some tips for cutting down that bottom line:

✔ **Use cheaper resources.** Do you have a high-priced engineer on a task that could be performed by a junior engineer? Did you assign a high-priced manager to supervise a task that could be handled by a lower-priced line supervisor?

✔ **Lower fixed costs.** If you allowed for the travel costs of four plant visits, could you manage with only three? Could you book flights ahead of time and get cheaper airfares? Could you find a cheaper vendor for that piece of equipment you allocated $4000 to buy?

✔ **Cut down on the overtime.** Are resources that earn overtime overallocated? Try cutting down their hours or using resources on straight salary for those 14-hour days.

✔ **Do it in less time.** Resource costs are a factor of task duration times hourly wages or number of units. If you change tasks so that less work hours are required to complete them, they'll cost less. However, don't be unrealistic about the time it will really take.

Your Resource Recourse

Before you finalize your plan, you should consider one final area: resource workload. As you went about assigning resources to tasks in your project, you probably created some situations where resources are working round the clock for days on end. Your first step is to see how to spot those overallocations. Then you have to give those poor folks some help!

Checking resource availability

To resolve issues with resource assignments, you have to first figure out where the problems lie. You can do that by taking a look at a few views that focus on resource assignments.

The Resource Usage view (see Figure 10-11) and the Resource Graph view (see Figure 10-12) are useful in helping you spot overbooked resources.

First, keep in mind that resources are flagged as overallocated in these Resource views based on their assignment percentage and calendars. A resource based on a standard 8-hour-day calendar assigned at 100% to a task will work 8 hours a day on it. If you assign that same resource at 50% to a task happening at the same time, the resource will put in 12-hour days (8 plus 4) and be marked as overallocated.

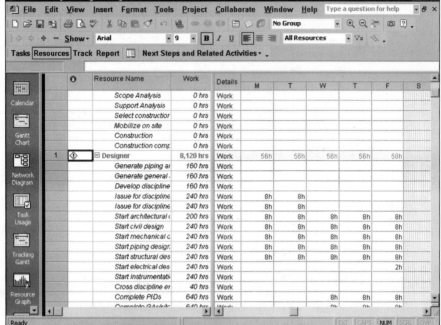

Figure 10-11:
The Resource Usage view spells out workflow resource by resource.

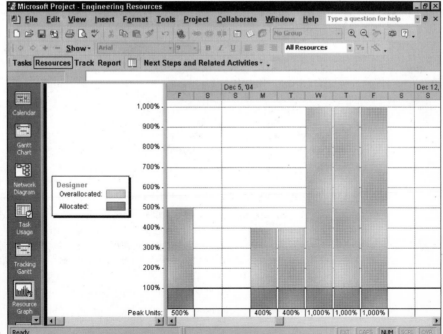

Figure 10-12:
The Resource Graph view gives you a visual clue to overworked resources.

In the Resource Graph view, work is summarized in the Peak Units row, and all work in the part of the bar graphic that's above the 100% mark is highlighted. In the Resource Usage view, any overallocated resource has a yellow diamond with an exclamation point in the Indicator column. The total hours that the resource is working each day on his or her combined tasks is summarized on the line that lists the resource's name.

Deleting or modifying a resource assignment

So, you discover that poor Henrietta is working 42 hours on Tuesday and 83 hours on Friday. What to do?

You have a few options:

- ✔ **Remove Henrietta from a few tasks to free up some time.**

- ✔ **Change Henrietta's resource calendar to allow for a longer workday — for example, 12 hours.** Keep in mind that this means a 100% assignment will have Henrietta working 12 hours on any one task in a day. If you stretch a resource's workday, you should probably reduce the resource's assignments. For example, if someone frequently puts in 16 hours on two tasks in one day based on an 8-hour calendar and two 100% assignments, try changing to a 12-hour calendar and 50% assignments (6 hours on each of the two tasks, totaling 12 hours a day). However, if the person typically works an 8-hour day and 12- or 16-hour days are the exception, you shouldn't change the resource's base calendar because it will have an impact on all assignments for that resource.

    Keep in mind that the two previous options may lengthen the tasks that the resource is assigned to if you either remove the resource or reduce the resource's assignment.

- ✔ **Change Henrietta's availability by upping her assignment units to more than 100% in the Resource Information dialog box.** For example, if you enter 150% as her available units, you're saying it's okay for her to work 12 hours a day, and Project will then consider her fair game and not overallocated until she exceeds that 12 hours.

- ✔ **Ignore the problem.** I don't mean this facetiously: Sometimes someone working 14 hours for a day or two during the life of a project is acceptable, and there's no need to change the resource's usual working allocation to make that overwork indicator go away. (However, consider telling Henrietta it's okay to order pizza on the company on those long workdays.)

Getting some help

When one person is overworked, it's time to look for help. You can free up resources in several ways.

One way is to assign someone to help out on a task, and reduce the over-booked resource assignment now that he or she is not needed for as many hours. Reduce the resource's work assignment on one or more tasks — say, reducing 100% assignments to 50%. You do this in the Task Information dialog box on the Resources tab or by selecting the task and clicking the Assign Resources tool to open the Assign Resources dialog box shown in Figure 10-13.

Figure 10-13:
You can change assignment units for a resource on a particular task.

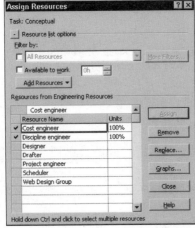

Note that you can quickly check a work graph for any resource by clicking the Graphs button in the Assign Resources dialog box.

You'll also find that by adding resources to some tasks, you'll shorten their duration. That means you might free up your resource in time to eliminate a conflict with a later task in the project.

Try changing the work contour for the resource. By default, Project has a resource work on a task at the same level for the life of the task. You can modify the work contour, for example, so that a resource puts in the most effort at the start of a task, which frees up the resource's workload later when a conflict with another assignment might occur.

Getting your resources level

Resource leveling sounds something like the St. Valentine's Day massacre, but it's not. Resource leveling is a calculation that Project goes through to try to resolve resource overallocation in your project. It works in two ways: by delaying a task until the overbooked resource frees up or by splitting tasks. Splitting a task involves essentially stopping it at some point, thereby freeing up the resource, and then resuming it at a later time when the resource is available.

You can make these same types of changes yourself or let Project do the calculation. Project will first delay tasks that involve overallocated resources to use up their slack. When no more slack is available on these tasks, Project makes changes based on any priorities you've entered for tasks, dependency relationships that are affected, and task constraints, such as a Finish No Later Than constraint.

But don't worry: You can turn on leveling to see what changes Project would make, and then clear the leveling to reverse its actions if you don't like them.

To level resources in your project, follow these steps:

1. **Choose Tools⇨Level Resources.**

   The Resource Leveling dialog box appears, as shown in Figure 10-14.

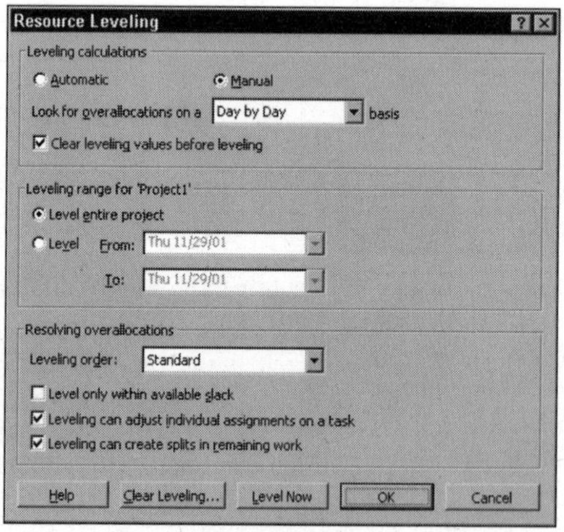

Figure 10-14:
You can
control
some
aspects
of the
resource-
leveling
calculation.

2. **Make a choice between allowing Project to do Automatic or Manual leveling.**

   Automatic tells Project to level every time you change your plan. The Manual option requires that you go to the Resource Leveling dialog box and click Level Now.

3. **If you choose to level automatically, be sure to check the setting in the Clear Leveling Values Before Leveling option depending on whether or not you want previous leveling actions reversed before you level the next time.**

4. **Check Level Entire Project, or click Level and fill in a date range by making choices in the From and To boxes.**

5. **In the Leveling Order box, click the arrow and make a selection.**

   Standard considers slack, dependencies, priorities, and constraints. ID Only delays or splits the task with the highest ID number — in other words, the last task in the project. The Priority, Standard choice uses task priority as the first criteria in making choices to delay or split tasks, rather than slack.

6. **Check any of the three check boxes at the bottom to control how Project will level.**

   You can level within available slack, meaning that no critical tasks are delayed and your current finish date for the project is retained. You can level by adjusting resource assignments, allowing Project to remove or change assignments. Finally, you can level by splitting tasks only for unstarted work in the project, which can put some tasks on hold for a period of time until resources are freed up for work.

7. **Click Level Now to have Project perform the leveling operation.**

To reverse leveling, go to the Resource Leveling dialog box (Tools⇨Level Resources) and click Clear Leveling.

To level or not to level?

Resource Leveling has pros and cons. It can make changes that you might not want it to make — for example, taking a resource off a task where you absolutely need that person's unique skills. It frequently delays your project's finish date, which might not be acceptable to you (or your boss).

The safest setting for Resource Leveling — that is, the one that makes the least drastic changes to your timing — is to level only within slack.

This setting may delay some tasks, but it won't delay your project completion date.

If you just can't live with everything Resource Leveling did, the capability to turn Resource Leveling on and off is your best ally. You can turn the feature on and look at the things it did to resolve resource problems, and then turn it off and manually institute the portions of the solution that work for you.

Getting in the Mix

One final word about all the solutions suggested in this chapter to deal with time, cost, and overallocation problems. To be most successful you'll probably have to use a combination of all these methods. Solving these problems is often a trial-and-error process, and although you might initially look for one quick fix, in reality the best solution might come through making a dozen small changes. Take the time to find the best combination for your project.

Chapter 11

Making Yourself Look Good

Some old chestnut would have you believe clothes make the man. Well, in the same spirit, there are times when presentation makes the project. Having a project that looks good serves two purposes. It impresses people with your professionalism (sometimes to the point where they'll overlook a little cost overrun), and it allows people looking at your project to easily make out what the different boxes, bars, and lines indicate.

Project uses default formatting that is pretty good in most cases. But you may have certain company standards for reporting that require that baseline data be yellow and actual data be blue, for example, or that you add more frequent gridlines to help your nearsighted CEO read Project reports more easily.

Whatever you need, Project provides tremendous flexibility in formatting various elements in your plan.

Putting Your Best Foot Forward

Microsoft has decided to capitulate to the artist in all of us by allowing us to modify shapes, colors, patterns, and other graphic elements in our Project plans. This gives you great flexibility in determining the way your plan looks.

When you print Project views, you can print a legend on every page. The legend helps those reading the plan understand the meaning of the various colors and shapes you've set for elements.

One important thing to realize is that all the views and formatting choices that Project offers you don't exist only on the screen. You can print your project or reports about your project. What is displayed when you print is what will print. So knowing how to make all kinds of changes to what's on your screen allows you to present information to team members, managers, vendors, and clients in hard copy.

It's useful to be able to print in color, so that all the various colors used for graphic elements such as taskbars and indicators will show up. If you print in black and white, you may find that certain colors that look good on screen aren't as distinct when you print. Being able to modify formatting allows your project to look good in both color and black and white, both on screen and in print.

Formatting Taskbars

Taskbars are the horizontal boxes that represent the timing of a task in the chart pane of Gantt Chart view. You can format each bar individually or change global formatting settings for different types of taskbars.

You can change several things about taskbars:

- ✔ **The shape that appears at the start and end of the bar; you can change the shape's type and color.** Each end can be formatted differently.

- ✔ **The shape, pattern and color of the middle of the bar.**

- ✔ **The text that you can set to appear in five locations around the bar: left, right, above, below, or inside the bar.** You can include text in any or all of these locations, but keep in mind that too many text items can become impossible to read. This text helps readers of your plan to identify information, especially on printouts of large schedules where a task may appear far to the right of the Task Name column identifying it by name in the sheet area.

When you track progress on a task, a progress bar is superimposed on the taskbar. You can format the shape, pattern, and color of the progress bar. The goal is to contrast the progress bar with the baseline taskbar, so you can see both clearly.

By formatting taskbars, you can help readers of your plan identify various elements, such as progress or milestones. If you make changes to individual taskbars, people who are accustomed to Project's standard formatting might have trouble reading your plan.

To make formatting settings for various types of taskbars, follow these steps:

1. **Right-click the chart area outside any single taskbar and then click Bar Styles.**

   The Bar Styles dialog box appears, as shown in Figure 11-1.

2. **In the spreadsheet along the top in the Name column, click the type of task that you want to modify (Task, Split, Progress, and so on).**

   For example, if you want to modify the styles used for all summary tasks, click Summary. The choices in the Bar tab in the bottom half of the dialog box change based on the task type you click on.

3. **Click in the Show For . . . Tasks column for the task type you want to modify and then select criteria for the task, such as Critical or Finished.**

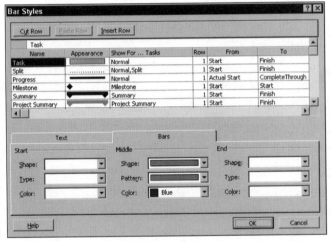

Figure 11-1:
You can modify the look of taskbars and the text you display along with them.

4. **Click the Bars tab to display it, if necessary, and then do the following:**

   a. **Click any of the Shape lists to modify the shape of either end or the middle of the taskbar.**

      Shapes on either end might be an arrow, a diamond, or a circle. Shapes in the middle consist of a bar of a certain width.

   b. **Click any of the Color lists to modify the color used on either end or the middle of the taskbar.**

      The Automatic choice is the default color for this type of taskbar element.

   c. **Click either of the Type lists to modify the type of formatting for the shape on either end of the taskbar.**

      This setting controls how such a shape is outlined: framed with a solid line, surrounded by a dashed line, or filled in with a solid color.

        d. Click the Pattern list to select another pattern for the middle of the bar.

   5. Click the Text tab (see Figure 11-2), and then do the following:

        a. Click any of the text locations.

          An arrow appears at the end of that line.

        b. Click the arrow to display an alphabetical list of possible data you can include, and then click a field name to select it.

        c. Repeat Steps 5a and 5b to choose additional text locations.

   6. Click OK to accept all new taskbar settings.

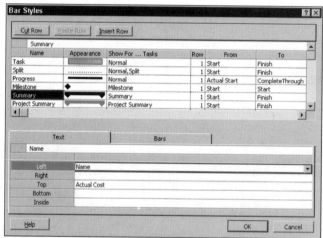

Figure 11-2:
You can place text in up to four locations around taskbars.

Gantt Chart Wizard

What would formatting be without a wizard to help you to make all your settings quickly? Gantt Chart Wizard allows you to make formatting settings to the entire Gantt Chart, including what information to display (standard, critical path, baseline, or several combinations of these), one piece of information to include with your taskbars, and whether or not you want to display lines to show dependencies among tasks.

If you choose to make custom settings while using Gantt Chart Wizard, you will be allowed to make choices for many of the settings you see in the Bar Styles dialog box, but those choices will affect all taskbar elements of that type in the project, not just individual taskbars.

If you want to make the same types of changes to an individual taskbar rather than to all taskbars of a certain type, right-click the taskbar and then click Format Bar. A Format dialog box appears with the same Text and Bar tabs found in the Bar Styles dialog box.

Formatting Task Boxes

Network diagram task boxes use different shapes to help you spot different types of tasks. For example:

- ✔ **Summary tasks** use a slightly slanted box shape and include a plus or minus symbol, depending on whether the summary task's subtasks are hidden or displayed. Click the symbol to hide or display subtasks.
- ✔ **Subtasks** are in a simple rectangular box.
- ✔ **Milestones** are shown in diamond-shaped boxes with blue shading.

You can change the formatting of each task box individually or by type. To change the formatting of task boxes displayed in the Network Diagram view, do this:

1. **Right-click the task box you want to change and then click Format Box, or right-click anywhere outside the task boxes to change formatting for all boxes of a certain style and then click Box Styles.**

   The Format Box dialog box appears.

2. **To modify the border style, make your selection in the Shape, Color, and Width lists.**

3. **To modify the background area inside the box, make a selection in the Color list, or Pattern list, or both (at the bottom of the dialog box).**

4. **Click OK to save your new settings.**

When you modify the formatting of individual boxes in the Network Diagram view, the standards of slanted summary tasks and shaded milestones will no longer be a visual guide to all tasks. If you make changes and decide you'd like to put a task box back to its default setting, click Reset in the Format Box dialog box.

Adjusting the Layout

In addition to displaying particular columns and formatting taskbars, you can make certain changes to the layout of your view. These options vary a great deal depending on what view you're working with: The layout of the Calendar and Network Diagram views is quite different than the layout choices offered in Gantt Chart view.

To display the Layout dialog box for a view, right-click the area, such as the chart area of the Gantt chart or anywhere on the Calendar or Network Diagram view, and then click Layout. The appropriate dialog box appears. Figure 11-3, 11-4, and 11-5 show the various layout choices available in the different views.

In general, the settings in these Layout dialog boxes deal with how the elements on the page are arranged and how dependency link lines are displayed.

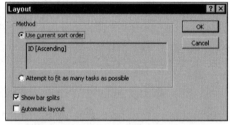

Figure 11-3:
The Layout dialog box for Calendar view.

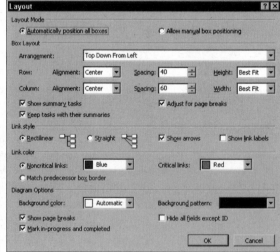

Figure 11-4:
The Layout dialog box for Network Diagram view.

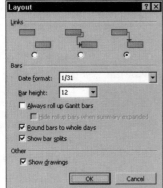

Figure 11-5:
The Layout
dialog box
for Gantt
Chart view.

Table 11-1 shows you the layout settings. You could probably spend a week redoing all these settings to see what they look like, and I could spend a few days writing about the various options. The tools Project offers to modify the formatting of elements such as taskbars and task boxes provide wonderful flexibility.

Table 11-1	Layout Options	
Layout Type	*Option*	*Use*
Calendar view	Use Current Sort Order	Project uses the latest sort order you've applied to tasks
	Attempt to Fit as Many Tasks as Possible	Ignores the sort order and fits as many tasks in a date box as possible
	Show Bar Splits	When a task includes a period of inactivity, that task can be shown as split into different parts over time
	Automatic Layout	Project modifies the layout based on the insertion of additional tasks

(continued)

Table 11-1 *(continued)*

Layout Type	Option	Use
Network Diagram view	Layout Mode area	Allows automatic or manual positioning
	Box Layout area	The settings in this section arrange and align boxes, adjusting alignment, spacing, and height and modifying how summary tasks are displayed
	Link Style area	Modifies the style for dependency link lines and labels
	Link Color area	Sets the color for links both on and off the critical path
	Diagram Options area	Controls the background color and pattern for boxes, and how page breaks and progress on tasks are indicated
Gantt Chart view	Links	Style of lines indicating dependency links
	Date Format	Modifies the format of the date used to label taskbars
	Bar Height	Sets the height of taskbars in points
	Always Roll up Gantt Bars	When checked, taskbar details roll up to the highest-level summary task
	Round Bars to Whole Days	When you have portions of days, allows bars to represent the nearest whole-day increment

Layout Type	Option	Use
	Show Bar Splits	When a task includes a period of inactivity, that task can be shown as split into different parts over time
	Show Drawings	When you've included drawings, they are displayed on the screen and in the printout

Now that you've seen the many options available for modifying view layouts, I have some advice: Stick with default settings unless you have a specific reason to make a change (such as when you want to highlight certain types of information for a project presentation). And when you don't need that layout change anymore, go right back to the default settings. Or, if you want to make changes, make them globally across your organization and stick to them. That will make it much easier for those reading your project plan to interpret the different kinds of information presented in views. Generally speaking, changing the way Project displays information at this point will just make your learning curve about how Project represents information slower and confuse those who know Project's default settings.

Modifying Gridlines

Just as phone numbers are broken up into several shorter sets of numbers to help you remember them, visual elements are often broken up to help you understand information. Tables use lines, calendars use boxes, football fields use yard lines, and so on.

Several views in Project include gridlines to indicate certain things, such as the break between weeks or the status date (that is, the date as of which progress has been tracked on a project). These lines help the reader of your plan discern intervals of time or breaks in information (for example, gridlines can be used to indicate major and minor column breaks). You can modify these gridlines in several ways, including changing the color and style of the lines and the interval at which they appear.

To modify gridlines, use the Gridlines dialog box, as follows:

1. **Right-click any area of a view that contains a grid (for example, the chart area of the Gantt Chart view or the Calendar view) and then click Gridlines.**

   The Gridlines dialog box appears, as in Figure 11-6.

2. **In the Line to Change list, click the gridline you want to modify.**

3. **Use the Normal Type and Color lists to select a line style and color.**

4. **If you want to use a contrasting color at various intervals in the grid to make it easier to read, do the following:**

   a. **Select an interval at which to include a contrasting line.**

      This setting is typically used with a different style or color from the Normal line setting to mark minor intervals for a grid. Note that not all types of gridlines can use contrasting intervals.

   b. **Choose the Type and Color of that line from the lists.**

5. **Click OK to save your settings.**

Figure 11-6:
The possible lines you can change will vary somewhat from one view to another.

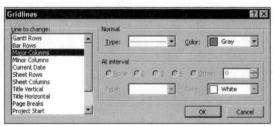

Note that you make choices for modifying gridlines one by one, and there is no reset button to put these settings back the way they were. Also note that gridlines modified in one view don't affect gridlines in any other view.

When a Picture Can Say It All

Words and numbers and taskbars and task boxes are fine, but what if you want to add something of your own? For example, you may want to draw attention to a task by drawing a circle around it, or you may want to include a simple drawing to show a process or working relationship in your plan.

You can use a Drawing toolbar to draw images in the chart area of the Gantt Chart view. Follow these steps to add a drawing:

1. **Display the Gantt Chart view.**

2. **Choose Insert➪Drawing.**

   The Drawing toolbar appears, as shown in Figure 11-7.

3. **Click the drawing tool that represents the type of object you want to draw, such as an oval or a rectangle.**

4. **Click at the location on the chart where you want to draw the object, and drag your mouse until the item is drawn approximately to the scale you want.**

5. **Release the mouse button.**

Figure 11-7:
This Drawing toolbar contains some tools it has in common with other Office family products you may have used.

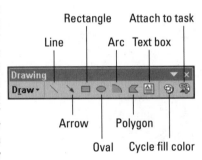

At this point, you have a few options:

- ✔ If you drew a text box, you can click in it and type whatever text you like.

- ✔ You can resize any object you've drawn by selecting it and then clicking any of the nodes around its edges to enlarge or shrink it.

- ✔ You can move the mouse over the object until the cursor becomes a four-way arrow, and then click the object and drag it elsewhere on the chart.

- ✔ You can use the Cycle Fill Color to choose a color for a selected object. Each time you click this tool, it displays another color in the available palette. Just keep clicking the tool until the color you want appears.

✔ If you have several drawings or objects that you want to layer on your page, you can click the Draw button on the Drawing toolbar and choose an order for a selected object, bringing it to the front of other images or sending it behind them.

✔ Finally, you can attach a drawn object to any task by moving it next to a task and then clicking the Attach to Task Drawing tool.

Part IV
Avoiding Disaster: Staying on Track

The 5th Wave   By Rich Tennant

"And tell David to come in out of the hall. I found a way to adjust our project budget estimate."

In this part . . .

So you've drawn up a project plan and your tasks are underway. Now what? Is there still some role for Microsoft Project in your life? You bet. This is when all the inputting you did to create a project plan really pays off. In this part, you work with setting a baseline for your project against which you can track progress. Then you use an army of Project tools that help you track your schedule and budget.

But what happens when you hit a snag in your project? You're not alone: Project helps you resolve schedule, budget, and resources problems that are as inevitable in ongoing projects as ants at a picnic. First, you discover how Project views help you see what's going on with your project, and then you can use Project to correct the things you find. You also explore the variety of reports you can use to communicate the status of your project to others.

The last chapter in this part clues you in to how to get better and better with Project as you learn from one project to the next and use features such as macros and templates to automate future work.

Chapter 12

It All Begins with a Baseline

*W*hen you go on a diet (and I know you all have at one time or another!), you step on the scale the first day to check your weight. Then, as your diet progresses, you have a benchmark against which you can compare your dieting ups and downs.

Project doesn't have a weight problem, but it does have a method of benchmarking your project data so that you can compare the actual activity that takes place on your tasks to your original plan. This saved version of your plan data is called a *baseline,* and it includes all the information in your project, including task timing, resource assignments, and costs.

Project also provides something called an interim plan. An *interim plan* is more of a timing checklist. It includes only the actual start and finish dates of tasks and the estimated start and finish dates for tasks not yet started.

This chapter shows you when, why, and how to save a baseline and interim plans for your project.

All about Baselines

Saving a baseline is like freezing a mosquito in amber: It's a permanent record of your estimates of time, money, and resource workload for your project at the moment you consider your plan final and before you begin any activity. A baseline is saved in your original Project file and exists right alongside any actual activity you record on your tasks.

You can use baselines to debrief yourself or your team at any point in a project. This is especially useful at the end of a project, when you can compare what really happened against your best guesses those many weeks, months, or even years ago. You can then become a much better user of Project, making more accurate estimates up front. You can also use a baseline and the actual activity you track against it to explain delays or cost overruns to employers or clients using a wide variety of reports and printed views.

Finally, you can also save and clear baselines for only selected tasks. So, if one task is thrown way off track by a major change, you can modify your estimates for it and leave the rest of your baseline alone. Why throw out the baby with the bathwater?

What does a baseline look like?

After you've saved a baseline and tracked some actual activity against it, you get both baseline and actual sets of data as well as visual indications of baseline versus actual.

Figure 12-1 shows the Gantt Chart view for a project displaying baseline and actual data. In the sheet area, you can display columns of data for baseline estimates and actual activity, such as baseline finish and actual finish. In the chart area, the black line superimposed on the taskbar represents your baseline estimate. This black line indicates actual activity on that task.

Figure 12-2 shows the Network diagram view. Here, progress on tasks is represented by a single slash for tasks where some activity has been recorded and an X over tasks that are complete. A notation of percent completed is included in each task box not marked as complete.

You can change the way different graphic elements are represented by reformatting. See Chapter 11 for more about formatting taskbars and task boxes.

How do I save a baseline?

Like a mother reminding a kid to eat all his vegetables, Microsoft has built in a little nudge to remind you to save a baseline. Whenever you save a file that doesn't have a saved baseline, Project displays the dialog box shown in Figure 12-3, asking whether you want to save the project with a baseline. The default is to save the file without a baseline.

Actual progress bar

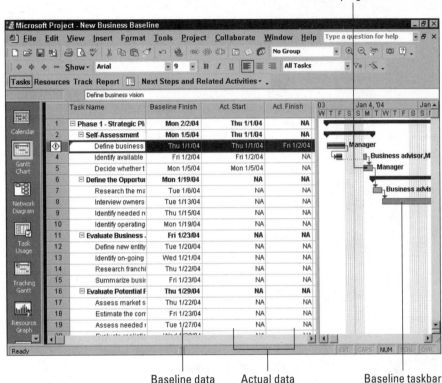

Figure 12-1:
You can stay constantly aware of variations between your plan and reality with both data and graphics.

Baseline data   Actual data   Baseline taskbar

You can also save a baseline at any time by displaying the Save Baseline dialog box. One setting in this dialog box is a new feature in Project 2002 and requires a little explanation. The setting concerns how Project rolls up data to summary tasks when you set a baseline. By default, after you've saved a baseline the first time, a summary task's baseline data isn't updated if you make changes to a subtask below it, even if you delete a subtask. However, you can change that functionality by making a choice about how the baseline rolls up data. You can choose to have modifications rolled up to all summary tasks or only from subtasks for any summary tasks you've selected. This second option works only if you have selected summary tasks but not selected their subtasks.

If you get sick of seeing the Save Baseline dialog box, next time it appears, click the Don't Tell Me About This Again check box.

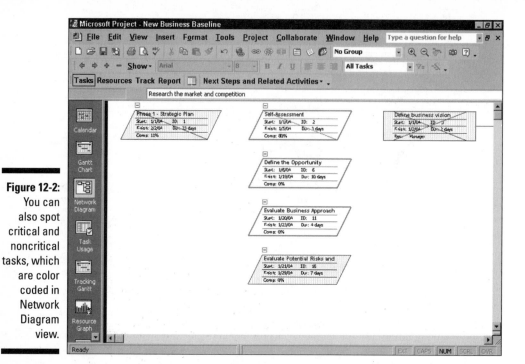

Figure 12-2:
You can
also spot
critical and
noncritical
tasks, which
are color
coded in
Network
Diagram
view.

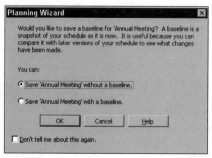

Figure 12-3:
You don't
need to
save a
baseline
until your
plan is
pretty much
final.

You can save a baseline at any time by following these steps:

1. If you want to save a baseline for only certain tasks, select them.

2. Choose Tools⇨Tracking⇨Save Baseline.

The Save Baseline dialog box appears with the Save Baseline option selected, as shown in Figure 12-4.

3. Click Entire Project or Selected Tasks.

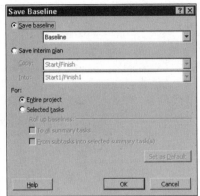

Figure 12-4:
This dialog box is used for baselines and interim plans.

4. **Make selections for how the baseline rolls up, or summarizes, changes to task data.**

   You can have changed data summarized in all summary tasks or only for the summary tasks you've selected.

5. **Click OK to save the baseline.**

What if I want more than one baseline?

I know you love to hear about new features in Project 2002 that make the cost of upgrading worthwhile. Here's one: You can now save your baseline up to 11 times during the life of your project. That's 11 potentially catastrophic events you can adjust for by resaving your baseline!

Multiple baselines can help you see the progress of your planning over the life of a longer project. They are also a sneaky but effective way of showing your boss that, yes, you really did anticipate that budget overrun — even though you didn't include it in your original saved plan. (I'm not advocating this, but it works as long as your boss didn't keep a copy of the original plan.)

The Save Baseline dialog box includes a list of these baselines, with the last date saved for each, as shown in Figure 12-5. When you save a baseline, you can save without overwriting an existing baseline by simply selecting another of the baselines in this list before saving.

If you save multiple baselines or interim plans, you can view them by displaying columns in any sheet view for those plans. For example, if you want to display information for a baseline you saved with the name Baseline 7, you would insert the column named Baseline 7 in your Gantt Chart view sheet.

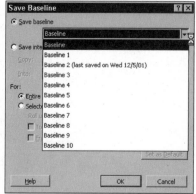

Figure 12-5:
Each
baseline
to which
you've
saved
something
includes
the last
saved date
in this list.

How do I clear and reset a baseline?

Okay, if you read the first part of this chapter, you know that I said that a baseline is intended to be a frozen picture of your project plan that you keep sacrosanct and never change. Well, that's the theory. In practice, things can happen that make an original baseline so obsolete that it's less than useful. It's not even worth keeping as one of your 11 possible baselines.

For example, if you have a project that takes four years from beginning to end, you might want to save a new baseline every year because costs go up or resources change. Then you can see incremental versions of your estimates that reflect the changes you made based on changes in the real world. Or, what if you start your project with a wonderful, well-thought-out baseline plan, but a week later the entire industry shuts down with a massive strike that goes on for three months. All your original estimates of timing would be bogus, so it's better to save a new baseline and move ahead after the strike is resolved.

To clear the existing baseline, follow these steps:

1. **If you want to clear the baseline for only certain tasks, select them.**

2. **Choose Tools⇨Tracking⇨Clear Baseline.**

   The Clear Baseline dialog box appears with the Clear Baseline Plan option selected by default, as shown in Figure 12-6.

3. **In the Clear Baseline Plan box, select the baseline that you want to clear.**

4. **Click to clear the baseline for the entire project or for selected tasks.**

5. **Click OK.**

   The selected tasks or project baseline are cleared.

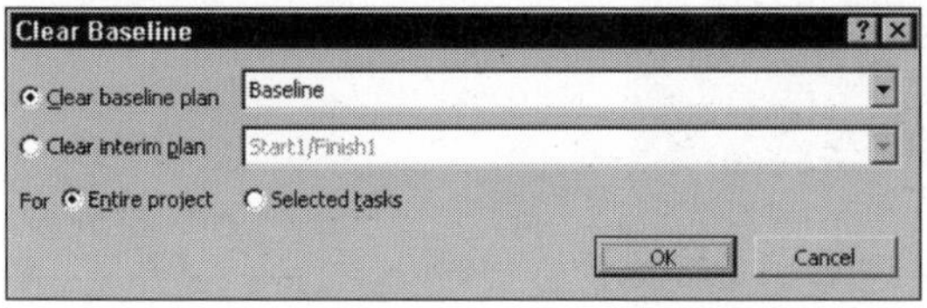

Figure 12-6:
Use this to
clear the
baseline or
interim plan.

In the Interim

An interim plan is sort of like baseline lite. With an interim plan, you save only the actual start and finish dates of tasks that have had activity tracked on them as well as the baseline start and finish dates for all unstarted tasks.

Why save an interim plan rather than a baseline? An interim plan saves only timing information. If that's all you need, why save all the data about resource assignments and costs and so on? (Keep in mind that you'll end up with a huge file if you save ten baselines.)

Another issue with a baseline is that because there's so much data, the baseline can become obsolete at some point. An interim plan can be saved to record date changes but not overwrite your original baseline.

Finally, although you're allowed to save up to eleven baseline plans, if you need more than that, consider using some interim and some baseline data to expand the number of sets of data you can save.

Saving an interim plan

Interim plans and baselines are saved using the same dialog box. The difference is that with an interim plan, you have to specify where the data is coming from.

To save an interim plan, do this:

1. **If you want to save an interim plan for only certain tasks, select them.**
2. **Choose Tools➪Tracking➪Save Baseline.**

   The Save Baseline dialog box appears, as shown in Figure 12-7.
3. **Select Save Interim Plan.**
4. **In the Copy box, select the set of data that you want to copy to the interim plan.**

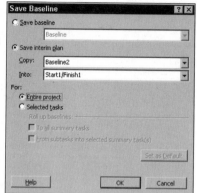

Figure 12-7:
You can
copy
settings
from any
saved
baseline to
an interim
plan.

5. **In the Into box, select the fields in which you want to store the interim plan data.**

6. **Click to save the entire project or selected tasks.**

7. **Click OK to save the plan.**

By using the Copy and Into boxes in the Save Baseline dialog box, you can save up to ten interim plans based on baseline or actual data.

Clearing and resetting a plan

Ten interim plans may seem like a lot now, but in the thick of a busy and ever-changing project, it may actually end up falling short of what you need. Because you have only ten interim plans to save, you may need to clear one at some point and resave it.

Project piggybacks baseline and interim plan settings, so you actually choose a Clear Baseline menu command to clear an interim plan. This can be frightening to those who think that clicking a Clear Baseline command will send their baseline into oblivion. Don't worry — it won't!

To clear an interim plan, follow these steps:

1. **If you want to clear only some tasks in an interim plan, select them.**

2. **Choose Tools⇨Tracking⇨Clear Baseline.**

   The Clear Baseline dialog box appears, as shown in Figure 12-8.

3. **Click the Clear Interim Plan option, and then choose the plan you want to clear in the accompanying list.**

Figure 12-8:
You can
clear and
reset interim
plans as
often as you
like during
the life of
your project.

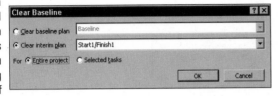

4. **Click to clear the specified interim plan for the entire project or for any tasks you have selected.**

5. **Click OK to clear the plan.**

You can now save new information to that interim plan, if you like.

You may want to save a backup of various versions of your file with interim and baseline data. If you clear a baseline or an interim plan, that data is gone forever!

Chapter 13

On the Right Track

● ●

In This Chapter

▶ Using the Tracking toolbar

▶ Recording actual activity on tasks

▶ Specifying percentage of work complete

▶ Updating fixed costs

▶ Using Update Project to make big-picture changes

● ●

*A*fter a project moves out of the planning stage and into action, it's like a constantly changing game in which there are rules, goals, and a general timeframe, but no one really knows which team will win (and sometimes where the ball is) till it's over.

Whether a task happens as planned or wanders off in an unexpected direction, your job at this stage of the game is to record that activity, which is referred to as *tracking*.

Tracking starts when your team reports their activity on the project. Then you or someone who is assigned to deal with tracking has to manage inputting that activity task by task.

When you have tracked activity, you'll be amazed at what data Project returns to you. Some will be good news, some bad, but all of it will be useful in managing your project throughout its lifetime.

Gathering Your Data

The first step in tracking progress on your project is to get information about what's been going on. The amount of data you collect will be determined by what you need to track and at what level of detail. For example, some people don't even create and assign resources to tasks because they use Project only to create a timeline for their activities, not to manage resource time or tally costs. Others use resources and want to track their total work on tasks, but not to the level of detail of hourly work performed. For some people, simply marking one task 50% complete and another 100% complete and letting Project assume all resources put in their estimated amount of work is fine. Your tracking method will be determined by the amount and type of information you need to monitor.

So, the first thing you have to do is identify the best tracking method for you.

A method to your tracking madness

Microsoft has identified four tracking methods:

- **Task-total method**
- **Task-timephased method**
- **Assignment-total method**
- **Assignment-timephased method**

You can begin to understand these by looking at the difference between task and assignment tracking. You can track information at the *task* level, indicating total work or costs for the task up to the present or as of a status date you select. Or you can track costs by *resource assignment,* which is the more detailed way of tracking.

For example, suppose that the *Test Electrical Components* task is estimated to take 12 hours of work, according to your project baseline. Three resources, Engineer, Electrician, and Assistant, are assigned at 100% of their time. Tracking by task, you can simply note that the task is 75% complete, which translates into 9 hours of work finished. Project will assume that the three resources split that work up equally.

In reality, however, the Engineer put in 1 hour, the Electrician put in 6, and the Assistant put in 2. If you want more detailed tracking so that totals of work for each resource assignment are accurately tracked, you would track the work at the resource assignment level.

But here's where the timephased variable comes in: Whether you choose to track work on a task or work by individual resources on the task, you can also make the choice to track by specific time increments, which Microsoft calls *timephased* tracking.

So, with our *Test Electrical Components* task, you can use a task approach of tracking 9 hours of work to date or use a timephased approach to record those hours on a day-by-day basis. With a resource assignment approach, you can go to the very deepest level of tracking detail by tracking each and every resource's work hour by hour, day by day.

Let your Project make the rounds

You can use the Send to feature on the File menu of Project to send your project to others and have them update their own activity. You can do this by either e-mailing a file or selected tasks as a file attachment, or you can route one file and have people make their changes in one place.

The challenge with the first method is that you need to manually incorporate the changes in the various files into a single file.

The challenge with the second approach is getting people to do the updating accurately and forward the file to the next person on the routing slip in a timely fashion. Generally, the best use of e-mail for updating projects is simply to have team members send an e-mail with their activity to the person updating the project, and let that person make all the changes in one central location.

Finally, if you want Project to keep an eye on costs, be sure to track fixed costs that have been incurred on each task.

Going door to door

How do you get all the information about what work has been performed, by whom, and when? Well, the first method is the one you've probably been using for years: Hunt down the people on your project and ask them. Ask them in the hallway, in your weekly one-on-one meeting, or over lunch. Give each person a call, or have everyone turn in a form.

This is not rocket science, but you still have to determine upfront what information you want, when you want it, and what form it should be in. The simpler you can keep manual reporting of progress on a project, the better, because people will actually do it. The more routine you can make it — such as every Friday, on a set form turned into the same person, and so on — the easier it will be.

If you need only a summary of where the task stands — say 25, 50, 75, or 100% complete — have the person in charge of the task give you that informed estimate. If you need total hours put into a task to date, that's what resources have to report. If you need a blow-by-blow, hour-by-hour, day-by-day report, you're likely to collect some form of timesheet from resources.

You can probably get information about fixed costs that have been incurred from your accounting department or by getting a copy of a purchase order or receipt from the resource that spent the money.

Consider a third-party add-on product such as Timesheet Professional (`http://timesheetprofessional.com`) for reporting resource activity. You make Timesheet available to every resource on the project. The resources record their work time on it, and you can use Timesheet's tools to automatically update your project. If you're using Project Professional edition, Timesheet's features are incorporated into Project Server.

Where Does All This Information Go?

After you've gathered information about task progress, fixed costs, and resource hours, you can input that information in several ways. You can use various views and tables to enter information in sheets of data; you can input information in the Task Information dialog box; or you can use the Tracking toolbar.

Doing things with the Tracking toolbar

Microsoft provides a toolbar for everything, so why should tracking be any different? The Tracking toolbar can be used to perform updates on selected tasks in any sheet view. Figure 13-1 shows the Tracking toolbar and the tools it has to offer.

The Tracking toolbar allows you to open the Project Statistics dialog box or display the Workgroup toolbar. You can use other tools to make specific updates to selected tasks:

- ✔ Selecting a task and clicking the **Update as scheduled tool** automatically records activity to date as you anticipated in your baseline.

- ✔ The **Reschedule work tool** reschedules all tasks that begin after the status date you set, or the current date if you didn't set a status date.

- ✔ The **Add progress line tool** turns on a kind of drawing tool. When you select the tool and then click the mouse cursor over a spot on the chart area, a progress line is placed at that point on the timescale. A progress line indicates visually to someone reviewing the project which tasks are ahead of schedule and which ones are behind schedule, by means of a line that connects in-progress tasks.

- ✔ By clicking a **Percentage complete tool** (0% to 100%), you can quickly mark a task's progress by the percentage of work completed.

- ✔ The **Update tasks tool** displays a dialog box containing tracking fields that you might recognize from the Task Information dialog box as well as some other fields you can use for updating your project.

Project statistics

Update as scheduled

Reschedule work

Add progress line

Percentage complete

Update tasks

Workgroup toolbar

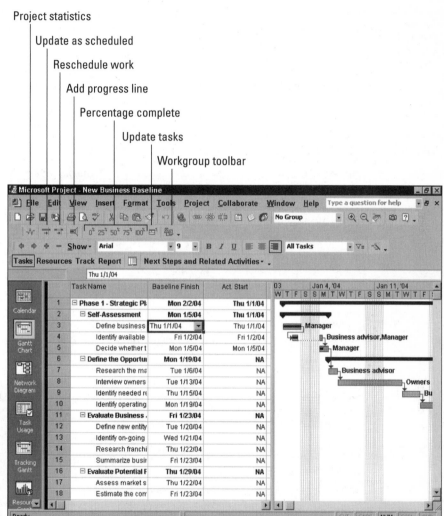

Figure 13-1:
Select a
task and
click on one
of these
tools to
update it.

You can also choose Tools⇨Tracking⇨Update Tasks to display the tracking fields from the Update Tasks dialog box; this is the same dialog box that the Update tasks button on the Tracking toolbar displays.

For everything there is a view

By now, you probably know that Project has a view for everything you want to do. For example, the Task Sheet view and the Task Usage view shown in

Figures 13-2 and 13-3, respectively, allow you to update either task or resource information easily. So many variations are available, you might think that Microsoft charged by the view!

Depending on the method of tracking you need (see "A method to your tracking madness" earlier in this chapter), different views serve different purposes. Table 13-1 shows the best view to use for each tracking method.

Table 13-1	Tracking Views	
Tracking Method	*Best View to Use*	*Table or Column Displayed*
Task	Task Sheet	Tracking table
Task timephased	Task Usage	Actual Work column
Assignment	Task Usage	Tracking table
Assignment timephased	Task Usage	Actual Work column

When you find the right view with the right columns displayed, entering tracking information is as simple as typing a number of hours, a dollar amount for fixed costs, or a start or finish date in the appropriate column for the task you're updating.

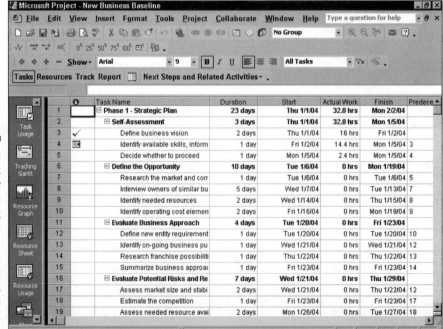

Figure 13-2: The Task Sheet view with the Actual Work column inserted is a great place for tracking work, start, and finish dates.

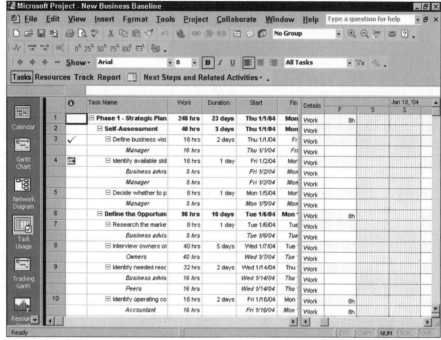

Figure 13-3:
The Task
Usage
view allows
you enter
specific
resource
hours on
task day-by-
day on your
project.

Tracking your work for the record

You need to input several types of information to track progress on your project. First, you have to tell Project as of when you want to track progress: By default, it records information as of the current date based on your computer's calendar settings, but if you want to record progress as of, say, Arbor Day, you can do that, too.

You can record actual start and finish dates for tasks, the percentage of a task that is complete (for example, a task might be 75% complete), and actual work performed (that is, the number of hours that resources put in on each task). If you think that the task will take less or more time than you anticipated, based on progress to date, you can modify the remaining duration for the task. You can also enter fixed-cost information for expenditures incurred, such as equipment rental or consulting fees.

Progress as of when?

If you don't know what day of the week it is, you can't very well gauge whether you're making the right amount of headway through your week's work. Well, tracking is like that: The first thing you have to do is establish a *status date;* that is, the date as of which you are tracking progress.

By default, Project uses the calendar setting of your computer as the current date when you enter actual activity information. However, sometimes you'll want to time travel. For example, suppose that your boss asks for a report showing the status of the project as of the last day of the quarter, December 31. You gathered all your resources' timesheets up through that date, but you didn't get around to inputting those updates until three days after the end of the quarter. You can deal with this by setting the status date in Project to December 31 and then entering your tracking data.

After you've set the status date and entered information, Project uses that date to make calculations such as earned value (the value of work completed to date). Also, any task-complete or percentage-complete information records as of that date, and progress lines in the chart area reflect that timing. Any reports or printouts of views that you generate give a picture of the status of your project as of that date.

Here's how to set the status date:

1. **Choose Project⇨Project Information.**

   The Project Information dialog box appears, as shown in Figure 13-4.

2. **In the Status Date box, click the arrow to display the calendar.**

3. **If you want to set the status date in another month, use the right or left arrow at the top of the calendar to maneuver to that month.**

4. **Click the date you want.**

5. **Click OK.**

Now you're ready to start inputting tracking data.

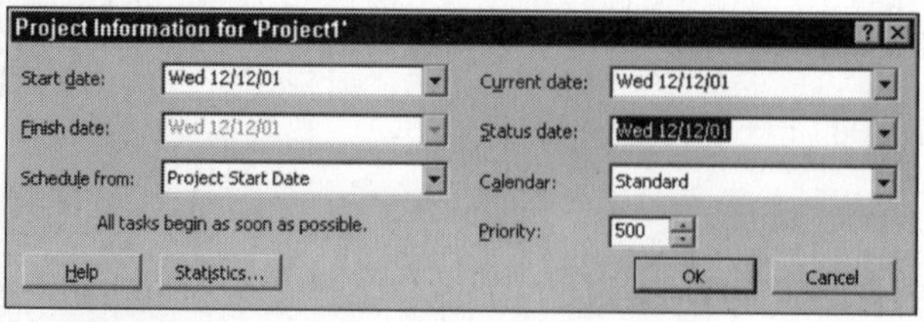

Figure 13-4:
When you
first open
this dialog
box, the
status date
is not set;
your project
is controlled
by the
current
date.

Percentage complete: How to tell?

When people ask me how to figure out whether a task is 25%, 50%, or even 36.5% complete, I usually refer them to their own intuition. If your boss asks you how things are coming on that report, you typically go through a quick internal calculation and come back with a rough estimate with no problem. A rough estimate based on your experience and the information your resources provide you about their progress is often good enough.

You can also calculate percentage complete in more precise ways. For example, if you estimate that a task should take 10 hours of effort, and your resources report performing 5 hours of effort, you could say you're 50% there. But be careful. Just because people have spent half the allocated time doesn't mean that they have accomplished half the work.

You could go by costs: If your original estimates said that your four resources assigned to a 4-day task would tally $4000 of costs and the time your resources report spending on the task add up to $3000, you could guess that the task is 75% finished. But again, just because you've spent three-quarters of the money doesn't mean you've accomplished three-quarters of what you set out to do.

When a task's deliverable is measurable, that helps a lot. For example, if you have a task to produce 100 cars on the assembly line in 4 days and you've produced 25 cars, you might be about 25% finished with the task. Or if you were supposed to install software on 10 computers in a computer lab and you've installed it on 5 of them, that's an easy 50%.

But not every task can be calculated so neatly. The best rule of thumb is to trust your instincts and review what your team is telling you about their progress.

Can tracking get too detailed?

Does it make sense to track 2.25% of progress every other day on a two-month task? Probably not. Except on the lengthiest tasks, entering a percentage more finely broken down than 25, 50, 75, and 100% complete probably isn't worth it. That's partly because tasks longer than a few weeks should probably be broken down into subtasks for ease of tracking, and partly because one of the main purposes of tracking is reporting. If your boss or board or client doesn't really want to know when you hit your 33.75% complete point, why track it?

On the other hand, if (for some reason known only to you) your project must include a six-month task and you can't break it into subtasks, you might use percentages such as 10, 20, 30, 40, 50, and so on so that you don't wait a month between updates with (apparently) no progress to show.

The simplest and quickest way to update percent complete on a task is to click the task to select it in any view, and then click the 0%, 25%, 50%, 75%, or 100% button on the Tracking toolbar. Alternately, you can double-click any task to open the Task Information dialog box, and then enter the percent complete there. You can also select a task and click the Update Tasks button on the Tracking toolbar to open the Update Task dialog box and make the change there. If you want to enter a percentage in increments of other than 25%, you'll have to enter it in the Task Information or Update Task dialog box or the Percent Complete column in any sheet view.

When did you start? When did you finish?

If you note that a task is complete and don't enter an Actual Start date, Project, ever the optimist, assumes you started on time. If you didn't start on time and you want to reflect the actual timing, you should modify the Actual Start date. If you finished late, you should enter the Actual Finish date. However, be aware that if you don't modify the task duration and enter an earlier finish date, the start date will be calculated to have occurred earlier.

You have several options of where to track this information. You can use the Update Tasks dialog box, which appears when you click the Update Tasks button on the Tracking toolbar (see Figure 13-5). You can also display a sheet view with Actual Start and Actual Finish columns, such as the Tracking Gantt view with the Tracking table displayed or the Gantt View with the Tracking table displayed. Then use the drop down calendar in the Actual Start or Actual Finish dates columns to specify a date.

A few conditions could cause a warning message to appear when you enter an actual start or finish date: for example, if the actual start date falls before the start date for the project, or if it causes a conflict with a dependent task. When this warning message appears, you usually have the options of canceling the operation or forcing the conflict to exist or the task to start before the project starts. If you want to cancel the change, correct what's causing the problem, and then go back and enter the actual information you can. Or you can force the conflict, and let it stand.

John worked 3 hours, Maisie worked 10

If you want to get to the blow-by-blow level of tracking, you'll need to record exactly how many hours each resource put in on your tasks. This can be about as much fun as typing the New York City phonebook into a database, but it has some benefits. After you've tracked actual hours, you can get tallies of total hours put in by each resource in your project by day, week, or month.

If you have to bill clients based on resource hours (for example if you're a lawyer), you have a clear record to refer to. If you're tracking a budget in detail, resource hours multiplied by their individual rates will tally an accurate accounting of costs as finely as day by day.

If you don't enter specific hours, Project just averages the work on the task based on the total duration. For many people, that's fine; for others, more detail is better. If you're in the detail camp, specify actual resource hours as a total by task or day-by-day through the life of each task.

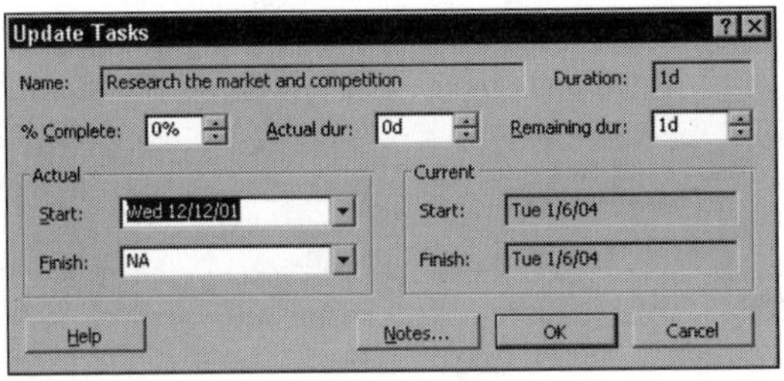

Figure 13-5:
Click the
arrow in the
Start or
Finish boxes
and choose
a date
from a
drop-down
calendar.

To enter resource hours, follow these steps:

1. **Display the Resource Usage view, which is shown in Figure 13-6.**

2. **In the Resource Name column, scroll down to locate the resource you want to track.**

   The tasks that each resource is assigned to are listed underneath the resource name.

3. **Enter the hours put in by the resource:**

   a. **If you want to enter only total hours, locate the task name under the resource listing, and click the Work column.**

   b. **If you want to enter hours on the task day by day, scroll in the chart pane to locate the timeframe for the task. Click the cell for a day that the resource worked and enter a number. Repeat this for each day that the resource worked on that task.**

If the hours you enter for a resource total more or less than the baseline estimate for that resource on that task, here's what happens:

✔ When you enter an amount and press Enter, the Work column total recalculates to reflect the total hours worked on that task.

> ✔ The hour notation on that date is displayed in red, showing some varia-
> tion from baseline hours.
>
> ✔ A little pencil symbol appears in the ID column for that task, indicating
> that the assignment has been edited.

Note that you can easily look up the total hours put in by each resource on
the project by checking the summary number of work hours listed next to
the resource in the Resource Name column of the Resource Usage view.

Uh-oh, we're into overtime

When you enter 16 hours of work on a single day for a resource, even though
that resource is based on a calendar with an 8-hour day, Project doesn't
recognize any of those hours as overtime. This is one case where you have to
lead Project by the hand and actually tell it to specify overtime work.

When you enter hours in the Overtime Work field, Project interprets that as
the number of total Work hours that are overtime hours. So, if you enter 16
hours of work on a task in the Work column, and then enter 4 in the Overtime
Work column, Project assumes that there were 12 hours of work at the
standard resource rate and 4 hours at overtime rates.

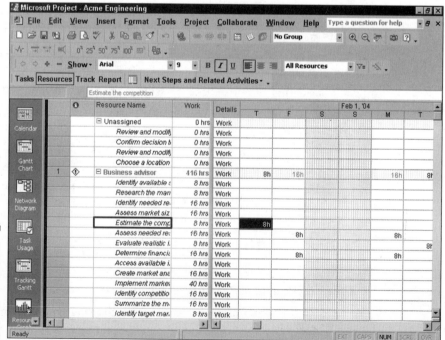

Figure 13-6:
Track
resource
activity day-
by-day in
this view.

To enter overtime hours, follow these steps:

1. **Display the Resource Usage view.**

2. **Right-click a column heading and then click Insert Column.**

   The Column Definition dialog box appears.

3. **In the Field Name box, click Overtime Work.**

4. **Click OK to display the column.**

5. **Click in the Overtime Work column for the resource and task you want to modify, and then use the spinner arrows to specify the overtime hours.**

Note that if you specify overtime, Project assumes that effort-driven tasks are happening in less time. After all, if the task was to take three 8-hour days (24 hours of work) to complete, and you recorded that the resource worked 12 hours for two days in a row, Project figures that all the effort got accomplished in less time. The duration for the task will actually shrink. If that's not what you want, you have to go in and modify the task duration yourself.

Specifying remaining durations

A lot of tracking information has a weird and wonderful relationship in Project. For example, Project will try to help you out by calculating durations based on other entries you make. Suppose that you enter actual start and finish dates. Project figures out the task duration based on those dates. (This works in reverse too: If you enter the task duration, Project recalculates the finish date to reflect that.)

Sometimes you'll want to enter a duration rather than have Project base it on other information you input. For example, you might have entered a start date and 20 hours of work on a task that had a baseline of 16 hours of work. What Project can't know is that the scope of the task changed, and now the task is not complete and will also take another 20 hours of work. You have to tell Project about that.

To modify the duration on a task in progress or completed, follow these steps:

1. **Display the Gantt Chart view.**

2. **Choose View⇨Table⇨Tracking.**

   The Tracking table is displayed.

3. **Click in the Actual Duration column for the task you want to modify, and then use the arrows to adjust the actual duration up or down.**

4. **If you want to enter a remaining duration, click in the Remaining Duration column and type a number as well as an increment symbol.**

   For example, you might type 25d (d is the increment symbol for days).

If you enter a percentage of completion for a task and then modify the duration to differ from the baseline, Project automatically recalculates the percentage complete to reflect the new duration. So, if you enter 50% complete on a 10-hour task and then modify the actual duration to 20 hours, Project considers that 5 hours (50% of 10 hours) as only 25% of 20 hours.

Entering fixed-cost updates

Fixed costs are costs that aren't influenced by time, such as equipment purchases and consulting fees. Compared to the calculations and interactions of percentage completions and start and finish dates for hourly resources, fixed-cost tracking will seem like simplicity itself!

Here's how to do it:

1. **Display the Gantt Chart view.**

2. **Right-click in a column heading and then click Insert Column.**

   The Column Definition dialog box appears.

3. **In Field Name box, select Fixed Cost.**

4. **Click OK.**

5. **Click in the Fixed Cost column for the task that you want to update.**

6. **Type the fixed cost, or a total of several fixed costs, for the task.**

That's it! However, because Project lets you enter only one fixed-cost amount per task, consider adding a note to the task itemizing the costs you've included in the total.

Consider using some of the 30 customizable Text columns for itemized fixed-cost entry. Rename one Equipment Purchase, another Facility Rental, and so on and enter those costs in those columns.

Update Project: Sweeping Changes for Dummies

If it's been a while since you tracked activity and you want to update your schedule, Update Project might be for you. It allows you to track chunks of activity for a period of time. Update Project works best, however, if most tasks happened pretty much on schedule.

This is not fine-tuned tracking: It's akin to getting your bank balance, drawing a line in your checkbook, and writing down that balance as gospel rather than accounting for your balance check by check. (I know you've done this) This assumes that all your checks and deposits probably tally with what the bank says as of that date; so going forward, you're back on track.

Here are the setting choices Update Project offers you:

- ✔ **Update Work as Complete Through.** You can update your project through the date you specify in this box in one of two ways. Set 0% – 100% Complete lets Project figure out the percent complete on every task that should have begun by that time; by making this choice, you tell Project to assume that the tasks started and progressed exactly on time. The Set 0% or 100% Complete Only works a little differently. This setting says to Project, just record 100% complete on tasks that the baseline said would be complete by now, but leave all other tasks at 0% complete.

- ✔ **Reschedule Uncompleted Work to Start After.** This setting reschedules tasks that aren't yet complete to start after the date you specify in this dialog box.

To use Update Project, do this:

1. **Display the Gantt Chart view.**

2. **If you want to update only certain tasks, select them.**

3. **Choose Tools⇨Tracking⇨Update Project.**

   The Update Project dialog box appears, as shown in Figure 13-7.

Figure 13-7:
You can update only selected tasks or the entire project.

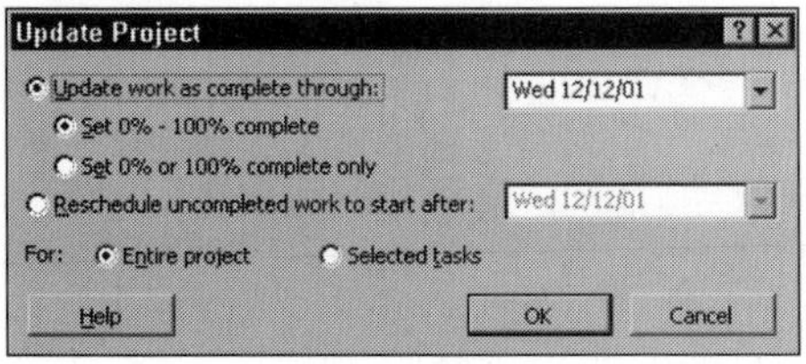

4. **Choose the Update method you prefer: Set 0% – 100% Complete or Set 0% or 100% Complete Only.**

5. **If you want a status date other than the current date, set it in the box in the upper-right corner.**

6. **If you want Project to reschedule any work rather than updating work as complete, click the Reschedule Uncompleted Work to Start After option and then select a date from the list.**

7. **Choose whether you want these changes to apply to the entire project or only selected tasks.**

8. **Click OK to save the settings and have Project make updates.**

If you want, you can use Update Project to make some global changes, such as marking all tasks that should be complete according to baseline as 100% complete, and then go in and perform more detailed task-by-task tracking on individual tasks that are only partially complete.

Chapter 14

A Project with a View: Observing Progress

Some people use Project just to paint a pretty picture of what their project will entail, and then put the plan in a drawer. That's a mistake. After you've entered all your project data, saved a baseline, and then tracked actual activity on your project, you get an amazing array of information back from Project that helps you to stay on time and on budget.

When you have tracked some actual activity on tasks, Project allows you to view baseline estimates right alongside your real-time plan. Project alerts you to tasks that are running late and how the critical path shifts over time.

Project also provides detailed budget information. In fact, the information you can get about your costs will make your accounting department's heart sing. The information is detailed and uses terms accountants love such as earned value and cost variance as well as lovely acronyms such as BCWP and EAC.

So keep that project file close at hand — and take a look at how Project can make you the most informed project manager in town.

Look at What Tracking Did!

You've diligently entered resource work hours on tasks, recorded the percentage of progress on tasks, and entered fixed costs. Now what? Well, all that information has caused several calculations to go on and updates to be reflected in your project. Time to take a quick look at the changes all your tracking has produced in your Project plan.

Getting an indication

A lot of information in Project just sits there waiting for you to hunt it down. But one tool that Project uses to practically jump up and down and say, "look at this" is *indicator icons*. You've seen these icons in the Indicator column and probably wondered what the heck they were for. Well, these little symbols give you a clue to important facts about each task, sometimes serving to alert you to problems or potential challenges.

Figure 14-1 shows several of these indicators, some of which relate to the results of tracking your project.

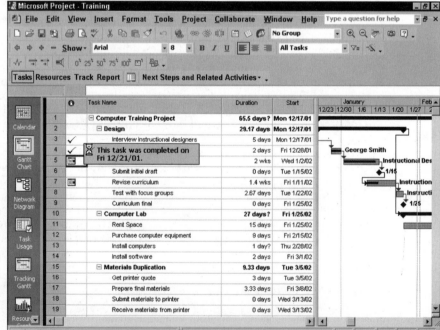

Figure 14-1:
The checkmarks here mean that the tasks are complete.

Here are some of the common icons that show up during a project:

Icon	Indicator	Meaning
✓	Completed tasks	The task is marked 100% complete
◇!	Resource conflict	A resource should be leveled
◆!	Late tasks	The task will not meet its deadline
▦	Missed constraint	The task hasn't been completed within the constraint timeframe

When you hold your mouse cursor over an indicator, a box describing its meaning appears.

To get a list of icons and their meanings go to Help, click the Index tab, and type the word *icon* in the Type Keywords box. Click search, and then click About Indicators.

Lines of progress

Progress lines offer an additional visual indicator of how you're doing. As you can see in Figure 14-2, a progress line zigzags between tasks and forms left-or-right-pointing peaks. These peaks indicate late or early tasks based on the status date you use when tracking. A progress line that points to the left of a task indicates that the task is running late. Progress lines that point to the right show that, wonder of wonders, you're running ahead of schedule. (Treasure these — they don't seem to appear often in most projects!)

Displaying progress lines

By default, Project doesn't display progress lines. You need to turn them on, and while you're at it, you might as well control the settings for when and how they appear. Here's how to make settings for and display progress lines:

1. **Display the Gantt Chart view.**

2. **Choose Tools⇨Tracking⇨Progress Lines.**

   The Progress Lines dialog box appears, as shown in Figure 14-3.

3. **If you want Project to always show a progress line for the current or status date, click Always Display Current Progress Line and then click At Project Status Date or At Current Date.**

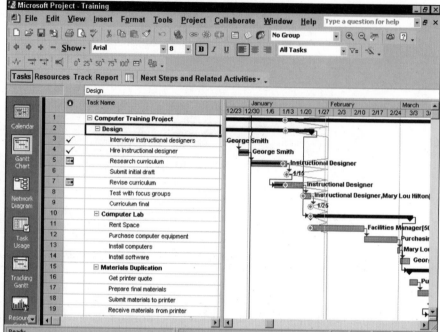

Figure 14-2: The circle indicator shows the direction of each progress line peak; here, we're behind schedule all the way!

Figure 14-3: These two tabs allow you to control just about everything about progress lines.

4. **If you want progress lines to be displayed at set intervals, do the following:**

   a. **Click Display Progress Lines at Recurring Intervals, and then click Daily, Weekly, or Monthly.**

   b. **Specify the interval settings.**

For example, if you select Weekly, you can choose every week, every other week, and so on, as well as which day of the week the line should be displayed on the timescale. Figure 14-4 shows a project with progress lines at regular intervals.

5. **Choose whether you want to display progress lines beginning at the Project Start or on another date.**

   To use the Project Start date, simply click the Project Start option to the right of Begin At. To select a project start date, click the second option and then click a date in the calendar drop-down list.

6. **If you want to display a progress line on a specific date, click Display Selected Progress lines and then choose a date from the Progress Line Dates drop-down calendar.**

   You can make this setting for multiple dates by clicking subsequent lines in this list and selecting additional dates.

7. **Finally, you can choose to display progress lines in relation to actual or baseline information.**

   If a task has been tracked to show 50% complete and you choose to have Project display progress lines based on actual information, the peak appears relative to the 50% actual line, not the complete baseline taskbar.

8. **Click OK to save your settings.**

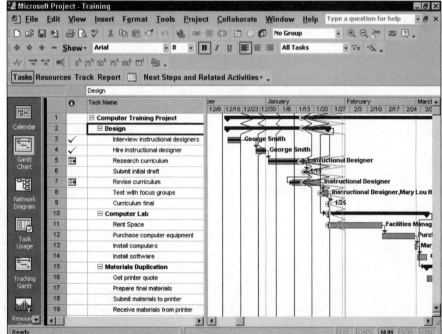

Figure 14-4:
Multiple progress lines can get rather busy, but do show you clearly how delays grew over time.

You can use your mouse to add a progress line. On the Tracking toolbar, click the Add Progress Line tool button. Then click the Gantt chart at the location on the timescale where you want the line to appear in the chart.

Formatting progress lines

In keeping with the almost mind-boggling array of formatting options Project makes available to you, you can modify how progress lines are formatted.

As with any changes to formatting, you're tampering with the way Project codes visual information for readers. You should be cautious about formatting changes that will make your plan difficult to read for those who are used to Project's default formatting.

To modify progress line formatting, follow these steps:

1. **Choose Tools➪Tracking➪Progress Lines.**

2. **Click the Line Styles tab, if necessary, to display the options shown in Figure 14-5.**

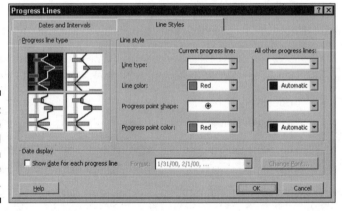

Figure 14-5: Select line styles and colors with these settings.

3. **In the Progress Line Type display, click a line style sample.**

4. **In the Line Type box, click a style from the samples shown.**

   Note that there are two settings you can make here: one for the Current Progress Line and one for All Other Progress Lines.

5. **You can change the line color, progress point shape, and progress point color by making different choices in those boxes.**

6. **If you want a date to display alongside each progress line, click the Show Date for Each Progress Line option, and then select a date in the Format box.**

7. **If you want to change the font used for the displayed date, click the Change Font button and make your changes.**

8. **Click OK to save your settings.**

When worlds collide: Baseline vs. actual

One of the most obvious ways to view the difference between your baseline estimates and what you've tracked in your project is through taskbars. When you've tracked some progress on tasks, the Gantt Chart shows a black bar superimposed on the blue taskbar that represents your baseline. For example, in Figure 14-6, Task 3 is complete; you can tell this by the solid black bar that extends the full length of the baseline taskbar. Task 5 is only partially complete; the black, actual task line only partially fills the baseline duration for the task. Task 8 has no recorded activity on it — there is no black actual line at all, only the blue baseline taskbar.

Learn by the Numbers

Visual indicators such as taskbars and indicator icons are useful to alert you to delays or variances between estimated and actual performance, but they're inexact. To get the real lowdown on how far ahead or behind you are down to the day or penny, you need to give the numbers a scan. The numbers Project provides reveal much about whether you're on schedule and within your budget.

Two tables you can display in the Gantt Chart bring your situation into bold relief. The Cost and Variance tables provide information about dollars spent and variation in timing between baseline and actual activity.

The Cost table is shown in Figure 14-7. Here you can review data that compares baseline estimates of fixed costs and actual costs. These two sets of data are presented side-by-side in columns. In the project shown in Figure 14-7, so far in the project you've spend $34,100 and your baseline estimate was $30,640, giving you a variance of $3,460 over your budget.

To display the Cost table, choose View➪Table➪Cost.

Figure 14-8 shows the Variance table. This table is to your scheduling what the Cost table is to your budget. It shows the variance between baseline start and finish dates and task durations as well as the timing that actually occurred after your project got going.

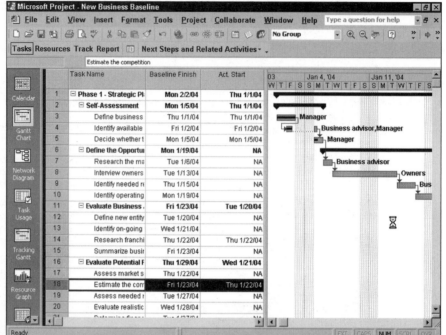

Figure 14-6:
The solid
line on
taskbars
represents
actual
activity in
your project.

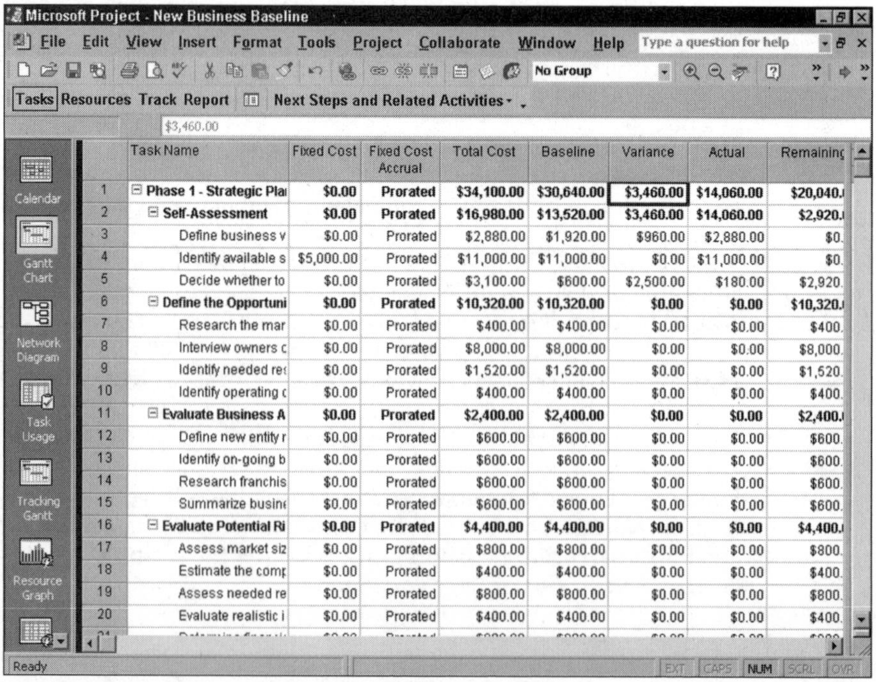

Figure 14-7:
The
Variance
column
shows the
difference
between the
total cost
and the
baseline.

Figure 14-8:
Use this
table to see
what delays
are doing
to your
schedule.

	Task Name	Start	Finish	Baseline Start	Baseline Finish	Start Var.	Finish Var.
1	⊟ Phase 1 - Strategic Pl	Tue 1/6/04	Thu 3/11/04	Thu 1/1/04	Mon 2/2/04	3 days	28 days
2	⊟ Self-Assessment	Tue 1/6/04	Fri 1/16/04	Thu 1/1/04	Mon 1/5/04	3 days	8.8 days
3	Define business	Fri 1/9/04	Tue 1/13/04	Thu 1/1/04	Fri 1/2/04	6 days	7 days
4	Identify available	Tue 1/6/04	Thu 1/8/04	Fri 1/2/04	Mon 1/5/04	2 days	3 days
5	Decide whether t	Thu 1/15/04	Fri 1/16/04	Mon 1/5/04	Mon 1/5/04	8 days	8.8 days
6	⊟ Define the Opportu	Wed 1/21/04	Mon 2/9/04	Tue 1/6/04	Mon 1/19/04	11 days	15 days
7	Research the ma	Wed 1/21/04	Wed 1/21/04	Tue 1/6/04	Tue 1/6/04	11 days	11 days
8	Interview owners	Thu 1/22/04	Wed 1/28/04	Wed 1/7/04	Tue 1/13/04	11 days	11 days
9	Identify needed r	Wed 2/4/04	Thu 2/5/04	Wed 1/14/04	Thu 1/15/04	15 days	15 days
10	Identify operating	Fri 2/6/04	Mon 2/9/04	Fri 1/16/04	Mon 1/19/04	15 days	15 days
11	⊟ Evaluate Business .	Fri 2/27/04	Wed 3/3/04	Tue 1/20/04	Fri 1/23/04	28 days	28 days
12	Define new entity	Fri 2/27/04	Fri 2/27/04	Tue 1/20/04	Tue 1/20/04	28 days	28 days
13	Identify on-going	Mon 3/1/04	Mon 3/1/04	Wed 1/21/04	Wed 1/21/04	28 days	28 days
14	Research franchi	Tue 3/2/04	Tue 3/2/04	Thu 1/22/04	Thu 1/22/04	28 days	28 days
15	Summarize busir	Wed 3/3/04	Wed 3/3/04	Fri 1/23/04	Fri 1/23/04	28 days	28 days
16	⊟ Evaluate Potential F	Mon 3/1/04	Tue 3/9/04	Wed 1/21/04	Thu 1/29/04	28 days	28 days
17	Assess market s	Mon 3/1/04	Tue 3/2/04	Wed 1/21/04	Thu 1/22/04	28 days	28 days
18	Estimate the corr	Wed 3/3/04	Wed 3/3/04	Fri 1/23/04	Fri 1/23/04	28 days	28 days
19	Assess needed r	Thu 3/4/04	Fri 3/5/04	Mon 1/26/04	Tue 1/27/04	28 days	28 days
20	Evaluate realistic	Mon 3/8/04	Mon 3/8/04	Wed 1/28/04	Wed 1/28/04	28 days	28 days

If you created a slack task to help you deal with delays that might come up, the total variance shown here will tell you how many days you might have to deduct from the duration of the slack task to get back on track. Read more about making adjustments in your plan to deal with delays and cost overruns in Chapter 15.

Acronym Soup: BCWP, ACWP, EAC, and CV

In any view, you can insert several columns of data to give you some calculated analyses of what's going on in your project budget. Much of this data will mean more to an accountant than to most in-the-trenches project managers. But if only to make your accountant feel more comfortable, you should become familiar with some of the most common calculations. Also, many organizations require information on these numbers in project reports:

✔ **BCWP (budgeted cost of work performed).** Referred to in some circles as earned value, BCWP is essentially a calculation of the value of the work that you've completed expressed in dollars. For example, if a task has $2,000 of costs associated with it and you record that the task is 50% complete, the earned value for that task is $1,000 (50% of the baseline estimated costs).

✔ **ACWP (actual cost of work performed).** This calculation looks at actual costs, including tracked resource hours or units expended on the task plus fixed costs. Where BCWP looks at the baseline value of work, ACWP looks at actual tracked costs.

✔ **EAC (estimate at completion).** This is a total of all costs on a task. For a task in progress, EAC calculates the actual costs recorded to date plus the remaining baseline estimated costs.

✔ **CV (cost variance).** This represents the difference between planned costs (that is, costs included in the baseline for a task) and the combination of actual costs recorded to date plus any remaining estimated costs. This number is expressed as a negative number if you're under budget and as a positive number if you're like the rest of us (over budget).

Studying these numbers can help you see what it has cost to get where you are today on your project.

Calculations behind the Scenes

While you're happily entering resource hours and fixed costs into your project, Project is busy making calculations that can shift around task timing and resource workload in your plan. These calculations relate to how tasks are updated, how the critical path is determined, and how earned value is calculated. If you're a control freak, you'll be happy to know that you can, to some extent, control how Project goes about making these calculations.

Going automatic or manual

By default, Project is on automatic as far as calculations go. When you make a change to your plan, Project recalculates totals, the critical path, and so on without you lifting a finger. However, you can change that setting and have Project wait for you to manually initiate calculations. You do this in the Calculation tab of the Options dialog box (Tools⇨Options). Figure 14-9 shows the settings available there.

If you change the Calculation mode to Manual, you must click the Calculate Now button in this dialog box to have Project perform all its calculations. You also have the choice here of setting different modes for only the current project or for all open projects.

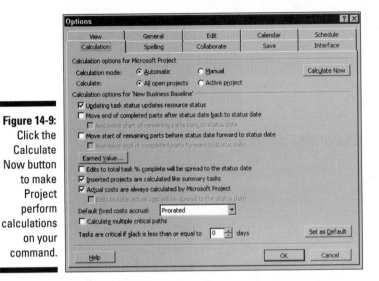

Figure 14-9:
Click the
Calculate
Now button
to make
Project
perform
calculations
on your
command.

So why would you choose to use manual calculation? You might want to make a lot of changes and not have Project take the milliseconds required to recalculate between each change, slowing down your entry work. You can put things on manual, make all your changes, and then use the Calculate Now button to make all the changes at one time.

In addition, because it's not always easy to spot all the things that have been recalculated when you make a series of changes, it might be easier to make all the changes in manual mode, print your Gantt Chart view, and then recalculate and compare the two. This shows you the cumulative calculations that occurred when all your changes were made so you can see whether or not you're happy with the revised plan. This feature is useful in trying out what-if scenarios.

Another calculation setting that you can arrange to occur automatically or manually is resource leveling. Choose Tools➪Level Resources, and you can make settings in the Resource Leveling dialog box for automatic calculation. With this active, Project automatically runs the leveling calculation whenever a resource becomes overallocated in your project.

Earned value options

Your first question about earned value probably is, "Why does Project use *BWCP* in its column names but *earned value* in the Options dialog box?" Don't ask. Just be glad I taught you both terms in a previous section ("Acronym Soup: BCWP, ACWP, EAC, and CV").

The second question you probably have is, "What do the settings you can make to the earned value calculation do to your project?" Well, start by looking at Figure 14-10, which shows you what's behind the Earned Value button on the Calculation tab of the Options dialog box.

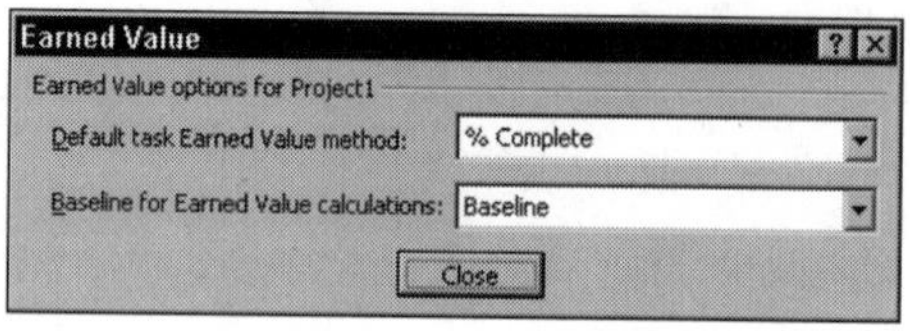

Figure 14-10:
Here are
two simple
settings to
use for
calculating
earned
value.

The Default Task Earned Value Method setting provides two choices:

- **% Complete.** This setting calculates earned value using the percent complete that you record on each task. This assumes that for a task that's halfway complete, half the work has taken place.

- **Physical % Complete.** Use this setting if you want to enter a percent of completion that is not based on a straight percent-complete calculation. For example, if you have a four-week task to do a mail survey, 50% of the effort might happen in the first 25% of the duration of the project — designing, printing, and mailing the survey. Nothing happens for two weeks while you wait for responses, and then there's a flurry of activity when the responses come back. So a straight calculation that 50% of the task is completed 50% of the way through wouldn't be accurate. If your projects have a lot of tasks like this, you might consider changing your settings to use this method. Then, you can display the Physical % Complete column in your Gantt Chart sheet, and enter what you consider more accurate percent-complete information for each task.

The second setting in the Earned Value dialog box is which baseline to use for calculations. Remember, earned value is the value of work complete expressed in dollars according to the baseline: A $2000 task at 50% complete has an earned value of work performed of $1000. Therefore, the baseline that you're calculating this against is key. Choose any of the 11 possible baselines you might have saved in your project here. When you've made these two choices, click Close to close the Earned Value dialog box.

You should explore one more option in the Options dialog box that concerns earned value calculation. The Edits to Total Task % Complete Will Be Spread to the Status Date option, which is not selected by default, affects how Project distributes changes in your schedule. With this option not selected, calculations go to the end of the duration of tasks in progress, rather than up to the status date or the current date. If you select this option, calculations spread changes across your plan up to only the status date or the current date. Selecting this choice helps you see changes to your project in increments of time, rather than across the life of tasks in progress.

If I were you, I'd leave the Edits to Total Task % option not selected for the most accurate reflection of your progress on your project.

How many critical paths is enough?

The last group of settings on the Calculation tab of the Options dialog box concerns critical path calculations.

The Inserted Projects Are Calculated Like Summary Tasks option is straightforward. If you insert another project as a task in your project, having this setting selected allows Project to calculate one critical path for your entire project. If you don't select it, projects you insert are treated like other projects and not taken into account in the master project critical-path calculations. If an inserted project will not have an impact on your project's timing, you might want to clear this option.

If following one project critical path is too tame for you, try getting critical with multiple paths. By selecting the Calculate Multiple Critical Paths option, you set up Project to calculate a different critical path for each set of tasks in your project. This can be helpful if you want to identify the tasks that, if delayed, will cause you to miss your final project deadline or the goals of a single phase in your project.

Finally, you can establish what puts a task on the critical path by specifying the number of days of slack critical tasks might have. By default, tasks with no slack are on critical path. But you can change this and be alerted that tasks with only one day of slack are critical, figuring that one day isn't much padding and these tasks are still in jeopardy.

If you want all the settings on the Calculation tab to pertain to all projects, click the Set as Default button before clicking OK to save the new settings in the Options dialog box.

Chapter 15

You're Behind: Now What?

· ·

In This Chapter

▶ Reviewing your plan versions and notes to understand what went wrong

▶ Trying out what-if scenarios

▶ Understanding how getting more time or more people will help

▶ Adjusting your timing going forward

· ·

*T*here comes a time in almost every project when you feel like the floor dropped out from under you. Suddenly — and this one just snuck up on you — you're $20,000 overbudget. Or you're going to miss that drop-dead deadline by two weeks. All the aspirin in the world isn't going to solve this one.

Of course, you have a general idea of what happened because you're smart, you kept in touch with your team, and you have Project and all its columns of data. Still, somehow things are off track and you need to take action at this point. First, you have to justify what occurred (abbreviated CYA), and then you have to fix things so that you can go forward and just maybe save your project, your job, or both.

How do you save the day when things go off track? What you have to do at this point involves analyzing your options and making some tough choices. This is stuff you did before you ever heard of Microsoft Project. But Project can help you try out some possible solutions and anticipate the likely results. After you decide what to do, you have to implement your solutions in Project.

Justifying Yourself: Notes, Baselines, and Interim Plans

If you've kept interim plans, multiple baselines, and task notes in Project, explaining to the powers-that-be how you got in this mess is much easier.

Interim plans and multiple baselines demonstrate how you made adjustments when major changes or problems occurred. Using these two items indicates to your boss that you were on top of things all the way and probably kept him or her in the loop by generating printouts or reports reflecting major changes as they occurred. (If you didn't, print them now from the interim plans or baselines you saved along the way to paint a picture of what happened).

A baseline saves all project data; an interim plan saves only the start and finish dates of tasks in the project. Chapter 12 deals with interim plans and baselines.

To view or print information from various baselines or interim plans, follow these steps:

1. **Display the Gantt Chart view.**

2. **Right-click the column heading area of the sheet pane and then click Insert Column.**

   The Column Definition dialog box appears, as shown in Figure 15-1.

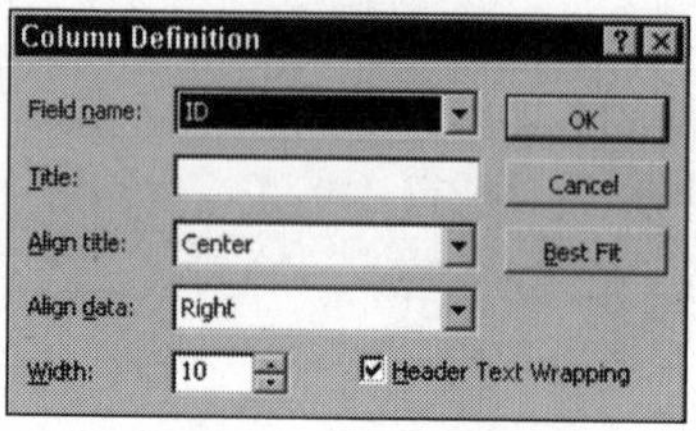

Figure 15-1:
Use this
dialog box
to insert
as many
columns as
you like in
any view
with a sheet
pane.

Column Definition		? X
Field name:	ID	OK
Title:		Cancel
Align title:	Center	Best Fit
Align data:	Right	
Width:	10	☑ Header Text Wrapping

3. **In the Field Name box, click a column name.**

   For example, you might select Start 1-10 and Finish 1-10 for any one of your interim plans or Baseline through Baseline 10 for baseline data.

4. **Click OK to display the column; if you need to, repeat Steps 1 through 3 to display additional columns.**

In addition to interim plans and baselines, task notes should include information about resource performance on a task, vendor problems, or late deliveries. Notes that are especially important to add are those you make when someone in authority over you has asked for a change and okayed more money or time to make that change.

To add a note to a task, either display the task note column in a sheet pane or double-click a task and add the note on the Notes tab of the Task Information dialog box.

What If?

Just as you can get too close to a problem to see a solution, you can get too close to your project to recognize what you need to do. Using Project's filtering and sorting features, you can slice and dice things a little differently to help you get a fresh perspective.

You can also use tools such as resource leveling to solve resource conflicts. Resource leveling might not always solve problems to your taste, but it's a good way to let Project show you one what-if scenario to solve most resource problems instantly.

Sorting things out

Sometimes when things won't sort themselves out, it's time to sort your tasks. Project allows you to sort tasks by several criteria, including start date, finish date, priority, and cost.

How can sorting help you? Well, here are a few examples:

- ✔ If you're trying to cut your costs, consider sorting tasks by cost. Then you can focus on the most expensive tasks first to see whether there's room to trim nice-to-have but pricey items.
- ✔ If you want to delete some tasks to save time, display tasks by priority and then look at the low-priority tasks as the first candidates for the waste bin.
- ✔ To review task timing, sort by Duration in descending order to see the longest tasks first.

If you want to apply a preset sorting order, simply choose Project➪Sort and then click an option in the submenu, such as by Start Date or by Cost.

If you want to see additional sort criteria or sort by more than one criterion, follow these steps:

1. **Choose Project➪Sort➪Sort by.**

   The Sort dialog box appears, as shown in Figure 15-2.

2. **In the Sort By list, select a criterion.**

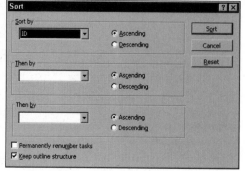

Figure 15-2:
This dialog
box allows
you to sort
by three
criteria in
ascending
or
descending
order.

3. **Click either Ascending to sort from lowest to highest or Descending to sort from highest to lowest.**

With a date field, the sorting order would be soonest to latest and latest to soonest, respectively; with a text field, alphabetical would be the order.

4. **If you want a second criterion, click the first Then By box and make a selection.**

For example, if you choose to sort first by Cost and then by Type, tasks are sorted from least expensive to most expensive, and within each cost level, tasks are sorted by type (Fixed Duration, Fixed Units, and Fixed Work).

5. **If you want to add a third criterion, click the second Then By box and make a selection.**

6. **Click Sort.**

To return to your original task order, choose Project⇨Sort⇨by ID. Tasks are now back in task ID number order, Project's standard sorting criterion.

Filtering

Chapter 10 deals with how you create and apply filters in Project. Now's a good time to call on your knowledge of those features. Especially in larger projects, where it's not always easy to scan hundreds of tasks and notice which are running late or overbudget, filters can hone in on exactly where your trouble lies.

You can choose to have tasks that don't meet filter criteria removed from your display or simply highlighted on screen.

Table 15-1 lists some filters that are useful when you're trying to identify and solve problems with your schedule.

Table 15-1	Filters to Isolate Problems
Filter Name	*What It Displays*
Critical	Tasks in the project that must be completed according to schedule to make your final deadline (critical path)
Cost Overbudget	Tasks that exceed budgeted expenditures
Incomplete Tasks	Tasks that haven't been marked as complete
Late/Overbudget Tasks	Tasks that are running later than their baseline estimate and are overbudget
Should Start by	Tasks that should have started as of a specified date
Slipped/Late Progress	Tasks that are running late and have no progress recorded
Update Needed	A task that should have had progress tracked by now
Overallocated Resources	Tasks that have resources assigned who are overbooked at some point during the life of the task
Slipping Assignments	Tasks that involve resource work that should have begun by now
Work Incomplete	Tasks that should have had all their work recorded by now
Work Overbudget	More work hours have been put in on the task than you had estimated

Don't see all of these choices in the More Filters dialog box? Remember, when you use this dialog box (Project⇨Filtered for⇨More Filters), you can click the Task option to see task-related filters and the Resource option to see resource-related filters.

Examining the critical path

One of the most useful filters is the one called Critical. This displays or highlights all tasks that are on the critical path. If you're running late, knowing which tasks can't slip helps you identify where there is no room for delay and, conversely, where you can delay noncritical tasks. You might use the Critical filter to help you determine how to free up overallocated resources or get a task that's running late back on track.

You can look at the critical path in any Gantt or Network Diagram view. Figure 15-3 shows the Gantt Chart view of a project with the critical path highlighted. Figure 15-4 shows the Network Diagram view with the same filter applied.

If you need a closer look at task timing consider modifying the timescale display to use smaller increments of time, such as days or hours. To do so, right-click the timescale itself and then click Timescale.

Use resource leveling one more time

If you performed manual resource leveling earlier in your project to solve resource conflicts, consider trying it again. With changes to tasks and tracked activity, resource leveling may be able to use new options to solve conflicts.

If resource leveling is set to automatic, Project automatically performs this calculation every time you modify your schedule. To see whether this is set to automatic or manual, choose Tools⇨Level Resources (see Figure 15-5).

How Adding People or Time Affect Your Project

It's part of corporate human nature to want to throw money and people at problems, and in some cases that instinct is on target. But you don't always have the ability to draw on endless supplies of resources or an endless amount of time to play with. Because of this, you may have to play around with a combination of options involving time and resources.

Hurry up!

Saving time in Project means doing things faster or adjusting the timing of things to suck up slack. But you'll find that this can be like an intricate puzzle: Correct one thing and something else pops up to cause you aggravation.

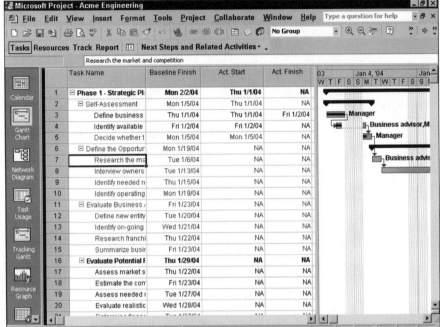

Figure 15-3:
The Gantt Chart view allows you see columns of data and a more precise timescale for each task.

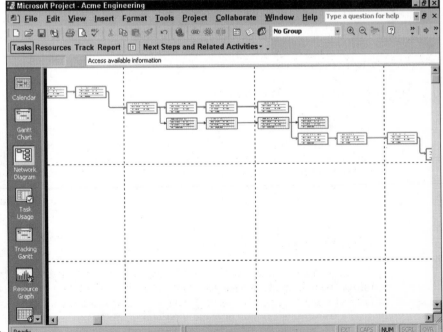

Figure 15-4:
The Network Diagram view gives you a feel for workflow and dependencies among tasks.

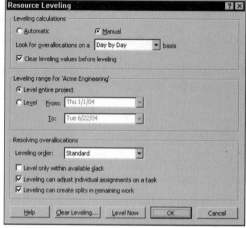

Figure 15-5:
Here's where you determine whether you or Project will control resource leveling.

To accomplish work faster, you have two options: Get more people to help out on tasks or modify the scope of tasks. Adding people adds money. So you might get back on track time-wise but it will cost you. Modifying the scope of the task might have an effect on its quality. If you do two inspections instead of three, or shorten your Q&A cycle by a week, you may run the risk of other types of problems down the road.

Changing the timing of tasks and shifting dependencies uses up slack to make up for delays but may leave you with no wiggle room. Next time a problem comes up, you'll be up against the wall with no slack to save you.

In reality, it's often a combination of small modifications in both areas that help you save the day.

Throwing people at the problem

With effort-driven tasks, things get accomplished when the specified amount of effort is expended. So, a task with a duration of 3 days based on a standard calendar will require 3 days times 8 hours a day to be completed, or 24 hours of effort. One resource performing this task working full time will take three days to complete it. Three resources working full time will take one day to complete 24 hours of work. When you add resources to such a task, Project automatically recalculates its duration.

But beyond simply adding resources to a task, you can also make modifications to existing assignments.

Changing how resources are assigned

On any given project, you might have dozens or even hundreds of resources working on tasks. All those people are working based on their working calendars, the percent you assigned them to tasks, and their ability to do the job. Take a look at how you assigned folks to begin with, and see whether you could save some time or money by modifying those assignments.

You can modify assignments in several ways:

- ✔ If someone is working at only 50% capacity on a task, consider upping the person's assignment units.

- ✔ If you have someone available who could perform a given task more quickly, switch resources on a task and then shorten its duration.

- ✔ Consider having some people work overtime or be overbooked at various points during the project. You may have modified an overbooked resource's assignments earlier to get rid of a conflict, but now you find that there's no choice but to have the resource work that occasional 12- or 14-hour day!

Remembering the consequences

Before you get carried away making changes to resources, think a minute. Adding resources to effort-driven tasks can shrink them, helping your project get back on track. But depending on the resources' hourly rates, it may cost you more.

Remember that three people working on a task won't necessarily geometrically shrink the duration of the task. That's because three people have to coordinate their efforts, hold meetings, and generally do the things people do when they interact that make their time a tad less efficient than when they work alone. If you add resources, Project shrinks the task geometrically: Consider going in and adding a little time to the task to accommodate the inefficiencies of multiple resources.

The other concern about adding resources to tasks is that it could cause more resource conflicts, with already busy people getting overbooked on too many tasks that happen in the same timeframe. But if you have the resources and they have the skills and the time, beefing up the workforce is definitely one way to perform some tasks more quickly.

To add resources to a task, you can use the Resources tab in the Task Information dialog box or select the task and click the Assign Resources tool button on the Standard toolbar.

Shifting dependencies and task timing

Time is a project manager's greatest enemy. There's never enough, and what there is gets eaten up like a bag of Quarter Pounders in a room full of hungry Little Leaguers.

Here are some ways you can modify task timing to save time:

- **Delete a task.** You heard me. If a task represents a step that could be skipped, just get rid of it. This doesn't happen often, but sometimes on rethinking your project you realize that a few things aren't necessary or have already been handled by someone else.

- **Adjust dependencies.** Couldn't the revision of the manual start a few days before all the feedback comes back? Could the electrical and plumbing go on at the same time instead of one after the other (assuming that the electrician and the plumber can stay out of each other's way)? Use the Predecessors tab of the Task Information dialog box shown in Figure 15-6 to modify dependencies.

- **Modify constraints.** Perhaps you set a task to start no earlier than the first of the year because you didn't want to spend money on it until the new fiscal year budget kicks in. To save time, consider whether you could allow it to start a week before the end of the year and just bill the costs in January. Examine any constraints such as this that you created to verify the timing logic.

- **Check external dependencies.** If you've inserted a hyperlinked task to represent another project and set dependencies with tasks in your project, check with the other project manager to see whether he or she can hurry up some things. Or if the timing relationship isn't absolutely critical, delete the hyperlink to the other project — it could be slowing you down more than you know.

Figure 15-6: Review a task's dependencies here, and modify the Lag column to include a negative number to allow tasks to overlap.

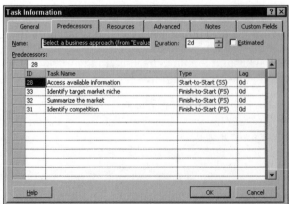

If you've set resource leveling to automatic, Project may be delaying some tasks until overbooked resources are freed up. Choose Tools⇨Level Resources and change the setting to manual.

When All Else Fails

Okay. You've monkeyed with resource assignments and shifted task dependencies around to save time, and deleted tasks and assigned cheaper workers to save money. But it's still not enough. This is the scenario where you have to say to your boss, "You can have it on time, you can have it on budget, or you can have quality work: Choose two."

If your boss throws money at you, go ahead and add resources to tasks, as discussed in the section of this chapter called "Throwing people at the problem." If she opts for time or quality, read on.

All the time in the world

If your boss is willing to give you more time, grab it. When you do, you have to update your project in a few ways:

- **Add to slack.** If you have a Slack task, you can simply add to its duration, giving more waffle room to all other tasks.

- **Modify task durations.** Take tasks that are running late and give them more time to be accomplished by increasing their durations or by pushing out their start dates to a later time.

- **Review your task constraints.** If you specified that some tasks couldn't finish any later than a certain date but now you're moving your deadline out three months, you might be able to remove or adjust those constraints accordingly.

After you've worked in the extra time provided to you, make sure that the new timing of tasks doesn't cause new resource conflicts, review the Resource Graph view, and then reset your baseline to reflect the new schedule. You reset a baseline by choosing Tools⇨Tracking⇨Save Baseline. When asked whether you're sure that you want to overwrite the existing baseline, reply Yes. Or choose Baseline 1-10 in the Save Baseline dialog box to save to a different baseline.

Don't forget to inform your team of the new timing and provide them with an updated version of your plan.

And now for something completely different

If your manager tells you to cut some corners and sacrifice quality, you have license to modify the scope of the project. You can cut out some tasks that might ensure higher quality, such as a final proofreading of the employee manual. You can hire cheaper workers. You can use cheaper paper or computer equipment.

In Project, this means you have to do the following:

Goal	*Action*
Take less steps	Delete tasks (click the ID of the task in Gantt Chart view and press Delete).
Use less expensive resources	Delete one set of resource assignments and assign other resources to tasks in the Assign Resources dialog box.
Use less expensive materials	Change the unit price for materials you've created in the Resource Sheet view, as shown in Figure 15-7.

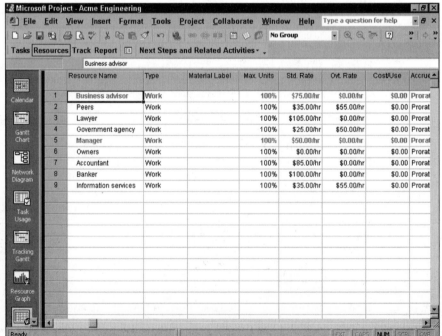

Figure 15- 7:
Use the Resource Sheet to quickly modify unit prices.

You can also take a more sweeping approach: Just redefine the goal of the project. If your goal was to launch a new product line, perhaps you can modify your goal to simply manage the design of the new product, and leave the launch to a later date or another project manager. If you were supposed to produce 10,000 widgets, could your company get along with 7500? To make these kinds of changes, you may have to slice-and-dice entire phases of your project or even start from scratch and build a new plan.

Consider saving your current project plan with a new name to give you a head start. Clear the baseline (Tools➪Tracking➪Clear Baseline), make your modifications, and then save a new baseline.

What Does Project Have to Say about This?

One final word of caution: When you take certain steps, such as deleting tasks or modifying dependency relationships, your action might just cause Project to alert you to a potential problem you hadn't thought of with a Planning Wizard dialog box, such as the one shown in Figure 15-8. If you make changes on your own instead of using the Planning Wizard, you may be more apt to back yourself into a problem situation.

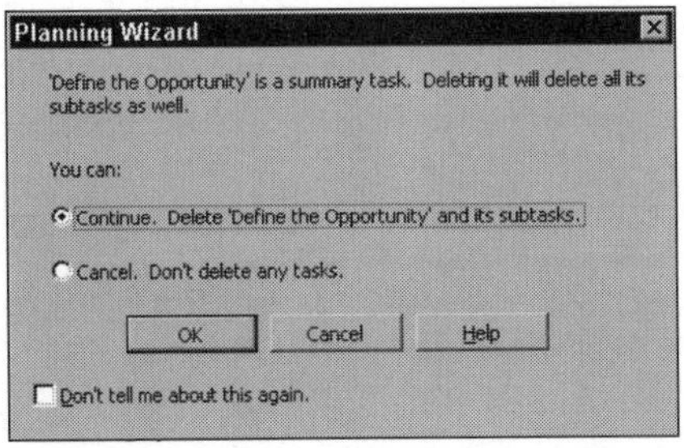

Figure 15-8:
The Wizard wants to be sure that you know that deleting a summary task takes all its subtasks with it.

Planning Wizard	✕
'Define the Opportunity' is a summary task. Deleting it will delete all its subtasks as well.	
You can:	
⦿ Continue. Delete 'Define the Opportunity' and its subtasks.	
○ Cancel. Don't delete any tasks.	
[OK] [Cancel] [Help]	
☐ Don't tell me about this again.	

These dialog boxes offer you options, typically to go ahead and proceed, to cancel, or to proceed but with some modification. Read these alerts carefully and consider the pros and cons of what will happen if you proceed.

Chapter 16

Spreading the News: Reporting

- -

In This Chapter

▶ Generating standard reports

▶ Creating custom reports

▶ Using graphics and formatting in reports

▶ Making printer settings

▶ Working with report legends

- -

*H*ere it is. The big payoff. The reward you get for inputting all those task names, entering all those resource hourly rates, tracking activity on dozens of tasks during those late-hour sessions in the first hectic weeks of your project. You finally get to print a report, getting something tangible out of Project that you can hand out at meetings and impress your boss with.

Reports help you communicate about your project, conveying information about resource assignments, how costs are accumulating, and what activities are in progress or coming up soon. You can take advantage of built-in reports or customize those reports to include the data that's most relevant to you.

Knowing that you'll want to impress people, Project has also made it possible to apply certain formatting settings to reports and add drawings to help get your point across.

Off the Rack: Standard Reports

Standard reports are already designed for you, offering a lot of choices regarding the information you can include. You don't have to do much more than click a few buttons to generate them. Essentially, you select a category of report, choose a specific report, and print it. If the plain-vanilla version of a report isn't quite right, you can modify standard reports in a variety of ways.

You can also print any view in Project; just display the view and click the Print tool button. The entire project is printed in whatever view you have on the screen at the time. Or you can choose File➪Print; in the Print dialog box, you can choose to print only certain pages of your project or only a specific date range from the timescale. Any filters or grouping you've applied will pertain.

What's available

Project has five categories of standard reports: Overview, Current Activities, Costs, Assignments, and Workload. Each category contains several predesigned reports, as you can see in the dialog box for Overview Reports shown in Figure 16-1, for a total of 22 standard reports.

Figure 16-1: In the Overview category, you can choose one of five reports.

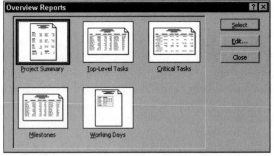

Standard reports vary in content, format (for example, a table versus a columnar report), and sometimes in page orientation (landscape or portrait). You can edit each report to change its name, the time period it covers, the table of information it's based on, and filters applied to it. You can also sort information as you generate the report and add formatting such as borders or gridlines.

Going with the standard

The standard report is simplicity itself. You could practically do this one in your sleep. Or better yet, you could create a macro to do it all with a single keystroke (more about macros in Chapter 17).

Follow these steps to generate any standard report:

1. **Choose View⇨Reports.**

   The Reports dialog box appears, as shown in Figure 16-2.

2. **Click the category of standard report you want, and then click Select.**

   A dialog box named after the category of report you selected appears, as shown in Figure 16-1.

3. **Click one of the standard reports shown here, and then click Select.**

   A preview of the report appears, like the one of Unstarted Tasks shown in Figure 16-3.

4. **To print, click the Print button.**

Figure 16-2:
All five categories of report, plus a custom report category, are accessible through the Reports dialog box.

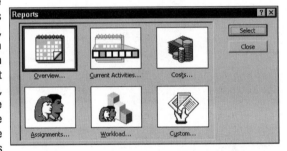

Clicking Close will return you to the Reports dialog box, which lists the category of reports. You'll have to start all over again if you do this.

When you click Print, with some reports an additional dialog box appears asking for a date range or other data specific to that report.

A standard report, with a twist

Some people are happy with the cookie-cutter standard reports that Project provides. But even though standard reports are prebuilt, you can still get in under the hood and tinker a little.

Page left

Page right

Page up

Page down

Zoom

One page

Multiple pages

Figure 16-3:
You may
have to click
a report
preview to
zoom in so
you can
read its
details.

You can edit three categories of things about a standard report:

- **Definition.** This includes the report name, the time period, the table of information, any filters applied, and whether or not summary tasks should appear.

- **Details.** Details can be included for tasks (such as notes or predecessors) and for resource assignments (such as notes or cost). You can also choose to show totals and add a border around the report or gridline between details.

- **Sort.** You can sort by up to three criteria in ascending or descending order.

When modifying standard report, you'll encounter some variations. For example, when you try to edit a Project Summary report, all you get is a text formatting dialog box. But the majority of reports are edited through one dialog box, as shown in the procedure that follows.

To edit a standard report, follow these steps:

1. **Choose View⇨Reports.**

   The Reports dialog box appears.

2. **Click a category of report, and then click Select.**

3. **Click a specific report, and then click Edit.**

   Depending on the type of report you chose, the Resource Report, Task Report, or Crosstab Report dialog box appears. The settings in these dialog boxes are the same, except for some default choices (for example, which filter is applied). Figure 16-4 shows a Task Report dialog box.

4. **Click the Definition tab, if it's not already displayed, and make your selections:**

   a. **If you want a new name for the report, type the name in the Name box.**

   b. **In the Period box, click the period of time to reflect in the report.**

   If rather than choosing Entire Project, you choose an increment of time in the Period box, such as week, you can set the Count counter to reflect the number of increments (for example, 3 for 3 weeks, which prints the report date in three week increments).

   c. **If you'd like a different table of information to be included, make a selection in the Table box.**

   d. **If you want to apply a filter to tasks, select one in the Filter box. To highlight tasks that match the filter's criteria, rather than simply not include tasks that don't meet the criteria, select the Highlight option.**

5. **Click the Details tab, which is shown in Figure 16-5, and make your selections:**

   a. **Click in various check boxes to include different types of information, such as task notes or resource assignment costs.**

   b. **If you want a border around these elements, click the Border Around Details option.**

   c. **If you want gridlines in the report, click the Gridlines Between Details option.**

   This gives your report more of the appearance of a table.

   d. **To include totals of dollar amounts or hours, click Show Totals.**

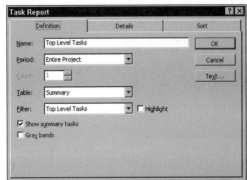

Figure 16-4:
You can
make three
tabs' worth
of settings.

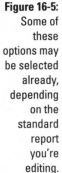

Figure 16-5:
Some of
these
options may
be selected
already,
depending
on the
standard
report
you're
editing.

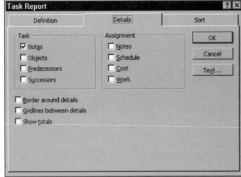

6. **Click the Sort tab, and make your selections:**

   a. **In the Sort By box, click a sort criteria, and then click either Ascending or Descending to choose a sort order.**

   b. **If you want to sort by additional criteria, repeat Step 6a with the Then By boxes.**

7. **Click OK to save your settings.**

8. **In the Reports dialog box, click Select to generate the report preview.**

You can find more details about sorting in Chapter 15.

Coming across crosstabs

Certain reports, called Crosstab reports, have slightly different settings when you edit them. Figure 16-6 shows the Definition tab of the Crosstab Report dialog box. A *crosstab report* tabulates a unique piece of data relative to column and row definitions. Essentially, the cell formed by the column and row intersection represents the unique data.

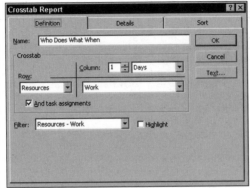

Figure 16-6:
Here you have to choose which three elements define the crosstab.

For example, you might have columns that list days and rows that list resources. The piece of information where the column and row intersects is resource work. The report would show the hours of work by each resource, by day.

When you edit a crosstab, you define the column, the row, and the piece of data being compared. On the Details tab for the crosstab, you can make settings to include row or column totals, to insert gridlines, and to display values of 0.

A Custom Job

Not impressed with the standard reports? Or perhaps none of those reports quite fits your information needs? That's okay. You can create as many custom reports as your heart desires.

A custom report starts out with a report type, which can be task, resource, monthly calendar, or crosstab. After you choose that basic category, you simply work with the same Reports dialog box that you use to edit a standard report.

Follow these steps to begin the process of creating a custom report:

1. **Choose View➪Reports.**

   The Reports dialog box appears.

2. **Click the Custom category, and then click Select.**

   The Custom Reports dialog box appears, as shown in Figure 16-7. You have two options: You can edit an existing report, or you can create a new custom report.

3. **Decide whether you want to base your custom report on an existing report or create a new report, and proceed accordingly.**

   a. **If you want to base your custom report on an existing report, select a report in the Reports list, and then click Edit.**

   b. **If you want to create a report, not based on any other report, click New. Click one of the categories in the dialog box that appears, and then click OK.**

4. **In the Reports dialog box, make choices to define your new report, and then click OK.**

   The choices in this dialog box are discussed in detail previously in this chapter in the section titled "A standard report, with a twist."

Figure 16-7:
The Custom
Reports
dialog box
lets you
start with an
existing set
of data.

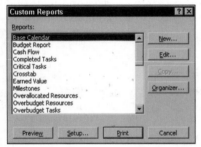

If you create a custom report based on an existing report, be sure to give it a unique name.

Spiffing Things Up

These days, image is everything. You and your project may be judged to some extent by how professional your printed information looks. Even if your project is a million over budget and four months behind, making your reports or other printouts look good can make delivering bad news easier.

To create impressive documents, make sure you cross the *t*'s of formatting text and dot the *i*'s of visual design.

Using graphics in Project

Wouldn't your company logo look spiffy in the header of your report? Or what about including a picture of the new product box in the Gantt Chart view of your New Product Launch project?

Graphics can add visual information or just plain make your plan look nicer. You can insert graphics in your project file by using three methods. You can

✔ Cut and paste a graphic from another file.

✔ Insert a link to an existing graphics file. Linking keeps your file smaller.

✔ Embed a graphic. Embedding lets you edit the graphic's contents in Project, using the tools of an image program such as Paint.

You can't add graphics willy-nilly, however. You can add graphics in only a few places: the chart pane of any Gantt view, a task note, a resource note, or a header, footer, or legend used in reports or printouts of views.

You might put pictures of resources in the resource note field so that you can remember who's who. Or you might include a photo of your corporate headquarters in the header of your report.

Remember, graphics files swell your Project file like a sponge in a pail of water. If you're thinking of using a lot of graphics, be sure they don't detract from the main information in your printouts, and try linking to them instead of inserting them in the file.

Follow these steps to begin the process of inserting a graphic in your Gantt Chart using object linking and embedding:

1. **Display the Gantt Chart view.**

2. **Choose Insert➪Object.**

   The Insert Object dialog box appears, as shown in Figure 16-8.

Figure 16-8:
You can
insert a
wide variety
of objects
using this
dialog box.

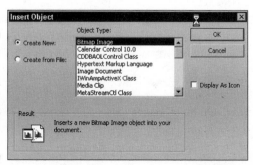

If you want to insert an existing graphics file, do the following:

1. **In the Insert Object dialog box, click Create from File.**

   The choices in the dialog box change to those shown in Figure 16-9.

2. **Type the file name in the File box or click Browse to locate the file.**

3. **If you want to link to the file, click the Link option and then click OK.**

   If you don't select this option, the object will be embedded in your file.

4. **If you want to insert the object as an icon, click Display as Icon.**

   When you display the object as an icon, those viewing your project on a computer can click the icon to view the picture.

5. **Click OK.**

   The image appears in the Gantt chart pane.

6. **You can then use the resizing nodes on the corners of the image to expand or shrink it, or click the image to move it around the pane.**

Figure 16-9:
Use the
browse
button to
locate the
file on a
network or
your hard
drive.

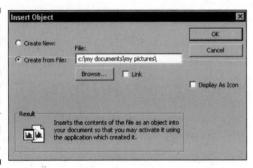

If instead of inserting an existing graphics file, you want to insert a blank graphics file, follow these steps:

1. **Click Create New.**

2. **In the Object Type list, click the type of object you want to insert.**

   For example, you might select Bitmap Image, Microsoft Word Picture, or Paintbrush Picture.

3. **If you want to insert the object as an icon, click Display as Icon.**

   When you display the object as an icon, those viewing your project on a computer can click the icon to view the picture.

4. **Click OK.**

   You see a blank object box with tools such as the one in Paintbox shown in Figure 16-10.

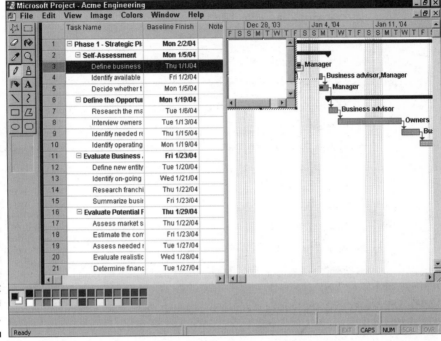

Figure 16-10:
When you
close this
window
you'll be
back in your
Project file;
double-click
on the
object to
open this
editing
environment
any time
you like.

5. **Use the tools of the program from which you inserted an object to make, draw, insert, or format the new graphic object.**

To insert an object into a notes field, open the Task or Resource Information dialog box, and then click the Insert Object tool. The Insert Object dialog box appears. Then just proceed as shown in the preceding steps. A similar tool is available in the Page Setup dialog box, where you can use the Header, Footer, or Legend tabs to insert objects.

Formatting reports

You probably cut your computing teeth by formatting text in word processors, so formatting reports will be a breeze. You have all the usual formatting options available to you whenever you generate a report in Project.

To edit report text, just do this:

1. **Choose View⇨Reports.**

   The Reports dialog box appears.

2. **Click a report category, and then click Select.**

3. **In the Reports category dialog box that appears, click the specific report that you want to generate.**

4. **Click Edit.**

   The specific report dialog box opens.

5. **Click the Text button.**

   The Text Styles dialog box appears, as shown in Figure 16-11.

6. **In the Item to Change box, click the item that you want to format.**

7. **Make your selections in the Font, Font Style, Size, or Color boxes.**

8. **If you want to format another item, select it in the Item to Change box and repeat Step 7.**

9. **When you're finished, click OK.**

10. **To view the report in preview, click OK again.**

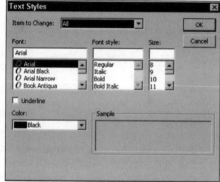

Figure 16-11:
This dialog box contains many familiar text settings.

As with any other business document, your goal in formatting text should be readability. Remember, in addition to dealing with neat columns of data, you also might be dealing with labels of dates or resource names wedged alongside taskbars in the chart pane. Keep the following points in mind when formatting Project text:

✔ Choose simple sans-serif fonts, such as Arial.

✔ If you're publishing your project on the Web, consider using Verdana, a font created for readability online.

✔ Consider your use of color. Will the printout be in color or black and white? Will the use of too many colors become confusing for the reader? Will certain colors, such as yellow, be difficult to read?

✔ Use a font size that is readable, without making it so big that the taskbar labels becomes too crowded.

✔ Avoid text effects that can make some text difficult to read, such as bold, italic, or underlining. Use such effects only to call attention to a few elements of your project.

Call the Printer!

The proof of the report is in the printing, but you should see to several adjustments before you click that button to Print. With Project, it's not just margins or page orientation that you need to set (though you do have to set those, too). You can also put useful information in headers and footers, and set legends that help your reader understand the many bars, diamonds, and other graphic elements many Project views display.

Working with Page Setup

The Page Setup dialog box can be used to control printouts of both reports and any currently displayed Project view. You get to this dialog box in slightly different ways:

✔ To make settings for printing the current view, choose File➪Page Setup.

✔ To modify the page setup for a report, you have to select Page Setup from the preview of the report. Choose View➪Reports, then click a report category, and then click a specific report. When you click Select to generate a specific report, the print preview appears. Click the Page Setup tool button that appears there.

The Page Setup dialog box, shown in Figure 16-12, contains six tabs. In the case of reports, all tabs might not be available to you. For example, reports don't contains graphic elements such as taskbars, so you can't set a legend to appear on them. Also, you have access to the View tab only when you're printing the currently displayed view.

When size is important

The Page tab contains some basic page settings that determine the orientation, the paper size, and the way the contents are scaled to fit the page. By making these settings, you are influencing how much can fit on each page and how many pages long your document will be.

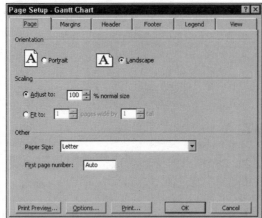

Figure 16-12:
You can
control
how your
document is
laid out and
is printed.

Here are the choices you have on this tab (shown previously in Figure 16-12):

✔ Portrait or Landscape orientation. No doubt you've dealt with these before. Portrait is like the Mona Lisa; Landscape is like . . . well, having the long edge of the paper running across the top!

✔ Scaling. You can use the Adjust To or Fit To setting. The Adjust To setting works by a percentage of the original size. The Fit To setting gives you some control over scaling to fit to the width of a single page or the height of a single page.

✔ The Other area is a catchall for two options: Paper Size and First Page Number. All the standard choices for paper size are available in the Paper Size list, including index cards and envelopes. First Page Number can be left as Auto (in which case the first page is numbered 1, the second page, 2, and so on), or you can enter a number there yourself.

Keeping things within the margins

I won't bore you by defining what a margin is. However, I will remind you that margins serve the dual purpose of controlling how much information can fit on each page and creating a border of white space that frames your document, making it cleaner looking and easier to read.

To set margins using the Page Setup dialog box, follow these steps:

1. **Click the Margins tab, which is shown in Figure 16-13.**

2. **Use the arrows to set the Top, Bottom, Left, and Right margins.**

   Click the up arrow for a wider margin and the down arrow for a narrower margin.

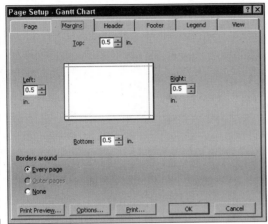

Figure 16-13:
As you
modify
margin
settings, the
preview
shows you
where they
will appear
on your
page.

3. **If you'd like a border representing the margin, use the Borders Around settings.**

   Here you can choose to print a border on Every Page, on only Outer Pages (this prints a border on the first and last pages only and is available only when printing a Network Diagram view), or None.

Setting margins to be less than ½ inch (.5) could cause your printed output to be cut off because printers can only print so close to the edge of a page.

Putting all the right stuff in headers and footers

Throughout the life of a project, you'll print many versions of your project, many reports, and many types of information using various tables. Headers and footers are a great feature to help you and your readers keep track of all this information.

You can use the Header (shown in Figure 16-14) and Footer tabs of the Page Setup dialog box to set and preview header and footer contents.

You can get to this area of the Page Setup dialog box also by choosing View⇨Header and Footer.

Here are the settings you can make on these tabs:

✔ Enter text to appear on the Left, Center, or Right of the header or footer by clicking on one of those tabs and typing the text.

✔ Format text using the tool buttons or quickly insert such things as the page number, the date, or a picture file.

✔ Select additional standard text to insert by using the General and Project Fields lists. The General list includes such things as Total Page Count, Project Title, and Company Name. The Project Fields list includes all the fields available in Project. You might use these to alert the reader to key fields to review or the nature of the printout. To add General or Project Field items, select them from their respective lists and then click Add to add them to the Left, Center, or Right tab.

Working with a legend

A *legend* acts as a guide to the meanings of various graphic elements, as shown in Figure 16-15. The Legend tab bears a striking resemblance to the Header and Footer tabs, except that the legend is generated automatically, so all you set here is the text that fits in the box to the left of the legend.

Format text font

Insert page number

Insert total page count

Insert current date

Insert current time

Insert file name

Insert picture

Figure 16-14:
The Header and Footer tabs are identical: One controls what appears at the top of your page, the other what appears at the bottom.

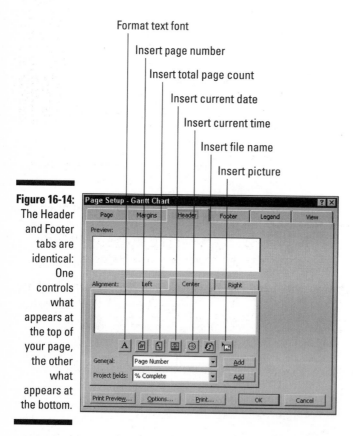

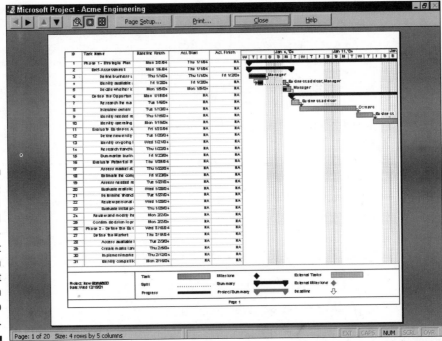

Figure 16-15:
The legend
is printed
automa-
tically, but
you can
insert
information
in the box to
the left of it.

The Legend tab of the Page Setup dialog box has only two settings that differ from the Header and Footer tabs:

- ✔ You can print the legend on every page or on a separate legend page, or you can decide to not print a legend.

- ✔ You can establish the width of the text area of the legend (the area where you can insert elements such as the page number or the date).

Unlike a header or footer, where you have to enter something to have anything appear, a legend prints by default. If you don't want a legend to print, you have to go into this tab and set the Legend On setting to None.

What to print?

If you're printing a currently displayed view, the View tab of the Page Setup dialog box appears, as shown in Figure 16-16.

You can make the following settings here:

- ✔ Print All Sheet Columns. Prints every sheet column in the view, whether or not it's currently visible on your screen. With this not selected, only the columns that show in your view will print.

- ✔ Print First # Columns On All Pages. Allows you to control a specific number of columns to print.

✔ Print Notes. Prints every task, resource, and assignment note. These are printed on their a separate notes page.

✔ Print Blank Pages. Choose this setting if you want blank pages, for example, a page that represents a time in your project when no tasks are occurring, to print anyway. If you want to view inactive as well as active periods for your project, choose this setting. If you want a smaller number of pages in your printout, don't choose this setting it.

✔ Fit Timescale to End of Page. Scales the timescale to allow you to fit more of your project on the page.

✔ Print Row Totals for Values Within Print Date Range. Adds a column containing row totals. Pertains to printouts of Usage views.

✔ Print Column Totals. Adds a column containing column totals. Pertains to printouts of Usage views.

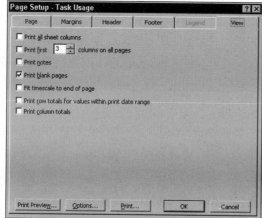

Figure 16-16:
This tab
is not
available if
you're
printing a
report.

Get a preview

There are movie previews, fall fashion previews, and in software, print previews. The print preview feature is accessible from many places in Project:

✔ Choose File⇨Print Preview (to preview the current view).

✔ Click the Print Preview button on the Standard toolbar.

✔ Click Print Preview on any tab of the Page Setup dialog box.

✔ Generate a print preview when you select a specific report to print.

Figure 16-15 shows a print preview. You can use the tool buttons here to do the following:

  ✔ Move around the pages of the report by using the Page Left, Right, Up, and Down arrows on the toolbar and the horizontal and vertical scrollbars.

  ✔ Read more detail by clicking the Zoom tool button and then clicking the report.

  ✔ Focus on a single page or all the pages of your report by using the One Page and Multiple Pages tool buttons.

  ✔ Modify margins and the orientation of the printout by displaying the Page Setup dialog box.

  ✔ Display the Print dialog box by clicking Print.

  ✔ Close the preview by clicking Close.

So, Let's Print!

Last but not least, I'll tell you how to actually print a document for which you've made all the wonderful settings discussed in this chapter. For this, you need to deal with the Print dialog box, which you've seen a million times in almost any other Windows program on the planet (see Figure 16-17).

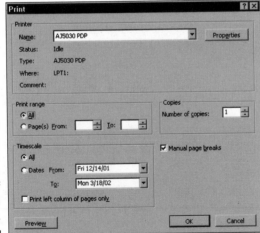

Figure 16-17:
Control the printer, the number of copies, and what prints.

Here are the settings you'll encounter in this dialog box:

  ✔ The first area of this dialog box concerns the printer you will use. You can choose a printer in the Name list, and click the Properties tab to control printer settings such as color quality and paper source.

  ✔ The Print Range area allows you to print All pages or to select a page range From one page number To another.

✔ The Copies area contains one simple setting: Click the up arrow here to print more copies or the down arrow to print fewer (but not less than 1).

✔ The Timescale settings are unique to Project: Here you can choose to print the entire timescale (the entire length of your project) or only a range of dates within your project. Along with Print Range, this setting helps control how much of your Project will print.

✔ If you want the leftmost column of the page to print on every page, select Print Left Column of Pages Only. For example, you might want the task ID number column to print on both pages when a printout width stretches over two pages.

✔ Finally, if you've inserted manual page breaks in your project, you can click the Manual Page Breaks option to include these breaks in your printed report. Leave this option blank if you want the Print feature to control where pages will break

When you've made all your settings and you're ready to print, just click OK.

Chapter 17

Getting Better All the Time

· ·

· ·

*H*ave you ever finished a project, and then wondered how the heck everything came together at the end? The total budget numbers mystically appear to be several thousand dollars too much, you missed your final deadline by three weeks, and somewhere along the line you lost track of three people who were supposed to be working on tasks. But you delivered your deliverable (somehow), and you can finally stuff your project file in the bottom of your drawer. Or can you?

Microsoft Project is not just a giant electronic to-do list; it's a way to manage your projects. But the by-product of that management is a fantastic tool that you can use to become a better Project user and a better project manager.

When you've sent out the last memo on your project and accepted your last kudos or criticism from your boss, take a moment to look over your Project plan one more time.

Learning from Your Mistakes

When I teach classes in using project management software, people are often a bit overwhelmed at all that a product such as Project can do. They're reeling from all the data that they have to input and all the information that Project throws back at them. They can't see straight for all the views, reports, tables, and filters that they can use to access information on their projects.

Here's the secret I tell them: You won't be perfect on your first project. You won't be perfect on your second project. But gradually, as you learn the ins and outs of Project and understand what you can get out of it, you'll become better and better and things will get easier and easier.

The best way to make that happen is to review every project to see what you did right and what you did wrong. Then, do it better in your next project.

It was only an estimate

You know what they say: If you don't study history, you're doomed to repeat it. And that's the last thing you want to do, at least as far as the mistakes you made in your last project.

Consider these strategies to debrief yourself on what happened in your last project:

- ✔ **Compare your original baseline plan against the final actual activity.** Even if you have interim baseline plans that adjusted for drastic changes, looking at the widest gap between what you expected to happen and what did can be the best way to see the areas where you tend to underestimate most.

- ✔ **Review the notes you made on your tasks to remind yourself of changes or problems that came up along the way.** Insert the column named Notes on your Gantt Chart sheet and read through all the notes at one time.

- ✔ **Note which resources delivered on their promises and which didn't; if you manage some of them, provide them with constructive feedback.** For those you don't manage, keep some notes on hand about how well or how fast they worked and make future assignments with those notes in mind.

- ✔ **Assess your own communications to others in saved e-mails or memos.** Did you give your team enough information to perform effectively? Did you keep management informed about changes or problems in a timely way?

Debrief your team

No Project project is the province of a single person. Even if no one else ever touched your Project plan, your team provided input for that plan through the hours of activity they reported and the information they provided to you during the course of your project.

- ✔ **Ask people how the process of reporting actual activity worked.** Did you use e-mail schedule notes, route files, or use the Project Server collaborative tools to get resource information? Should you consider the use of a third-party product such as Timeslips for automated resource activity tracking on the next project?

✔ **Would your team rate your communications as frequent and thorough enough?** Did you share enough of your project with resources, or did you inundate them with too much information? Did you send an entire Project file to people regularly when a simple report on a specific aspect of the project would have served you and them better?

✔ **Did you integrate activity on various projects successfully so that resources weren't overbooked or underutilized?** If people on your team report that there were conflicts with other projects, consider using Project tools such as hyperlinking to tasks in other projects or developing a master project in which you insert several projects into a master plan to view resource conflicts across them.

Building on Your Success

Although it's human nature to focus on all the things that went wrong with a project, the fact is that you probably did many, many things right. So before you start planning your next project, take the good stuff and put it somewhere where you can find it later.

Create a template

One option is to create a template. *Templates* are simply files you save that contain certain settings. When you open a template, you can save it as a Project document with a new name and have all those settings already built in.

Debrief yourself?

Don't forget to sit down and have a good talk with yourself about what went on during your project. Did your team give you the kind of information you needed to operate efficiently, or should you lay down more stringent ground rules for reporting in the next project? Were you overbooked throughout the project, and would it be wise to find someone to make updating entries for you the next time around? Did management give you information about company changes in a timely way so that you could make adjustments to keep your project on schedule?

It's often the case that in the heat of project battle, you don't have time to stop and change processes or get the help you need. Review the notes you kept in the Project notes areas to see what made you pull your hair out and institute changes before you begin the next project.

Project contains its own templates for common projects, but you can save any of your projects as templates. If you often use the same set of tasks in your projects, as people in many industries do, you'll save yourself the time of creating all those tasks again. In addition to any tasks in the project, templates can contain any or all the following information for those tasks:

✔ All the information for each baseline

✔ Actual values

✔ Rates for all resources

✔ Fixed costs

✔ Notation of tasks that you have published to Project Server

You can save all this information or only selected items. So, for example, if you created a lot of fixed costs, such as equipment, and resources with associated rates and will use those again in most of your projects, you could save a template with only fixed costs and resource rates.

To save a file as a template, follow these steps:

1. **With the file you want to save open, choose File⇨Save As.**

   The Save As dialog box appears, as shown in Figure 17-1.

2. **In the Save As Type list, click Template.**

   Project selects the Templates folder as the Save In location.

3. **Click Save.**

   The Save As Template dialog box appears, as shown in Figure 17-2.

4. **Click the check boxes for the information you want saved in the template.**

5. **Click Save.**

The file is saved in the template format with the MPT extension. When you open a new project, click General Templates in the New Project task pane. The Templates dialog box appears, and any templates you've saved will appear in the list on the General tab. Just open the template, and then save it as a Project file with a new name.

Master the Organizer

Project has this marvelously flexible nature that allows you to customize a lot of things. For example, you can create your own tables of data to display in views that contain sheets of data. You can create also your own filters, reports, and calendars. If you have any kind of a life, you don't want to spend your evenings recreating all that stuff for your next project. So, use the Organizer to copy them to other Project files instead.

Figure 17-1:
Microsoft
saves
templates
in a central
file called
Templates.

Figure 17-2:
Choose
which
information
about
values and
resource
rates will be
saved with
all the tasks
in the
project in a
template
format.

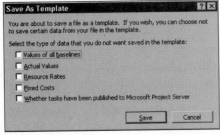

The Organizer allows you to take information in one file and copy it to another file. You can also rename the item.

Follow these steps to use the Organizer:

1. **Open the project that you want to copy things from and the project that you want to copy things to.**

2. **In the file you want to copy to, choose Tools⇔Organizer.**

    The Organizer dialog box appears, as shown in Figure 17-3.

3. **Click the tab for the type of information you want to copy.**

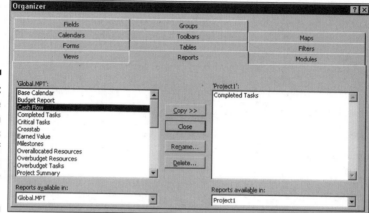

Figure 17-3:
You have
eleven
sheets
worth of
stuff you
can copy
here!

4. **If necessary, select other files to copy to or from.**

   The Global template is selected as the file to copy from by default and the file you used to open the Organizer is the file to copy to. To use other files, select another file in the Available In box on the left (copy from) or right (copy to) of the dialog box. These boxes contain the Global.MPT file and any other files you currently have open.

5. **Click an item in the list on the left that you want to include in the file on the right, and then click Copy.**

   The item appears in the list on the right.

6. **If you want to rename an item, click it and then click Rename. In the Rename dialog box that appears, enter a new name and then click OK.**

7. **To copy additional items on the same tab, repeat Step 5.**

8. **To copy an item on a different tab, repeat Steps 3 to 7.**

9. **When you've finished copying items from one file to another, click the X in the upper-right hand.**

   All the items have now been copied.

Handy little timesavers: Macros

If you were paying attention, you may have noticed that there were a lot of activities in your project that you did again, and again, and again. No, I'm not talking about all those cups of coffee you downed in the wee hours. I'm talking about things such as generating the same report every week, or inserting your five department projects into a single master schedule once a quarter to review resource allocations.

You don't have to reinvent the wheel to perform actions such as these. Instead, you can create a macro. A *macro* is simply a combination of keystrokes, text entries, and so on that you can record and play back any time you like.

Suppose that you generate and print a report on current activities every week. This requires the following keystrokes and entries:

1. Choose View⇨Reports.

2. Click Current Activities.

3. Click Select.

4. Click Tasks Starting Soon.

5. Click Select.

6. Type a unique date for tasks that start or finish after a point in time.

7. Click OK.

8. Type a unique date for tasks that start or finish before a point in time to complete the specified range.

9. Click OK.

10. Click Print to print the report.

If you record all those keystrokes, you'll go through a 10-step process. But once recorded, that process is reduced to 3 steps when you play them back with a macro (start your macro, enter the first part of the date range, and then enter the last part of the date range).

One great use I've seen for macros is to copy a range of tasks that's repeated again and again in your project — for example, a Q&A procedure that's repeated five times throughout a project. In recording the macro, just select the absolute range and copy it, go to the first blank task and paste it, five times. While the macro's running, you can go get yourself another cup of coffee.

Recording a macro

Recording a macro is a simple process: You just start recording, do whatever you usually do to perform the action, and then stop recording. You run macros by selecting them from a list of macros. You can edit them if you need a slightly different series of keystrokes at a later date.

Here's how you record a macro:

1. **Choose Tools⇨Macro⇨Record New Macro.**

   The Record Macro dialog box appears, as shown in Figure 17-4.

2. **In the Macro Name box, type a name.**

   Make the name descriptive of what the macro does.

Figure 17-4:
Macros you
record are
played back
using a
shortcut key
that you
designate
here.

3. **In the Shortcut Key box, type a letter.**

   Pressing Ctrl plus that key will play back the macro.

4. **If you like, edit or add to the description of the macro.**

   This is especially useful if you think others will use it.

5. **Select whether row and column references will be relative or absolute.**

   With relative references, if you select, say, the task in the third row displayed in a sheet and perform an action on it, Project selects the third task when you run the macro. With absolute references, Project selects a specific named task no matter what row it is in.

6. **Click OK to begin recording.**

   Remember that every keystroke you make during this time becomes part of the macro.

7. **When you've completed your keystrokes, choose Tools⇨Macro⇨ Stop Recorder.**

Remember these points about recording macros:

✔ Macro names have to start with a letter and can't contain spaces. Use the underscore to separate words in a macro name (Weekly_Report, for example).

✔ Several keystroke shortcuts are already used by Project for built-in functions, such as Ctrl+K to insert a hyperlink. Project displays a message telling you this if you choose such a shortcut and gives you an opportunity to choose another letter or number.

✔ If what you record includes entering specific information, such as a name or a date range, you're presented with a blank box to enter new information when you run the macro — even if you entered information while recording the macro.

Running and editing macros

To run a macro, your best bet is the shortcut key you entered when you created it. This two-keystroke combination runs the macro, pausing for you to fill in any requested information.

Alternately, you can choose Tools⇨Macro⇨Macros, click a macro in the list of macros shown in the Macros dialog box in Figure 17-5, and then click Run.

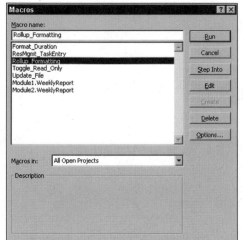

Figure 17-5:
The Macros
dialog box
lists all
available
macros in
any open
projects.

To edit a macro, you might want to simply re-record (this is sometimes the quickest way to do it). Or you can choose Tools⇨Macro⇨Macros. In the Macros dialog box, click the macro you want to modify and then click Edit. The Microsoft Visual Basic editor opens; your macro is displayed in Visual Basic code, as shown in Figure 17-6.

You can edit this code much as you edit text in a word-processed document, although you have to be familiar with the Visual Basic programming language to make most changes. However, you can make some edits without being a programmer. For example, if you see items in quotes, these are text entries or names of things such as reports. If you want to change a macro that generates the report named "Tasks Starting Soon" to generate the report "Tasks in Progress," just replace the existing report name with the new report name.

If you want to delete a piece of the process, you can usually figure that out from the code. For example, if you see the line `'If project is empty, alert the user and end the macro'` and you don't want the macro to include that step, just select it and press the Delete key.

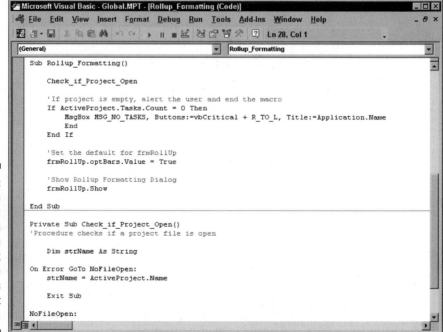

Figure 17-6:
This is
Visual Basic
code, which
uses certain
syntax
to code
keystrokes
and text
entry.

But monkeying around with Visual Basic for anything much more complex could mess up your macro. Because I don't want to write another book on Visual Basic at this point, I suggest that you keep your life and mine simple: Delete the first macro and walk through the procedure again, re-recording it as a new macro.

Part V
The Part of Tens

The 5th Wave   By Rich Tennant

"I hear some of the engineers from the mainframe dept. project managed the baking of this year's fruitcake."

In this part . . .

*P*ut anything in a list and it snaps into focus like a
nearsighted person putting on bifocals. In this part,
you get two useful lists of ten to make your project
management role easier.

Chapter 18 offers the ten golden rules of project management. Use these to make your experience with Microsoft
Project even more productive.

Chapter 19 lists ten useful Web sites that feature project
management software products that add functionality to
Project. Some of these are add-on products that integrate
with Project's functionality. Others are additional project-
management-related products that complement Project's
features.

Chapter 18

Ten Golden Rules of Project Management

In This Chapter

▶ Understanding how to put good project management practices to work using Microsoft Project

▶ Creating and tracking Project schedules more efficiently

▶ Learning from your mistakes

You've heard this one: You can have your deliverable on time, on budget, or done right — choose two. That's an example of some traditional project management wisdom. But how does that wisdom translate to the use of project management software?

Well, it's simple: You've learned that if you assign additional resources to a Project schedule, you add costs and time to your schedule because resources have costs attached and can work only based on their work calendars. So clearly, making changes that might improve quality, such as adding more or higher-priced resources, affects time and money. The adage is still true; it's just that you can clearly see the effect one action has on other aspects of your project with Project's many views and reports.

So what project management adages should you be aware of as you begin to use Project? Here are ten to tack up on your office wall.

Don't Bite off More Than You Can Manage

As I've mentioned elsewhere in this book (see Chapter 5), you must have an understanding of the goal of your project as well as the scope of its activities before you start to build a Project schedule. Don't plan a full marketing campaign if all you can anticipate at this point is what the market research phase will look like. Because the additional elements of a marketing campaign hinge on that market research, build your project in phases. That way, you'll have less reworking of later tasks that simply can't be anticipated when you begin. You'll also have less need to manipulate the baseline for later tasks because the odds are, if those tasks are too far in the future, they won't look anything like your original timing by the time you get there.

Here are some Project features that help you with this process:

- ✔ The capability to combine subprojects into a master project with linking
- ✔ The Network Diagram view, which helps you visualize phases of your project graphically
- ✔ The flexible nature of Project outlines, which allows you to hide or display different phases of a project

Get Your Ducks in a Row

Before you start creating your project, you would be wise to do your homework. If you don't have all the information you need when you sit down at your computer to work with Project, you'll find yourself constantly stopping in midplanning and running off to find that information. This isn't a very efficient way to work.

Here are some things to research before you sit down to build a project schedule:

- ✔ **Resource information.** This includes the full name, contact information, manager and manager's contact information, skills, cost, schedule, and timing conflicts. For equipment or facilities, find out their availability and cost.

- ✔ **Team structure.** Will everyone do his or her own tracking, or will someone else on the team input everyone's progress? Who will update the schedule for changes that might occur? Who should get copies of which reports? Should your team have access to the master schedule online? Does everyone on the team have the technology to communicate using collaborative features such as Project Server?

- ✔ **Management expectations.** Does management expect to see standard reports on a regular basis? Do you need to get budget approval at various phases in your project planning, and from whom? Are cross-divisional interests involved that require you to report to or get approval from multiple sources?

- ✔ **Company policies.** These include company work policies regarding resource hours and overtime, the holiday calendar, how your company charges overhead costs or markups to projects, and what information can and can't be shared with clients or vendors.

The Enterprise resource features new to Project 2002 help you call on company information stored on your server, such as enterprise resources, for consistency across projects.

Now you're ready to sit down and start inputting a Project project!

Plan for Murphy

You know he's out there: Murphy and his darn law! The fact is that most projects don't happen on time or on budget. This is especially true of lengthier and more complex projects. Your job is to do the most accurate planning you can and make prudent adjustments whenever a wrench is thrown into the works. Project gives you lots of tools to do that. But beyond all the automated features of Project, you can anticipate change by planning for it.

As described in Chapter 6, the critical path in a project is indeed critical. Every wise project manager builds extra time and even extra money into schedules. When the project comes in only a week late and only $5000 overbudget, only the project manager knows that it was really four weeks later and $25,000 costlier than what the first schedule reflected — the one with no allowance for Murphy.

Add time to the duration of every task if possible to account for shifts in schedule, and add a resource to every phase of your project that pads your budget just a bit to help you deal with overages. You can even name the extra resource *Murphy,* if you like!

Don't Put Off Until Tomorrow

Project management software can make many aspects of your life easier, but the thing that overwhelms most people when they begin to use Project is the amount of time you have to spend actually inputting data and keeping it up to date. It's true, those tasks can be cumbersome, but what you can get in the way of automated updating and reporting capabilities more than makes up for the work.

However, if you don't tend to the task of tracking progress on a project, you can wind up behind the proverbial eight ball. Track just as often as you can — at least once a week. This not only saves you from facing a mountain of tracking data to be entered but also means that you and your team are seeing the true picture of your project at any point in time. That way, you can spot disaster coming promptly and make adjustments accordingly.

Delegate, Delegate, Delegate!

Don't try to do everything on a project yourself. Although creating and maintaining your Project file on your own may seem to give you more control, doing so is just about impossible in larger projects. Of course, you don't want dozens of people going in and making changes to your plan, because you'd run the risk of losing track of who did what and when. But a few simple practices make a few fingers in the project pie helpful, not harmful:

- ✔ Designate one person to enter all tracking data into the master file for you, or automate tracking by using the Request Progress Information feature.

- ✔ Break your project into a few subprojects and assign people you trust to act as managers of those phases. Let them deal with their own tracking and adjustments, and then assemble the phase projects into a master project so that you can monitor their changes.

- ✔ Enlist the help of your IS person in setting up Project Server to provide enhanced collaborative features to your team.

- ✔ Set uniform procedures for your team upfront. Don't have one person report time on an inner-office memo sheet, somebody else e-mail you his progress, and have others use the Timesheet feature to communicate work performed on a task.

CYA (Document!)

Everyone knows the project management adage to CYA, but Project makes it a lot easier. Try using these features to document the details of your project:

- ✔ Use the Notes area (see Figure 18-1) for both tasks and resources to make a record of background information, changes, or special issues.

- ✔ Use the routing feature of Project to route schedules to people for review. This builds an electronic paper trail of where information went and who responded.

- ✔ Customize reports to incorporate all pertinent information and help you document trends and changes.

- ✔ Save multiple versions of your project, especially if you make changes to your baseline in later versions. This provides a record of every step in your project planning, which you can refer to when questions arise down the road.

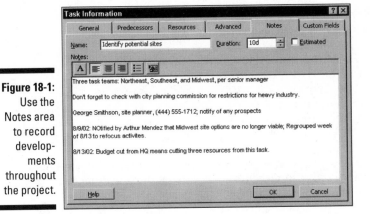

Figure 18-1:
Use the Notes area to record developments throughout the project.

Keep Your Team in the Loop

I've worked in offices where I spent more time trying to keep straight who I should keep informed about what than I did working. If I didn't include marketing and finance in every e-mail on a new product launch, I'd be called on the carpet the next day or worse: Some vital action step would fall through the cracks because someone didn't know that he or she was supposed to take action. Try these methods of keeping communication channels open:

- ✔ Use the Project features that allow you to integrate with Outlook or other e-mail programs to route Project files or other communications.

- ✔ Build address lists in your e-mail program specific to your project team so that every message goes to everyone, every time.

- ✔ Review progress with your team by meeting regularly, whether in person, over the phone, online in a chat area, or by using meeting software. Make sure each team member has the latest version of the Project schedule to refer to during these meetings.

- ✔ Use the Send to: Exchange Folder command to post the latest version of a project in a folder on your network so that others know what's going on.

- ✔ Display the work breakdown structure code on reports so that you can easily reference specific tasks in large projects and avoid confusion.

Measure Success

When you begin your project, you should have an idea of what constitutes success and a way to measure that success. Success can involve many things, such as

✔ Customer satisfaction

✔ Management satisfaction

✔ Being on budget

✔ Being on time

When you start your project planning, know how you'll measure your success. Will success in budgeting mean that you don't exceed your original estimates by more than 10 percent? Will your project be considered on time if you worked the estimated amount of weeks on it minus a two-month period when you went on hold for a union strike, or is the total working time less important than meeting a specific deadline? How will you measure customer satisfaction? Will management satisfaction be reflected by you getting a promotion or your division receiving more funding? Does a successful product launch include high sales figures after the launch, or was your project successful merely because you got it out the door?

Place milestones in your project (see Figure 18-2) that reflect the achievement of each type of success. When you reach each milestone, you can pat your team on the back. Knowing what success looks like helps you motivate your team to get there.

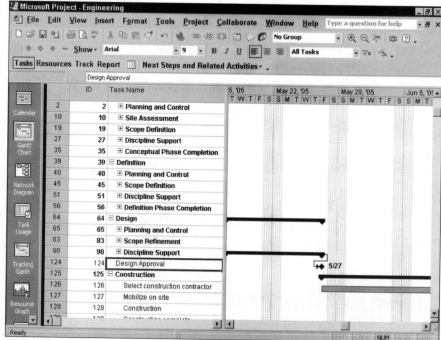

Figure 18-2:
Milestones provide markers along the way that give your team a feeling of achievement.

Have a Flexible Strategy

Stuff happens. There hasn't been a project in the world that didn't require accommodations for surprises along the way. The mark of a good project manager is that he or she is alert to these changes and makes adjustments to deal with them quickly.

This isn't always easy: It's really, really hard to be the messenger of bad news. But avoiding a problem in your project, hoping it will go away, has a nasty habit of snowballing. The following tools can help you stay alert to changes and make adjustments:

- ✔ The Resource Substitution Wizard helps you make changes when a one resource you'd counted on suddenly wins the lottery and disappears.

- ✔ Use the Portfolio Modeling feature (see Figure 18-3) to try what-if analyses on your project to anticipate how possible changes might affect you.

- ✔ Use various views to see the critical path on your project and track how much slack you have left. Adjusting tasks to efficiently use up their slack may keep you on schedule in a crisis.

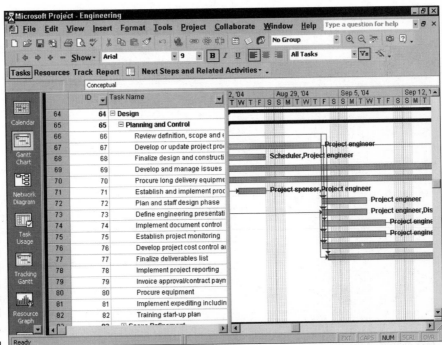

Figure 18-3: Critical path can be seen in several ways using Project's views and filters.

Learn from Your Mistakes

One of the greatest gifts Project offers you is the ability to look back when you've completed a project and learn from your mistakes. You can review your original schedule and every version after that to see how well you estimated time and money, and learn to do it better.

By using records of your project, you can spot trends. Where do you always seem to miss on timing? Do you always allow way too little time on market research and way too much time for Q&A? Do you always forget to budget in temporary help during rush times, or do you overstaff early on when you could get by with fewer people?

Use the wealth of information in Project schedules to educate yourself on your own strengths and weaknesses as a project planner and manager and to get better with each project you take on.

Chapter 19

Ten Project Management Software Products to Explore

In This Chapter

▶ Looking at add-on software

▶ Discovering software that integrates with Project-generated plans

▶ Reviewing separate software products that help project managers with project-related tasks

*Y*ou've probably figured out by now that project management software, just like a project manager, wears a lot of hats. Project does everything from allowing you to create tasks and assign resources, to tracking progress, analyzing cost overruns, and analyzing scheduling conflicts. It handles graphics, complex calculations, and interacts with the Web.

Software designers always have to make trade-offs between which features to include and how much functionality to include for each feature. Most of Project's features do everything you need, but others are less complete. For some features, you may need a more specialized tool in addition to Project. Third-party software partners work with Microsoft to create add-in software to provide Project with greater functionality, such as more graphic report generation. In other cases, software handles specialized functions that Project doesn't incorporate, such as managing the hundreds of drawings involved in construction projects.

Consider this the "when two heads are better than one" chapter. This chapter describes ten interesting software tools you can use with Project. Most offer some kind of free demo of their product on their Web site. Plenty of products are out there, so use this chapter as a starting point to considering ways to extend Project's functionality.

AMS Real Time Helps Keep Resources in Line

AMS Real Time, from Advanced Management Solutions (www.amsrealtime. com), is billed as an "enterprise project and resource management suite." Features that make this an interesting add-on to Project include the Workforce Browser, which helps you define and share information about resources across various projects and project managers. Also included are timesheets that people on your project can use to report their activity on multiple projects that you're tracking in Microsoft Project.

Another nice feature of this software is that it enables integration with enterprise resource planning (ERP) systems such as those manufactured by PeopleSoft and Oracle. In fact, when you use AMS Real Time with Project, an Enterprise menu is added to your standard Project menus so you can work from your familiar Project interface. Advanced Management Solutions even offers seminars on how to integrate Project with their software.

Cobra Squeezes the Most from Cost/Earned Value

WST Corporation (www.welcom.com), which makes its own complete project management package called Welcom, also produces Cobra, a cost/earned value management software package that you can use with Project plans. Tools offer functionality in estimating, what-if modeling of costs, and budget forecasting based on information in your Project schedule. An easy-to-use Integration Wizard helps you combine Project data with Cobra's costing software.

Cobra, which is shown in Figure 19-1, allows you to define certain budget calculations yourself, offering more flexibility than some of Project's costing features. In addition, the Chart Template Designer lets you play around with a variety of 3-D charts, which you can manipulate and rotate in several ways.

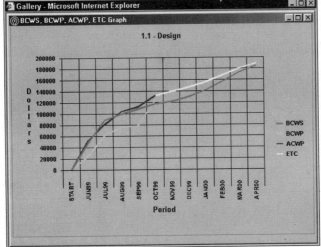

Figure 19-1:
3-D chart options are expanded when you use Cobra with your Project data.

Inspiration Helps Planning with Visual Thinking Tools

Inspiration is an interesting product, though it's not an add-on to Microsoft Project. Inspiration is a visual learning and visual thinking software package from Strategic Transitions (www.strategictransitions.com). It's used in educational and corporate settings to help you create visual models of ideas and processes. In some ways, it resembles the Network Diagram view in Project, providing a visual view of processes. But Inspiration is more robust and flexible. You can use collections of graphic symbols, photos, and animated symbols to create diagrams.

Templates make getting started with the product fairly easy. Try the checklist feature in Inspiration to help you start planning your task list in Project.

The software has a variety of uses, from novelists mapping out book ideas to corporate types brainstorming project goals (see Figure 19-2). Use the Webbing feature to map project phases and work processes before you start to build your Project schedule. You can use it for online brainstorming with your team to get their ideas, as well. Although there's no direct integration with Project, you can place links to Inspiration diagrams in your Project file, and cut-and-paste notes you've created here into Project task or resource forms.

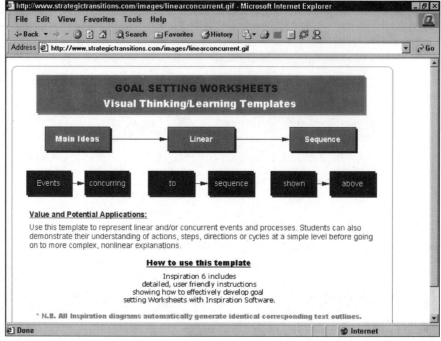

Figure 19-2:
Use various
forms and
captions in
Inspiration
to visually
brainstorm
projects.

Innate Integrates Projects Large and Small

Innate Timesheets and Innate Resource Manager from Innate Management Systems (www.innateus.com) are especially helpful if you're juggling multiple projects that range from small to large. You can use Innate to manage resources (see Figure 19-3) who work on smaller projects in your organization and are also busy on larger projects that you plan in Microsoft Project.

The Innate Resource Manager helps you scope out resource availability and prioritize resource assignments. Innate Timesheets is tracking software, but it offers more than Project does in this area. You can do productivity comparisons across several tasks or projects. You can also tap into sophisticated billing systems and integrate project information with accounting and payroll systems.

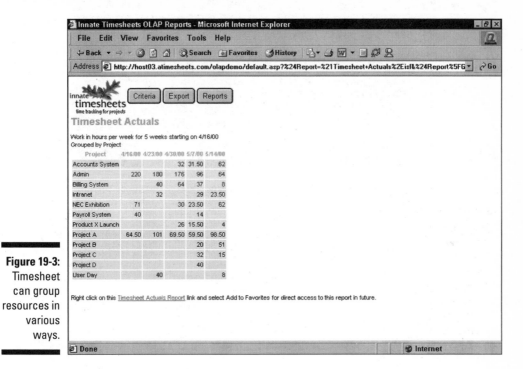

Figure 19-3:
Timesheet can group resources in various ways.

PlanView Models Your Workforce Capacity

PlanView, Inc. (www.planview.com) produces a software product that helps you sort through the various players in your project. This role-modeling feature in PlanView is intriguing. This feature creates three project roles:

✔ Stakeholders, such as clients and business partners who have a need to know. PlanView offers a scoreboard feature to help stakeholders see the overall productivity in a project.

✔ Managers, who must make decisions and manage people and processes. These people can use PlanView's tools to figure out the best deployment of resources in a project.

✔ Contributors are those working on the project who track their actual work on tasks. PlanView connects contributors' data into expense and billing features.

You can also define your own roles for people in your project.

PlanView is closely integrated with Microsoft Project, so you can share information about processes and people on a project between the two products. PlanView templates can also be used to give you a head start on your Project plan.

Projeca Streamlines Business Processes

Projeca, from Tenrox (www.projeca.com), puts the focus on business processes, such as performance analysis, resource planning, purchasing, and revenue and cost accounting. One of the best uses of this software for the Microsoft Project user is as a bridge to various enterprise and accounting packages such as SAP and ADP Payroll.

Projeca is a Web-based solution that can be very useful in a geographically diverse project team setting. You should take a look at this package also if you have need for RFI, quotation, and evaluation functions in your projects. Projeca offers a set of proposal management tools to help you get the project in the first place.

Project KickStart Gives Your Project a Headstart

Project KickStart from Experience In Software (www.experienceware.com) is a simple-to-use program with a wizard-like approach to helping you lay the groundwork for small to midsize project. If you need a little help getting started with a project, you can create your plan here in 30 minutes or less, and then use their hot link to port information over to Microsoft Project.

ProjectKickStart is designed to help you figure out your project strategy as you come up with a list of tasks. Planning icons remind you to map out the goals of your project and plan for obstacles. Libraries of typical goals and challenges make building them into your plan simple, and you can add your own specific company or industry phrases to the libraries. Links to Outlook, Word, and Excel also offer you some flexibility in sharing information among the Office family of products, which includes Project.

Project Manager's Assistant Organizes Drawings for Construction Projects

Originally aimed for the construction industry, Project Manager's Assistant from Crestsoft (www.crestsoft.com) is useful for any industry that uses a lot of drawings.

Essentially, this is a database product that helps you track drawings, issue copies, and manage changes over the life of the project.

Although the product doesn't integrate directly to Project, it's an additional software product that might prove useful to many project managers. For example, graphic designers and new product designers who generate drawings can catalogue them here.

If you manage scientific or engineering projects, you might also find this software useful for managing schematics or diagrams. By placing links to this database in your Project plan, you can make this information available to your project team.

TeamTrack Solves Mission-Critical Issues

TeamTrack from TeamShare (www.teamshare.com) offers "Web-architected workflow management solutions." In English, that means that the software helps you identify problems and defects in your processes and find solutions.

The software allows you to create visual maps for your processes and share that data among your team. The Web focus here means that people can get to the process data online without having Project running.

One nice feature of this software is that it notifies you when a problem occurs or deadlines have passed without activity. TeamTrack even helps you identify issues that may arise when "non-talking" systems communicate. In other words, if you integrate two pieces of software to share data, data may come into Project that causes a problem, and you won't even know it because you're not inputting it. TeamTrack flags such problems to help you avoid missing a critical situation before it's too late.

TeamShare's Web site offers a live online demo, shown in Figure 19-4.

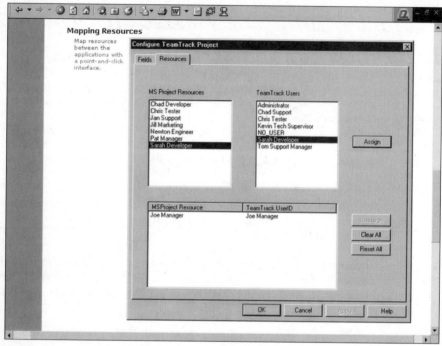

Figure 19-4:
You can
view project
issues
by role in
TeamTrack.

TimeSheet Professional Makes Tracking a Piece of Cake

Microsoft integrated some of TimeSheet's features into Project a few years ago. However, the fullest functionality comes from buying the TimeSheet Professional software package and using it with Project. The TimeSheet interface is simple to use, and the software is seamlessly integrated with Project for automated updating of your schedule.

This is a great product for gathering resource information on work performed on tasks. If every member of your team doesn't have access to Project, provide them with this much less expensive product for inputting their work time; then you can easily download all their data to update Project. In addition, you can get useful information on total project effort and estimates of costs by project completion.

Part VI
Appendixes

The 5th Wave   By Rich Tennant

"Get ready, Mona — here come the stats."

In this part . . .

*A*lthough an appendix is sometimes considered something that just dangles out there without purpose, the appendixes in this book should be very useful to Project users.

Appendix A provides information about Project Server, the workgroup software product that you can use along with the Professional edition of Microsoft Project. This appendix provides a useful overview of Project Server that will help you decide whether or not you need the features of that software for your organization.

Appendix B is a hodge-podge of additional resources, from add-on software products you can use with Project to enhance its functionality to project management books and associations.

Appendix A

Overview of Project Server

· ·

*O*ne of the substantial changes to Microsoft Project 2002 is the addition of so-called enterprise features, a great many of which require Microsoft Project Server 2002. These features allow you to share and update information across an *enterprise* (a fancy word for an organization).

Project Server is a companion product to Project, which means you have to fork over more money to get it. Project Server isn't built into Project, although Project has several built-in hooks to accommodate Server's functionality. For example, several commands listed on the Collaborate menu in Project won't work without some access to Project Server.

If you used Project 2000, you'll recognize much of the Project Server functionality — it used to be built into the product and was called Project Central. But times move on, and now you have to pay for what was once free.

Because using this companion product requires that you buy or license a separate software application and set up all sorts of server-type stuff, I haven't included detailed coverage of it in this book. But because you might be curious about its capabilities, I provide this brief overview.

What Can Project Server Do?

Project Server works with both Microsoft Project Professional and Enterprise versions. Server sets up an online project command central that can be used by people in your project to

- Communicate online, exchanging updates on progress and sending suggested new tasks to project managers
- Make, view, and accept or decline task assignments
- Update activity on tasks using a timesheet interface
- Request status reports and review project information
- Manage project documents, creating and comparing multiple versions of projects and setting up document libraries

Project Server uses a user model with three types of participants, and provides various information and access requirements accordingly:

- ✔ Managers, who oversee the day-to-day operations of a project
- ✔ Team members, who perform the work on the project
- ✔ Shareholders, such as clients and senior management, who require regular updating on project progress, often across several projects in an organization

One of the benefits of Project Server is that not every member of your team has to have Project installed to interact with it, as long as they have access to the Server, a browser, and appropriate permissions.

Manage documents and resolve issues

Think of Project Server's document management feature as enabling you to set up a public library for your project online. Document libraries can be project specific or contain more general documents that might be accessed by anyone in your company.

If you want to create and manage online document libraries, you'll have to set up SharePoint Team Services Server, which involves setting up something called a subweb. This is not something you would normally want to try yourself — call in your local IS professional, please.

After your document libraries are set up, you can publish documents to the libraries and assign permissions to regulate who can access what. You can even allow some users to create sublibraries for your project.

You can also use a feature called Issue Tracking. *Issues* are like big red flags that display an indicator on the document, project, or task that you attach them to. You can also set up Project Server to send e-mails alerting everyone that such a flag has been posted.

Make assignments and delegate tasks

Because the main focus of Project Server is to help you interact with your team members, one of its most useful features is the capability to post resource assignments and delegate work on tasks.

Members of a project team can interact and access data on Project Server using Microsoft Project Web Access. Yes, this is another product you have to license separately. Think of Web Access as being like all those views you can look at in Project — they're an online access interface for Project Server.

The folks on your team can access timesheets for their specific assignments and can get e-mail notification of those assignments. Team members can delegate assignments to others on the team. Then, the team member can review and approve status reports on work performed on the task before sending those reports on to the project manager.

Of course, you don't want everyone on a project to be able to pass the buck when it comes to assignments: The project manager has control over who can — and can't — delegate tasks in a project.

Track your progress

The other big perk in using Project Server is the functionality it gives your team members to track their activity on tasks and report their progress to you online. Project managers can request updates or send reminders shortly before updates are due.

Team members can use the Microsoft Project Web Access interface to enter actual activity into a timesheet. Web Access communicates directly with Project on the project manager's computer. As project manager, you can then make manual updates to your project plan or let Project make updates automatically.

Figure out what's going on with status reports

Status reports are essentially forms people on your project can complete explaining the status of their tasks. These aren't used to track and record actual work performed. Instead, they help team members describe what's going on with various tasks.

One of the nice things about status reports for you, as a project manager, is that you can assemble all the individual reports into a complete status report for the project. Then you can make that report available to shareholders to update them on the latest news.

What's Involved in Setting up Project Server?

Well, I wish I could tell you that Project Server is a plug-and-play solution, but it's a little more complicated than that. Here's what you have to do to start using Project Server through a company intranet or the Internet:

✔ Buy Microsoft Project Server and Microsoft Web Access licenses for the number of people in your organization who will use them.

✔ Project 2002 itself must be installed on the project manager's computer.

✔ Install and set up the Server product on a server computer that uses Internet Information Server (IIS) 5.0 or later as well as Microsoft Windows Server 2000 or later.

✔ The server computer must also have one of these Windows operating systems installed: Windows 98, Millennium, NT 4.0 (Service Pack 6), 2000 Professional, XP Home, or XP Professional.

✔ If you want to use document libraries, set up SharePoint Team Services Server and a subweb.

✔ Create accounts for all your team members, which may include setting up authentication (passwords) for greater security. On an intranet, everyone must have network access.

✔ Make sure all team members have browsers (preferably Internet Explorer 5.5) and access to the server. If you prefer, you can use the browser module that comes with Project Server.

If you don't want to mess with installing servers, consider Microsoft Project Central Service. This web-hosted solution has pretty much the same features as Project Server, but someone else deals with most of the setup. (However, you still have to set up team accounts and permissions.) You can get a license for the Microsoft Project Central service to store project data on a Microsoft Web site.

Appendix B

Project Management Resources

*B*ooks

Books on project management range from project management techniques to specific such as cost estimating. See whether one of these titles fits your learning needs.

Microsoft Project 2002 Bible by Elaine Marmel (published by Hungry Minds, Inc.) is helpful for those who want a comprehensive reference book on Project. For readers of *Microsoft Project 2002 For Dummies,* this book will provide more information on advanced features as well as a CD containing templates and trial versions of some useful third-party software add-ins.

If you want a book detailing project management standards and practices, *A Guide to the Project Management Body of Knowledge,* 2000 Edition (published by PMI) might be just the ticket. It is available in hardcover, paperback, or on CD from the Project Management Institute.

Cost Estimator's Reference Manual by Rodney Stewart, James Johannes, and Richard M. Wyskeda (published by John Wiley and Sons) is a 700+ page tome that outlines the methods and procedures used across a variety of industries to accurately estimate costs for project management. The step-by-step approach of this book is very helpful to those trying to learn tried-and-true methods of cost estimating.

Customer Driven Project Management by Bruce Berkley and James Saylor (published by McGraw Hill) discusses through numerous case studies how to involve customers in projects for success. This is a good study of the life cycle of any project in which a customer, internal or external to your organization, is involved.

Although *Managing High Technology Programs and Projects* by Russell Archibald (published by John Wiley and Sons) has a focus on high-technology projects, it offers methodologies useful to any project manager. One chapter covers project and scheduling software, but the focus here is on approaches to successful project management.

Education and Training

As with every other type of professional, ongoing training and accreditation can be important to your career advancement. Check out these schools and organizations for project management related training.

International Project Management Association Certified Project Manager Accreditation (http:\\www.ipma.ch/) has set out a four-tiered project management program concept that is the basis for project management accreditation. View the program and its requirements at this site.

Several schools offer specializations or degrees in project management, but I list University of Wisconsin Project Management Program (www.uwplatt.edu/~disted/project_management.htm) here because the University of Wisconsin is highly respected in the area of distance learning. If you want to study project management from home, this is worth checking into.

The Project Management Institute (http://pmi.org) offers several courses and seminars on project management. Check them out on this site.

Microsoft Web Sites

Microsoft offers several kinds of support for and information about Microsoft Project on the following Web sites, as well as links to third-party resources.

For information from Microsoft about updates to Microsoft Project, as well as product support, go to the Project home page (http://Microsoft.com/office/project/default.htm). Companies deploying Project on an organizational level can find advice and strategies for deployment on this site. Microsoft also maintains a list of Solutions Providers on this site — third-party companies that offer consulting or software add-ons for Project.

Although Microsoft Template Gallery (http://officeupdate.microsoft.com/templategallery) doesn't have many Project templates, it does have templates of interest to project managers. For example, you can find templates for vendor and contractor contracts, as well as a PowerPoint presentation to use when you want to give a project overview to colleagues.

To meet other users of Microsoft Project and share tips and tricks, go to the Microsoft Project Users Group (http://mspug.com/main.htm). This is an active online users group, so be prepared to learn and share!

Periodicals

Keep up on how people are using Microsoft Project and project management principles throughout the world by reading some of the following periodicals.

International Journal of Project Management, a publication with an international project management slant, is published eight times a year by Elsevier Science (http://www.elsevier.nl), a publisher of various technical journals. Topics covered include risk analysis, team building, cost and time allocation, dispute resolution, and project evaluation.

Projects @Work (http://www.projects@work.com) magazine is produced bi-monthly. It's touted as a magazine offering business and technology solutions for project management professionals. Its approach offers case studies of real-life project management scenarios.

PMTimes () is an electronic project management magazine. Look into the job vacancies area if you're in the mood for a career change, and try out the jobs search engine.

Project Management Journal (http://pmi.org/publictn/pmjournal), produced by the Project Management Institute on a quarterly basis, is sent to all members of the Institute. This publication is also available at some libraries, and you can order back copies on CD.

Project Management Organization Web Sites

Check out these sites if you're interested in how standards and tools for project managers are developing. Many of these offer discussion areas where you can tap into the accumulated knowledge and experience of fellow project managers.

The Project Management Institute (http://pmi.org/) was founded in 1969. The organization provides research, publications, and education in project management topics. They sponsor local chapters, as well as career advice for project management professionals.

American Society for the Advancement of Project Management (ASAPM) offers a magazine about project management, as well as learning and career assistance. They maintain a Web page about project management standards and a discussion area where you can share information with other project managers (http://www.asapm.org).

The International Project Management Association (http://www.ipma.ch/) is based in England. Its focus is on international project management issues. The group sponsors a World Symposium on Project Management every year, so if you want to wrangle a company-paid trip to Europe, this is the group to join (the 2002 conference is in Berlin).

The Project Management Forum site (http://www.pmforum.org) offers some practical tools for project managers, such as a virtual office and timesheet tracking for projects. The PM Road Warrior offers tools for project managers who travel a great deal, including currency converters, the time around the world, and free online faxing services. The Library on this site offers free access to published papers as well as information on journals and books on project management.

Other Resources

If you're hot and heavy into project management, one of the following resources might prove to be of interest. They range from annual conferences to online meetings sites.

Guide to Project Management Research Sites (http://www.fek.umu.se/irnop/projweb.html), maintained by a professor at Umea School of Business and Economics in Sweden, offers a listing of various sites with studies on project management. Links lead you to listings of project management software, sites that offer papers on management skills, educational resources, and more.

ProjectWorld Conference (www.projectworld.com) is held at various locations in North America every year. The event offers both project-management-oriented exhibitions and educational programs.

Webex Online Meeting Center (http://www.Webex.com) offers a virtual meeting service for project managers who have to gather resources from various locales to keep project communications open. They're a fee-based service that corporations use for meetings with employees, vendors, and clients and for training their own remotely located employees.

Glossary

actual: The cost of the percentage of work that has been completed on a task.

ACWP (actual cost of work performed): Cost of actual work performed to date on a project, plus any fixed costs.

ALAP (as late as possible): A constraint put on a task's timing to make the task occur as late as possible in the project schedule, taking into account any dependency relationships. *See also* dependency.

ASAP (as soon as possible): A constraint put on a task's timing to make the task occur as early as possible in the project schedule, taking into account any dependency relationships. *See also* dependency.

BAC (budget at completion): The total of all costs involved in completing a task. *See also* baseline cost.

base calendar: The default calendar on which all new tasks are based, unless a resource or task-specific calendar is applied.

baseline: The detailed project plan against which actual work is tracked.

baseline cost: The total planned costs for a project's tasks, before any actual costs are incurred.

BCWP (budgeted cost of work performed): Also called earned value, this term refers to the value of work that has been completed. For example, a task with $1000 of costs accrues a baseline value of $750 when it's 75 percent complete.

BCWS (budgeted cost of work scheduled): The percentage of the plan that's completed times the planned costs. This calculated value totals a task's completed work and its remaining planned costs.

calendar: The various settings for hours in a workday, days in a work week, holidays, and nonworking days on which a project schedule is based. You can set Project, Task, and Resource calendars.

circular dependency: A timing relationship among tasks that creates an endless loop that can't be resolved.

collapse: To close up a project outline to hide subtasks from view.

combination view: A Project view with task details appearing at the bottom of the screen.

constraint: A parameter that forces a task to fit a specific timing. For example, a task can be constrained to start as late as possible in a project. Constraints interact with dependency links to determine a task's timing.

cost: The amount of money associated with a project task when you assign resources, which are equipment, materials, or people with associated fees or hourly rates.

critical path: The series of tasks that must occur on time for the overall project to meet its deadline.

critical task: A task on the critical path. *See also* critical path.

crosstab: A report format that compares two intersecting sets of data. For example, you can generate a crosstab report showing the costs of critical tasks that are running late.

cumulative cost: The planned total cost to date for a resource's effort on a particular task. This calculation adds the costs already incurred on a task to any planned costs remaining for the uncompleted portion of the task.

cumulative work: The planned total work of a resource on a particular task. This calculation adds the work completed on a task to any planned work remaining for the uncompleted portion of the task.

current date line: The vertical line in a Gantt Chart indicating today's date and time. *See also* Gantt Chart.

CV (cost variance): The difference between the baseline costs and the combination of actual costs to date and estimated costs remaining (scheduled costs). The cost variance is either positive (overbudget) or negative (underbudget).

deadline date: A date you assign to a task that doesn't constrain the task's timing. However, if a deadline date is assigned, Project displays an indicator symbol if the task runs past the deadline.

dependency: A timing relationship between two tasks in a project. A dependency link causes a task to occur before or after another task or to begin or end at some point during the life of the other task.

detail task: *See* subtask.

duration: The amount of time it takes to complete a task.

duration variance: The difference between the planned (baseline) task duration and the current estimated task duration, based on activity to date and any remaining activity still to be performed.

EAC (estimate at completion): The total planned cost for resource effort on a specific task. This calculation combines the costs incurred to date with costs estimated for a task's remaining work.

earned value: A reference to the value of work completed. A task with $1000 of associated costs has a baseline value of $750 when 75 percent complete. *See also* BCWP.

effort driven: A task that requires an assigned amount of effort to be completed. When you add resources to an effort-driven task, the assigned effort is distributed among the task resources equally.

enterprise custom fields: Custom fields stored in a global file; these fields can be used to standardize Project plan content across an organization.

enterprise resources: A feature that allows you to save all resource information for resources used across an organization in one location.

estimated duration: A setting that indicates that you are using a best guess of a task's duration. When you enter an estimated duration for a task, you can then apply a filter to displays only tasks with estimated duration, which reflects the fact that they have questionable timing.

expand: To open up a project outline to reveal both summary tasks and subtasks.

expected duration: An estimate of the actual duration of a task based on work performance to date.

external task: A task in another project. You can set links between tasks in your project and external tasks.

finish date: The date on which a project or task is estimated to be or is actually completed.

finish-to-finish relationship: A dependency relationship in which one task must finish at the same time that another task finishes.

finish-to-start relationship: A dependency relationship in which one task must finish at the same time that another task starts.

fixed duration: The length of time required to complete a task remains constant no matter how many resources are assigned to the task. A half-day seminar is an example of a fixed-duration task.

fixed units: A cost where resource units are constant; if you change the duration of the task, resource units won't change. This is the default task type.

fixed work: A task where the number of resource hours assigned to a task determine its length.

float: *See* slack.

Gantt Chart: A standard Project view that displays columns of task information alongside a chart that shows task timing in bar-chart format.

gap: *See* lag.

generic resources: A type of resource that allows you to make skill-based assignments based on a skill/code profile.

grouping: The organization of tasks by a customized field to summarize costs or other factors.

ID number: The number automatically assigned to a task by Project based on its sequence in the schedule.

indent: To move a task to a lower level of detail in the project's outline hierarchy.

lag: The amount of downtime that can occur between the end of one task and the beginning of another. Lag is built into a dependency relationship between tasks when you indicate that a certain amount of time must pass before the second task can begin.

leveling: A calculation used by Project that modifies resource work assignments for the purpose of resolving resource conflicts.

linking: (1) To establish a connection between tasks in separate schedules so that task changes in the first schedule are reflected in the second. (2) To establish dependencies among project tasks.

material resources: The supplies or other items used to complete a task (one of two resource categories; the other is work resources).

milestone: A task of zero duration, which marks a moment in time or an event in a schedule.

network diagram: An illustration that graphically represents workflow among a project's tasks; one of Microsoft Project's standard views.

node: In Network Diagram view, a box containing information about individual project tasks.

nonworking time: The time when a resource is not available to be assigned to work on any task in a project.

outdent: To move a task to a higher level in a project's outline hierarchy.

outline: The structure of summary and subtasks in a project.

overallocation: When a resource is assigned to spend more time on a single task or a combination of tasks occurring at the same than that resource's work calendar permits.

overtime: Any work scheduled beyond a resource's standard work hours. You can assign a different rate than a resource's regular rate to overtime work.

percent complete: The amount of work on a task that has already been accomplished, expressed as a percentage.

PERT chart: A standard project-management tracking form indicating work-flow among project tasks. This is called a Network Diagram in Project. *See also* network diagram.

portfolio analyzer: A view that gives higher-level managers an overview of data across several projects to enable analysis and decision making.

portfolio modeling: A feature that allows you to model any changes to your project and see what impact those changes would have.

predecessor: In a dependency link, the task designated to occur before another task. *See also* dependency and successor.

priorities: A ranking of importance assigned to tasks. When you use resource leveling to resolve project conflicts, priority is a factor in the leveling calculation. A higher-priority task is less likely than a lower-priority task to incur a delay during the leveling process. *See also* resource leveling.

progress lines: Gantt Chart view bars that overlap the baseline taskbar and allow you to compare the baseline plan with a task's tracked progress.

project: A series of tasks that achieves a specific goal. A project seeks to meet the triple requirements of timeliness, quality, and budget.

project management: The discipline that studies various methods, procedures, and concepts used to control the progress and outcome of projects.

Project Server: A Web-based companion product of Microsoft Project that enables team members to enter information about their tasks into an overall project schedule without having Project installed on their own computers.

recurring task: A task that will occur several times during the life of a project. Regular project-team meetings or quarterly inspections are examples of recurring tasks.

resource: A cost associated with a task. A resource can be a person, a piece of equipment, materials, or a fee.

resource driven: A task whose timing is determined by the number of resources assigned to it.

resource leveling: A process used to modify resource assignments to resolve resource conflicts.

resource pool: (1) Resources that are assigned as a group to an individual task, such as a pool of administrative workers assigned to generate a report. (2) A group of resources created in a centralized location that multiple project managers can access and assign to their projects.

resource sharing: A feature that allows you to copy resources you've created in another project to your current plan.

Resource Substitution Wizard: A wizard that replaces an unavailable resource with another of similar skill and cost.

roll up: The calculation by which all subtask values are "rolled up," or summarized, in a summary task.

slack: The amount of time you can delay a task before the task becomes critical. Slack is used up when any delay in a task will delay the overall project deadline. Also called float.

split tasks: Tasks that have one or more breaks in their timing. When you split a task, you stop it part way, and start it again at a later time.

start date: The date on which a project or task begins.

start-to-finish relationship: A dependency relationship in which one task can't start until another task finishes.

start-to-start relationship: A dependency relationship in which two tasks must start at the same time.

subproject: A copy of a second project inserted in a project. The inserted project becomes a phase of the project in which it is inserted.

subtask: A task detailing a specific step in a project phase. This detail is rolled up into a higher-level summary task. Also called a subordinate task. *See also* roll up.

successor: In a dependency relationship, the later of two tasks. *See also* dependency.

summary task: In a project outline, a task that has subordinate tasks. A summary task rolls up the details of its subtasks and has no timing of its own. *See also* roll up.

task: An individual step performed to reach a project's goal.

template: A format in which a file can be saved. The template saves elements such as calendar settings, formatting, and tasks. New project files can be based on a template to save the time involved in reentering settings.

timescale: The area of a Gantt Chart view that displays units of time; when placed against those units of time, taskbars graphically represent the timing of tasks.

tracking: To record the actual progress of work completed and the costs accrued on a project's tasks.

variable rate: A shift in resource cost that can be set to occur at specific times during a project. For example, if a resource is expected to receive a raise or if equipment lease rates are scheduled to increase, you can assign variable rates for those resources.

WBS (work breakdown structure): Automatically assigned numbers that designate an outline structure for each project task. Government projects often require the use of WBS codes.

work breakdown structure: *See* WBS.

work resources: The people or equipment that perform work necessary to accomplish a task. *See also* material resources.

workload: The amount of work any resource is performing at any given time, taking into account all tasks to which the resource is assigned.

workspace: A set of files and project settings that you can save and reopen together, so that you pick up where you stopped on a set of projects.

Index

• S •